IMAGES
of Modern America

Lake Charles

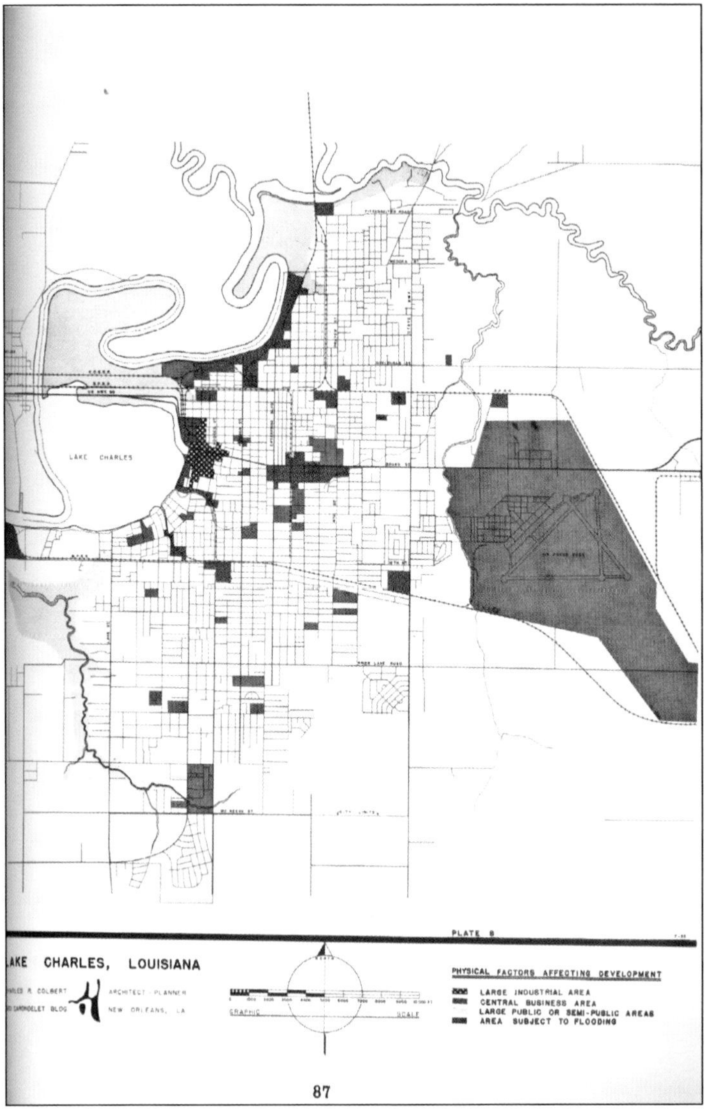

This mid-century map of Lake Charles was used to demonstrate factors affecting the future development of the city, including areas prone to flooding, central business areas, and the industrial area of the city near the lakefront. The city's layout changed dramatically during the following decades as US Interstate 10 and the I-210 Bypass facilitated growth to the south. (Courtesy of the Frazar Memorial Library Archives.)

On the Front Cover: Clockwise from the top left, the Calcasieu River Bridge (page 20, courtesy of www.monsoursphotography.net); the Lake Charles Yacht Club (page 68, courtesy of the Frazar Memorial Library Archives); a fishing pier on the lake (page 94, courtesy of Lindsey Janies); Riff's Department Store (page 11, courtesy of the Frazar Memorial Library Archives); and McNeese State University football players (page 64, courtesy of Dennis Thibodeaux).

On the Back Cover: From left to right, Chris Miller with his daughter, Candace, and the Bayou Roots (page 55, courtesy of www.visitlakecharles.org); Gumbeaux Gator (page 95, courtesy of www.visitlakecharles.org); and the Sallier Oak (page 95, courtesy of www.visitlakecharles.org).

IMAGES
of Modern America

Lake Charles

Jessica Hutchings

ARCADIA
PUBLISHING

ISBN 978-1-4671-1328-1

Published by Arcadia Publishing
Charleston, South Carolina

Printed in the United States of America

Library of Congress Control Number: 2014944515

For all general information, please contact Arcadia Publishing:
Telephone 843-853-2070
Fax 843-853-0044
E-mail sales@arcadiapublishing.com
For customer service and orders:
Toll-Free 1-888-313-2665

Visit us on the Internet at www.arcadiapublishing.com

Contents

ACKNOWLEDGMENTS

This book would not be possible without photographic contributions from many local contributors who are credited in the captions of this book. Unless otherwise noted, all images are from the Frazar Memorial Library Archives at McNeese State University. I especially appreciate Dennis Thibodeaux, a talented local photographer who indulged my numerous requests for photographs. Janet Allured, Dr. Pankaj Chandra, Adley Cormier, Charles Dickson, Paul Gonsoulin, Braylin Jenkins, Angie Manning, Erica McCreedy, and Rick Richard all kindly contributed their time and knowledge, for which I am most grateful. I am indebted to my colleagues in Frazar Library, especially those in the Reference Department: Walt Fontane, Barbara Houssiere, and Shandi Thibodeaux; thank you for your kindness and support. Our city is lucky to have the McNeese Archives, which is run by the capable and professional Pati Threatt, whom I appreciate greatly. I am grateful to Bob Richard, who provided a peaceful and supportive space to work when my life became chaotic. Finally, I would like to thank my mother, Carla Hutchings, for showing me that life is best handled with fortitude, humor, and love.

INTRODUCTION

Lake Charles, the seat of Calcasieu Parish and the fifth-largest city in Louisiana, is situated in the southwest corner of the state along the Calcasieu River and Contraband Bayou. Like many American cities following World War II, Lake Charles experienced a surge in population due to increased immigration to the United States during the 1940s, a decrease in the death rate, and a surge of births after the war, a nationwide trend that was eventually dubbed "the baby boom." In 1950, the city's population was about 41,000, reflecting not only the significant increase of residents during the previous decade but also the expansion of the city limits. Many at the time considered Lake Charles to be a "new city" due to the extensive rebuilding that occurred after the fire of 1910 and the 1918 hurricane that destroyed or damaged virtually every structure in the city.

Increased industrial activity along the Calcasieu River sustained the region's rise in population. Lake Charles is surrounded by natural resources, including sulphur, shell, lumber, oil, and natural gas. Its location on the West Gulf Coastal Plain is well suited to the cultivation of rice and crawfish. Complementing the area's natural and agricultural resources is the city's use of its strategic location. Prior to the war, Lake Charles had a solid backbone of infrastructure, including the Port of Lake Charles, which lies along the Calcasieu Ship Channel, a deepwater ship channel leading to the Intracoastal Waterway and the Gulf of Mexico, giving industries a fast and cheap method of transportation. The city was also already located along three rail lines and US Highway 90, which was supplanted by US Interstate 10 in 1952. Lake Charles Air Force Base, today's Chennault International Airport, lies three miles east of the city's core and supported a variety of military and industrial enterprises. The infrastructure coupled with the area's abundant resources made Lake Charles an agricultural, industrial, and transportation center in the mid-20th century.

During subsequent decades, Lake Charles experienced many of the same changes as other American cities. World War II veterans took advantage of the GI Bill of Rights and its low mortgage rates to move from the urban center of town to the new suburbs. Cars made living in the suburbs possible, because people could live farther away and drive to work instead of living near their workplaces or near public transportation. Lake Charles expanded east and south, and surrounding communities' populations increased, including Sulphur, Westlake, and Maplewood. New neighborhoods in the east included Oak Park and Greinwich, and the University and Sunset neighborhoods were built south of the city. Once focused on downtown Ryan Street and Broad Street, commercial activity moved further south on Ryan Street and to Highway 14. Downtown Lake Charles, with its narrow streets and lack of parking, was unaccustomed to the new, heavy traffic. Construction of Interstate 10 and the Interstate 210 Bypass were further disruptions to the traditional layout of the city, providing quick access to newer development in the south and the east.

The area's schools experienced dramatic changes during the second half of the 20th century. Since 1906, the Lake Charles City School Board operated separately from the Calcasieu Parish School Board. As the city grew and its limits expanded, the Lake Charles City School Board did not expand its boundaries; thus students residing in newly developed neighborhoods went to new schools operated by the Calcasieu Parish School Board. Because most of the people who moved to the suburbs were white, the Lake Charles City Schools for white students became underpopulated and the schools for African American students became overcrowded.

These events unfolded within the context of the civil rights movement. The 1954 *Brown v. Board of Education* decision declared that "separate but equal" institutions were unconstitutional; however, the decision did not instigate immediate change. The Civil Rights Act of 1964 ending segregation in schools, along with a local NAACP lawsuit, led Judge Edwin F. Hunter to order the desegregation of Lake Charles City Schools and Calcasieu Parish Schools in 1965. Formulating the plan for integrating the schools was contentious and difficult, especially when, at the same time, the Calcasieu Parish School Board wanted to reabsorb the Lake Charles City Schools. The parish finally absorbed the city system in 1966 and proceeded to take measures to integrate student populations, including merging and closing several schools.

As Southwest Louisiana's businesses and industries grew and changed, educational institutions were needed to train a skilled labor force to provide necessary technical expertise and support. McNeese State University provided a solid source of teachers, nurses, engineers, and other professionals, while SOWELA Community and Technical College provided vocational and technical training and Delta Tech provided clerical and basic medical training. As more women and minorities had access to postsecondary education after *Brown v. Board of Education* and the Civil Rights Act of 1964, the workforce eventually reflected these changes. Women and minorities not only participated in greater numbers during the late 20th century, they also held more leadership positions in the community.

The population of Lake Charles increased each decade of the 20th century until reaching a peak in 1970 with almost 78,000 people, just before the beginning of difficult economic times for the United States during the 1970s and early 1980s. As retail and commercial areas moved away from the city's center to the newer suburban developments with wider streets and parking lots, downtown Lake Charles lost business. As a measure to compete with the new retail areas, city officials enacted a redevelopment plan. Downtown streets were blocked and rerouted to create a pedestrian mall. Part of the lake nearby was filled in to create the Lake Charles Civic Center and a large parking lot that allowed quick access to the downtown retailers. However, the pedestrian mall could not compete with the Southgate Shopping Center or the new Prien Lake Mall. Downtown theaters, restaurants, hotels, and stores closed, and gradually, buildings were destroyed and never replaced. Many buildings that remained were left vacant and neglected for years.

Though Lake Charles experienced growing pains and turbulence along with the rest of the United States, the city has a unique history and culture that its citizens love to celebrate. Each year, Lake Charles hosts numerous festivals and events that bring people together to enjoy food, music, art, and culture. Contraband Days pays homage to the area's history of Jean LaFitte and bands of pirates, and the Mardi Gras festivities in Lake Charles are second in size only to those in New Orleans. The area cuisine reflects the region's Cajun heritage, as well as the local abundance of seafood and rice. The festive atmosphere, the tempting cuisine, and the natural beauty of the region have not only contributed to a high quality of life for its residents but have also drawn tourists to Lake Charles through the years. Near the end of the 20th century, Lake Charles embraced gaming as an avenue for generating economic activity, thus contributing even more to the local tourism industry.

Hurricane Rita signaled a harsh turning point for Lake Charles in 2005. The storm hit Southwest Louisiana just weeks after Hurricane Katrina devastated New Orleans. Citizens were evacuated, buildings all over the city were damaged or destroyed, and many people never returned. It took months to clear the streets of fallen trees and debris, and it took years before all of the blue tarps were replaced with new roofs on homes. Like New Orleans, many Lake Charles citizens lived in FEMA trailers while they put their homes back together. In the middle of the chaos, the citizens of the city went back to work, children returned to school, and life eventually regained normalcy.

Ten years later, although Lake Charles still bears scars from the storm, the city has experienced a gradual rebirth. As residents rebuilt their homes, city and industry leaders worked, and are still working, to rebuild Lake Charles in a sustainable way. Recent improvements since the hurricane include a downtown streetscape that complements the newly refurbished lakefront promenade. Downtown development has created a revitalized business district. Parks all over the city have seen new equipment, and roads have been widened and improved. Groups like the Calcasieu Preservation Society and Empire of the Seed have taken strides to prevent the further decay of some of the finest and oldest structures in Lake Charles. Industry leaders are bringing new business to Lake Charles by highlighting the city's infrastructure and other assets. The city is poised for growth and prosperity.

This book provides brief glimpses into our city's history since 1950, but there is so much more that can be told. Readers may want to consult the 2012 book Images of America: *Lake Charles* for information about Lake Charles history before 1950. I urge those who are interested in learning more about our city's history or about Southwest Louisiana to use the archives at Frazar Memorial Library by contacting the archivist, Pati Threatt. Also, the online archives of the *American Press* newspaper can be accessed with a subscription, and the powerful database can search local news all the way back to the 19th century. Both of these resources were invaluable to me as I worked on this project.

In addition to these information resources, I am grateful for those individuals who gave their time to discuss the history of the city with me. Janet Allured, Adley Cormier, Paul Gonsoulin, Braylin Jenkins, Angie Manning, Erica McCreedy, and Rick Richard all gave me information that helped focus my efforts. I am also grateful for Allured's careful reading of the manuscript and invaluable suggestions. I am responsible for any errors that may remain.

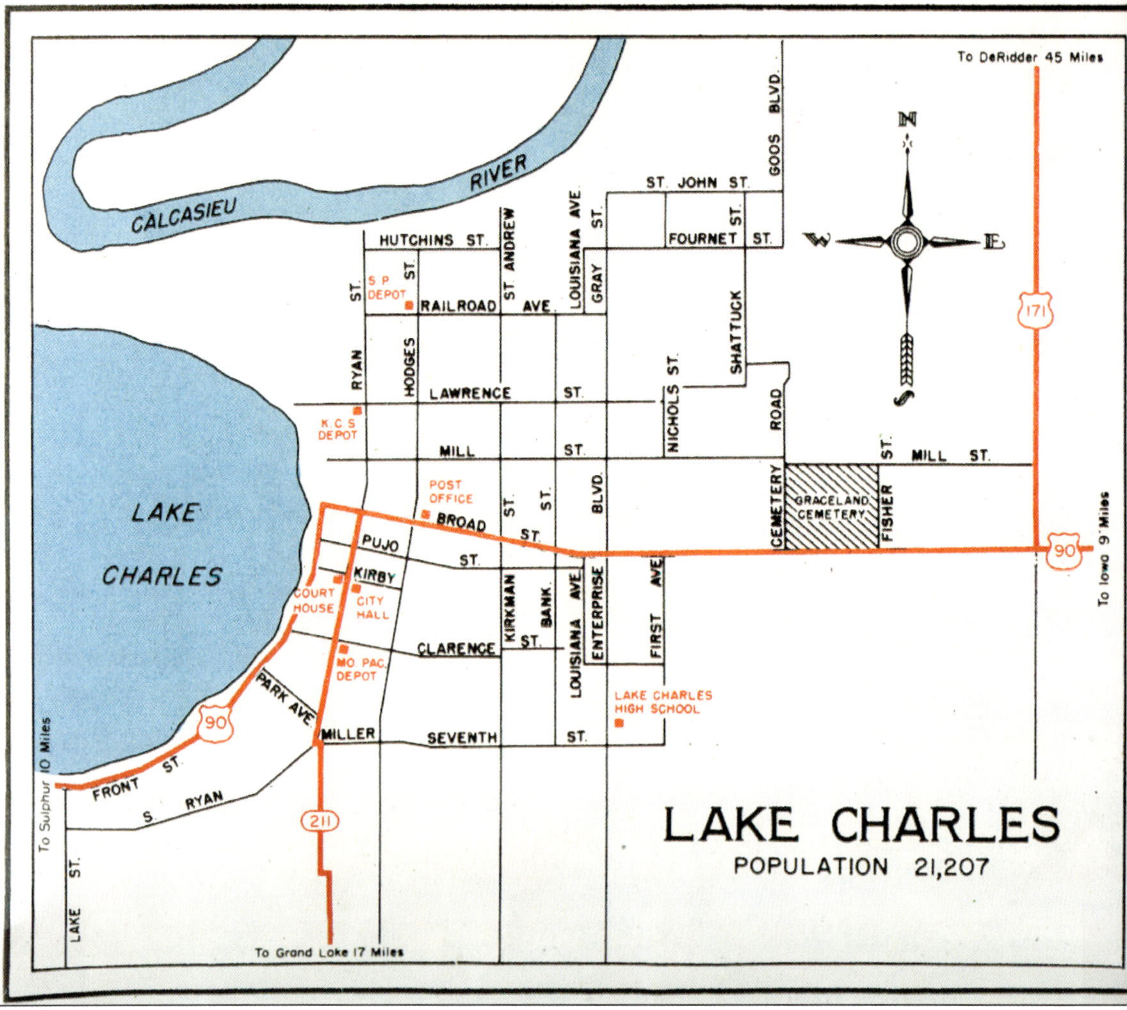

This 1948 map of Lake Charles depicts the city before the mid-century population increase and before Interstate 10 replaced US Highway 90 as the main east-west route through Lake Charles. During the years after World War II and the baby boom, people moved to Lake Charles and surrounding communities for new opportunities in burgeoning industries, and the city grew toward the south and the east. The grand entryways into Lake Charles were Broad Street from the east and Shell Beach Drive from the west, but now visitors are likely to exit Interstate 10 near the north end of the lake and drive through downtown on Ryan Street. Streets like Nelson Road, Prien Lake Road, and Highway 14 south of Interstate 210 now feature thriving commercial districts that did not exist prior to 1948. (Map courtesy of Rick Richard.)

One

Mid-Century Lake Charles

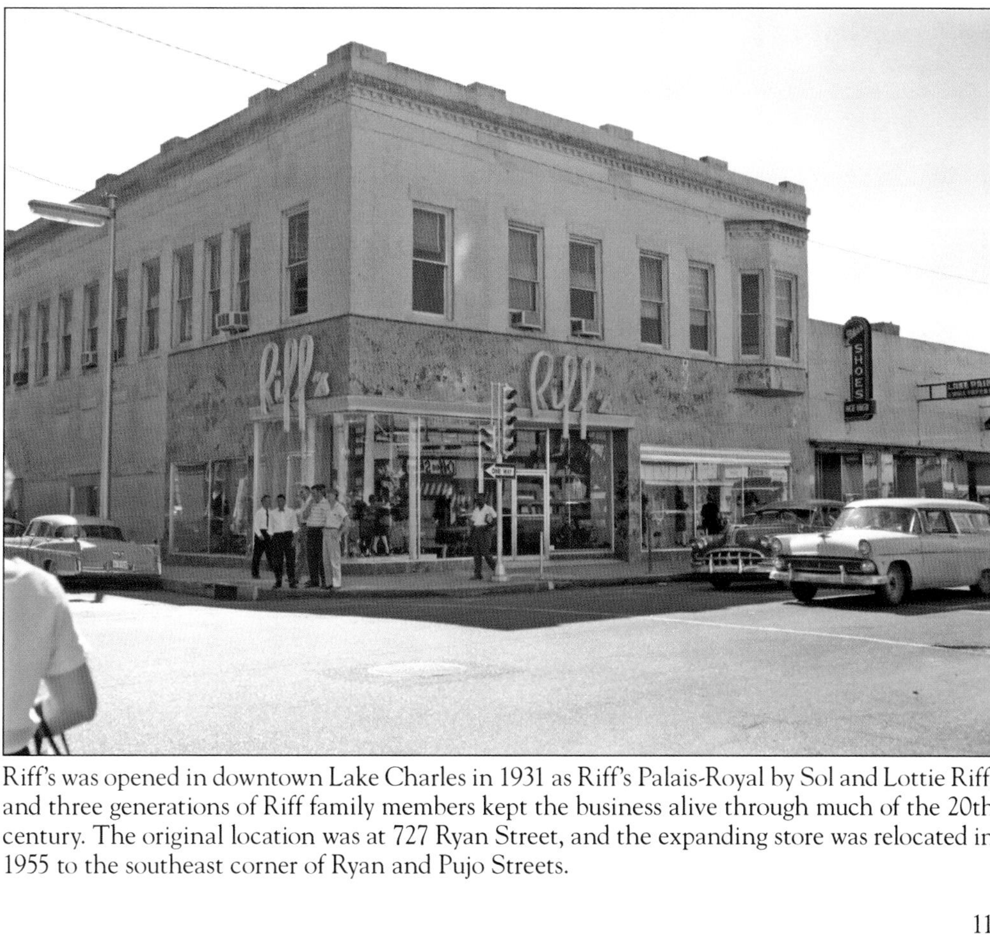

Riff's was opened in downtown Lake Charles in 1931 as Riff's Palais-Royal by Sol and Lottie Riff, and three generations of Riff family members kept the business alive through much of the 20th century. The original location was at 727 Ryan Street, and the expanding store was relocated in 1955 to the southeast corner of Ryan and Pujo Streets.

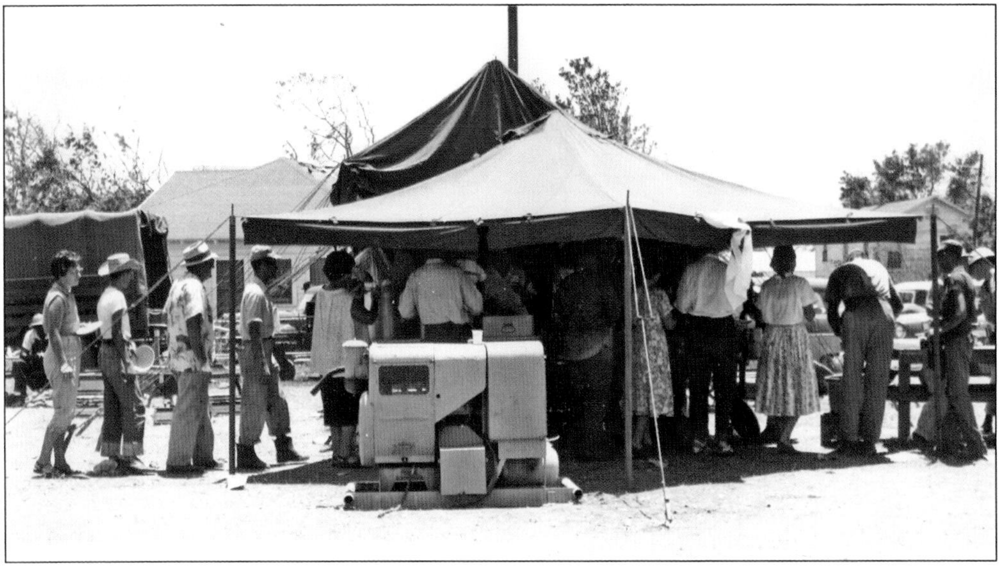

Hurricane Audrey hit the Southwest Louisiana coast on June 27, 1957, killing hundreds and causing tremendous property damage. Over 2,000 refugees from the destruction poured into Lake Charles and Sulphur during the days following the storm. As Audrey approached, the Red Cross set up an emergency committee to form immediate plans for providing food, clothing, and shelter to victims, and McNeese State College was one of the many school sites used for shelter. The above photograph depicts a line for food at a Red Cross tent in Lake Charles, and the picture below shows evacuees in the McNeese Arena.

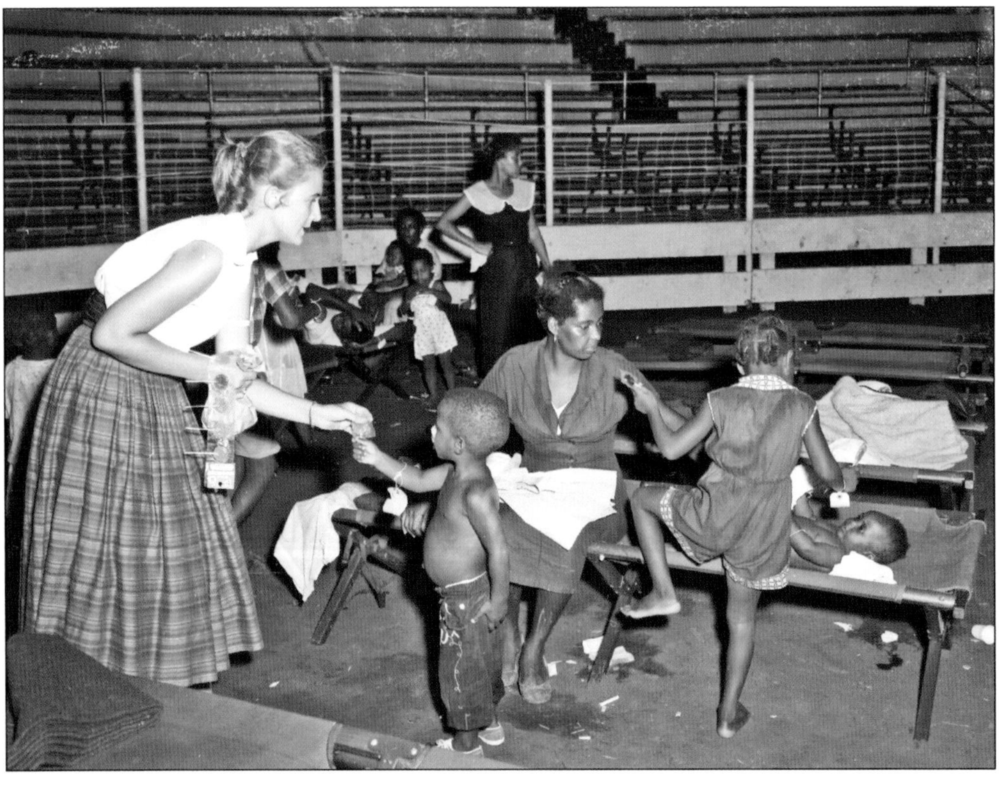

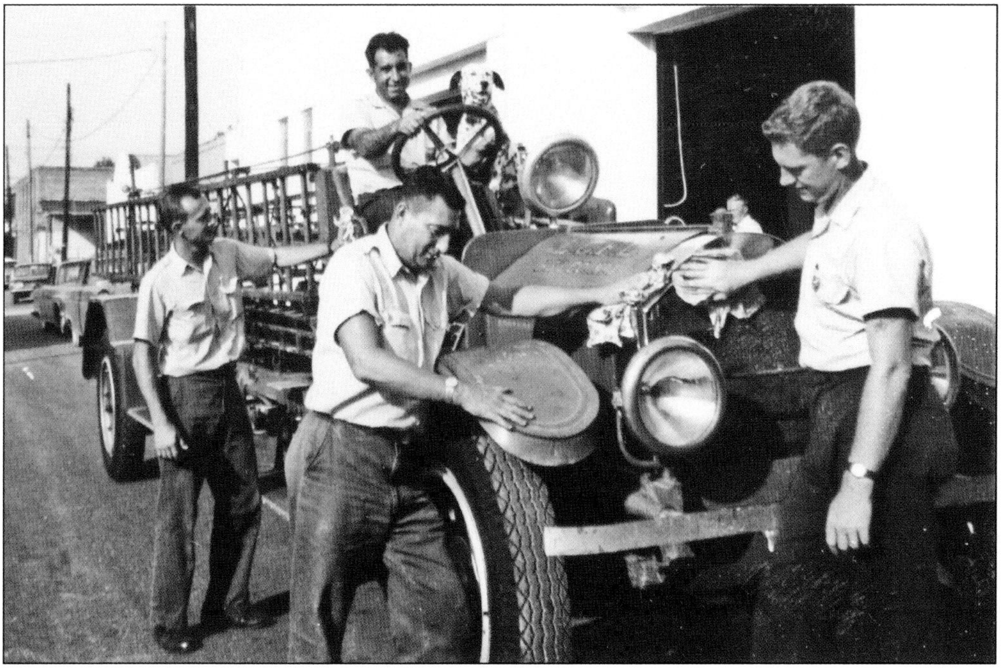

This photograph from around 1960 shows Lake Charles firefighters, from left to right, William Hinch, Arsen Hinton, Jack Reynolds, Capt. Joe LaRocca (seated), and Spot the dog cleaning the fire truck after extinguishing a fire that broke out on downtown Ryan Street. LaRocca's brother, Leon Paul LaRocca, served as assistant chief of the Lake Charles Fire Department for many years.

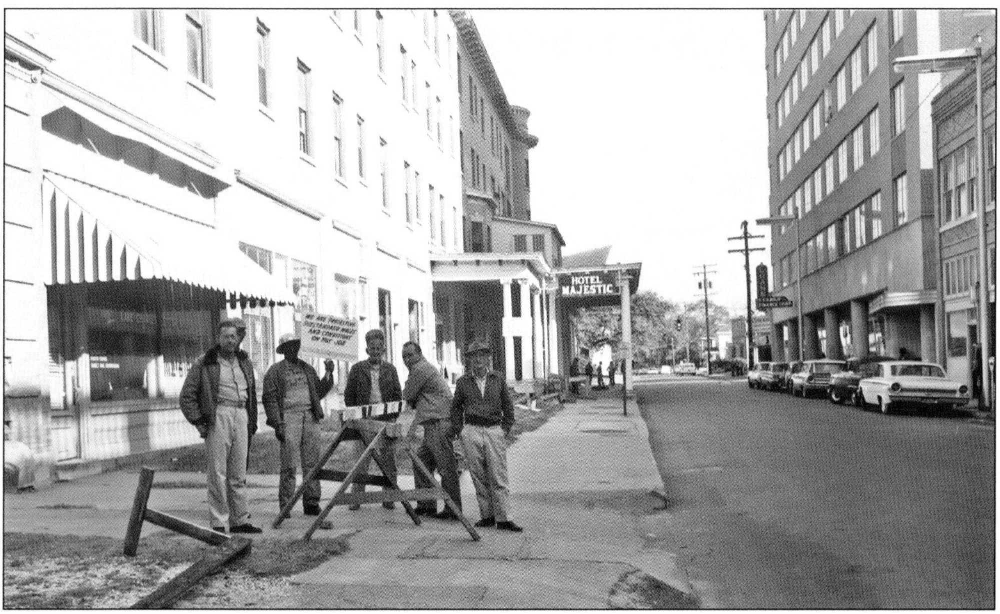

The Majestic Hotel, built on the northwest corner of Pujo and Bilbo Streets in 1904, hosted social affairs and distinguished guests. The modern hotel had its own power plant and water system, and each room had its own ceiling fan. This 1964 photograph shows demolition workers on strike. The sign on the Majestic Hotel behind the workers says, "All Materials in Hotel for Sale."

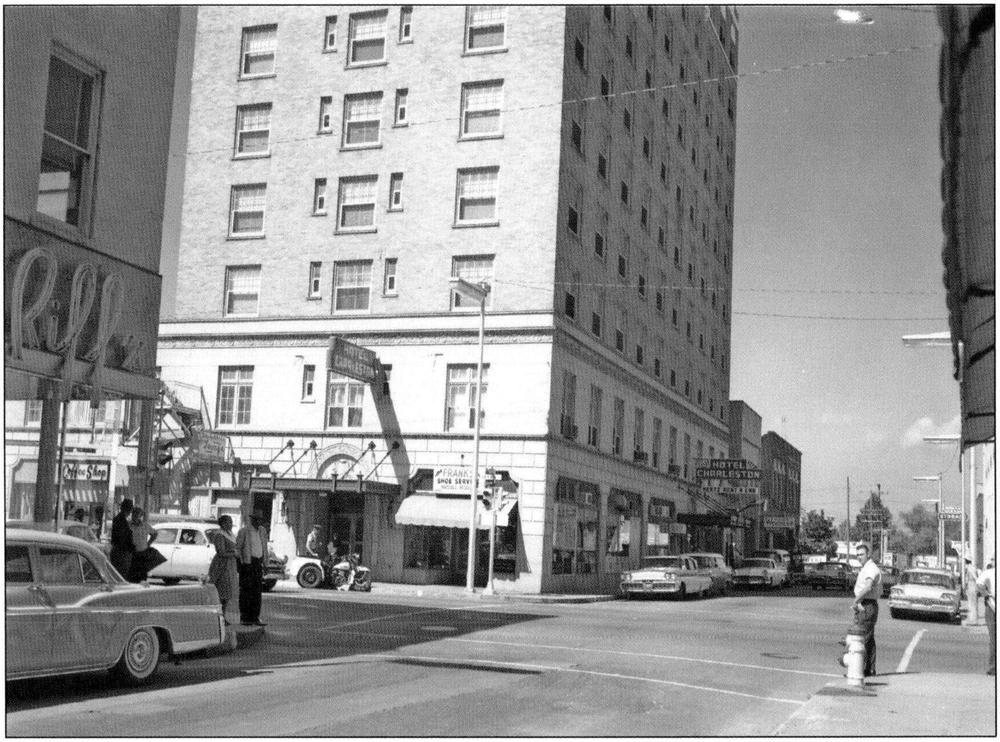

The Charleston Hotel was built in 1929 at the southwest corner of Pujo and Ryan Streets. The first skyscraper of Lake Charles featured a coffee shop, a barbershop, and a Spanish interior motif. The hotel closed in May 1973 due to fire code violations, and it was seized in 1974 for unpaid taxes.

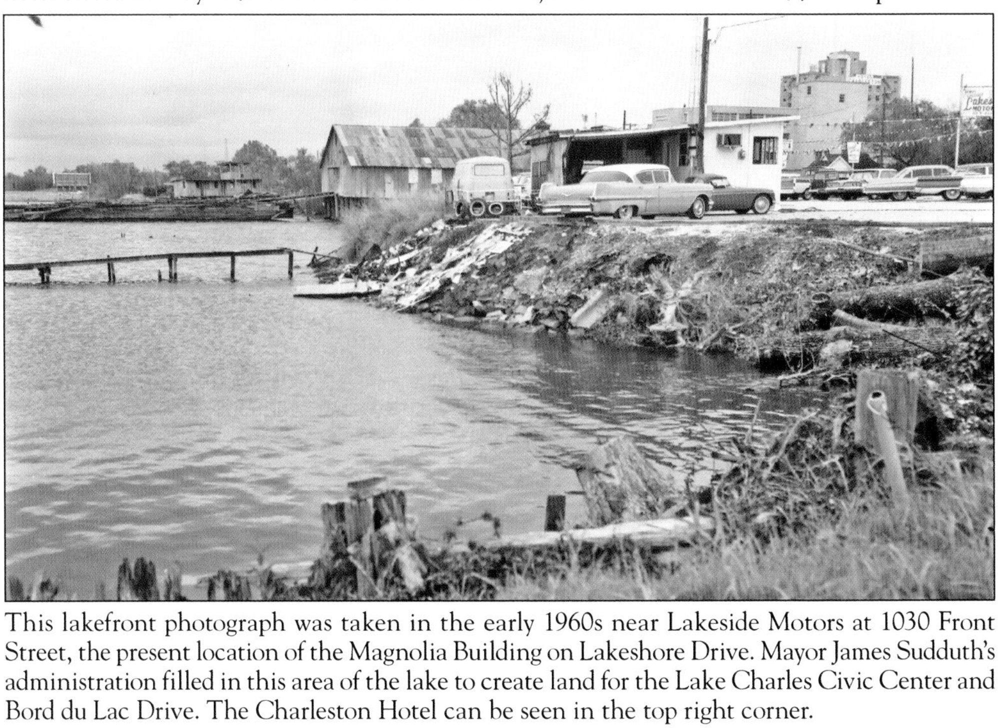

This lakefront photograph was taken in the early 1960s near Lakeside Motors at 1030 Front Street, the present location of the Magnolia Building on Lakeshore Drive. Mayor James Sudduth's administration filled in this area of the lake to create land for the Lake Charles Civic Center and Bord du Lac Drive. The Charleston Hotel can be seen in the top right corner.

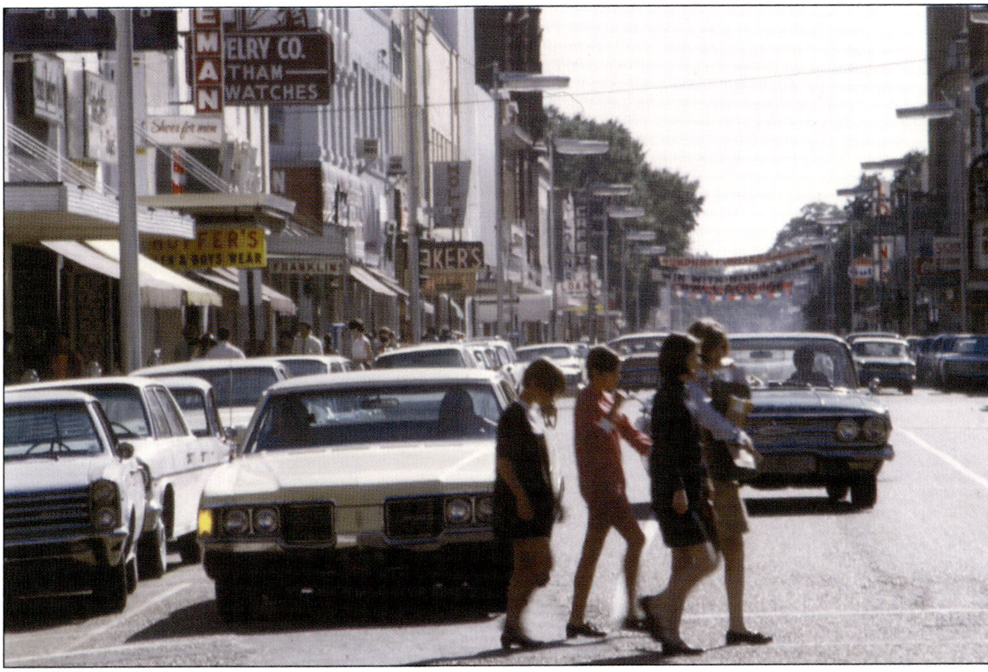

This 1968 photograph of downtown Lake Charles depicts a bustling commercial district on Ryan Street looking south between Division and Broad Streets. Subsequent decades brought blight to this area as businesses moved to Prien Lake Mall or other locations further south. Several downtown buildings were demolished, never to be replaced.

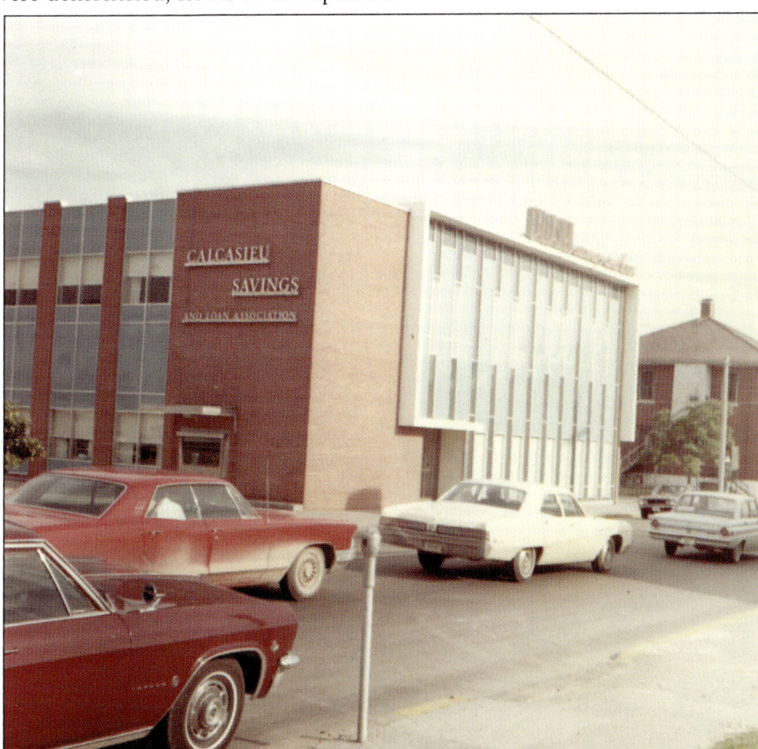

This 1969 photograph shows the Calcasieu Savings and Loan Association building at the intersection of Clarence and Ryan Streets. It opened in 1960, soon after the company's 50th anniversary. At the time of construction, the building was the most modern in Lake Charles; however, the bank stayed in the building for less than 20 years.

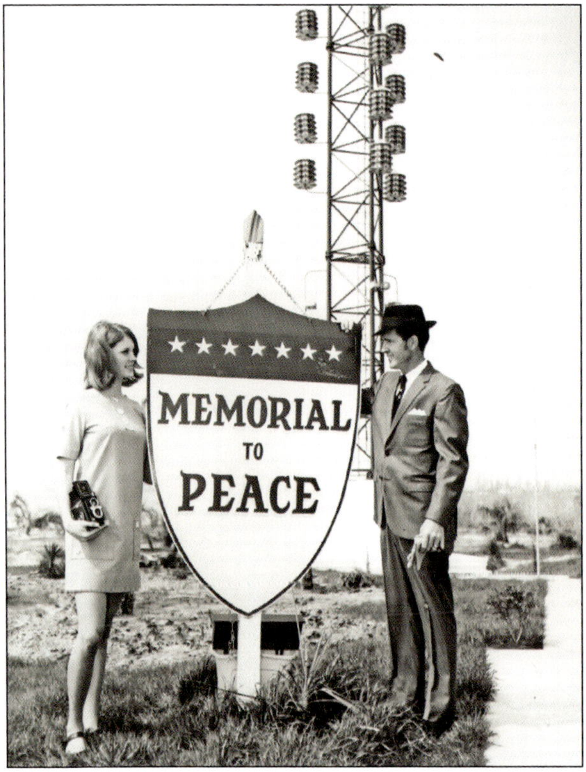

Dedicated on Veteran's Day in 1968, local businessman Gene Dolan worked with the Young Men's Business Club to bring the Memorial to Peace to the lakefront at the west end of Lawrence Street after the city obtained a permit from the State of Louisiana. The steel radar tower was brought from Chennault, and community members purchased 46 purple martin birdhouses to adorn the tower's rungs. The tower served to honor all Louisiana men and women who served or died in the Vietnam conflict. The area where the tower stood is now Veteran's Memorial Park, and the tower's original pedestal now holds a Vietnam-era Huey helicopter.

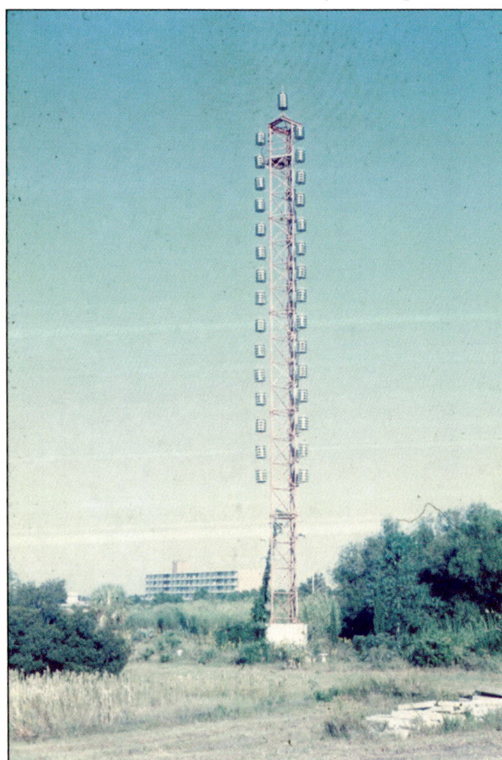

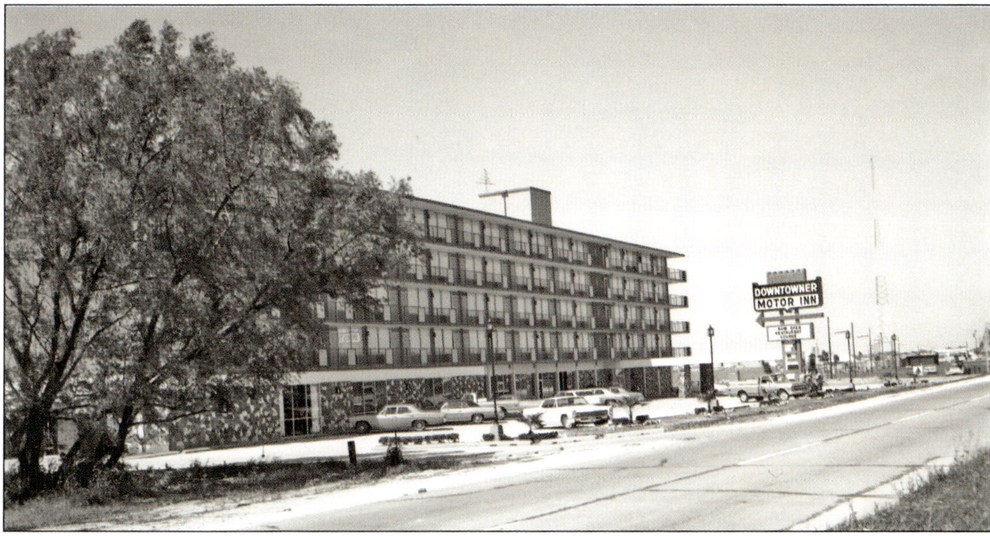

The Downtowner Motor Inn was a fixture on the north shore of Lake Charles from 1970 until it changed to Players Riverboat Casino Hotel in 1993. It featured expandable meeting rooms and the Tiffin Inn Restaurant and Lounge. The building was demolished in 1999 to make room for more casino parking.

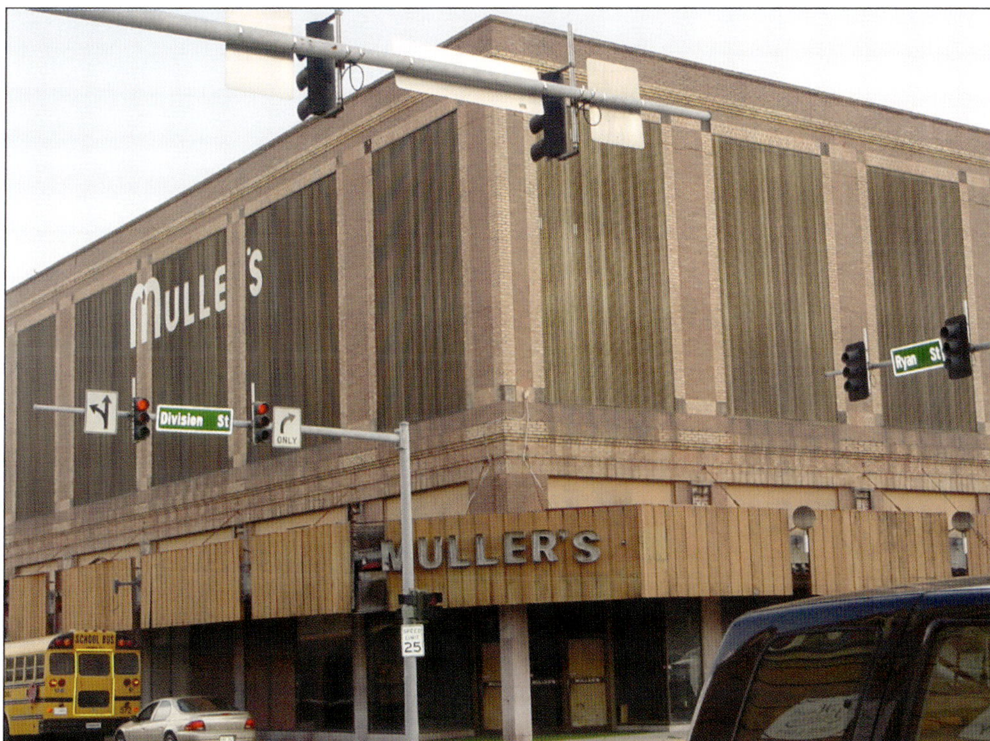

Julie Muller opened her downtown Lake Charles store in 1882, and she eventually grew her business to be the largest department store between Houston and New Orleans. This 2002 photograph depicts Muller's as it looked when it finally closed in 1985. The building reopened in 2007 as lofts, with the original "motor stairs" (escalator) still intact.

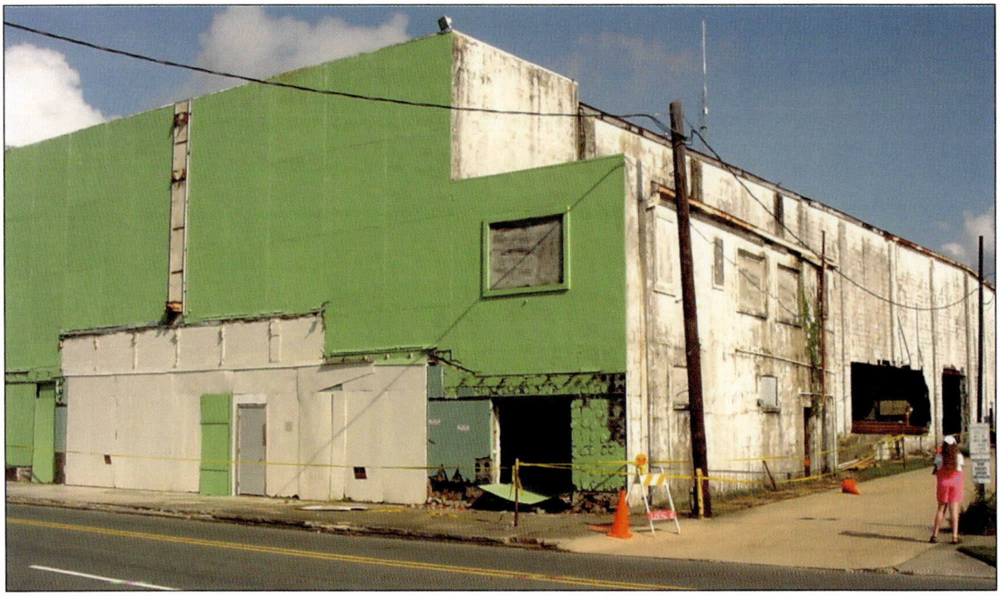

The Pitt Theater opened on Kirby Street in 1949, one of several downtown theaters that closed during the 1980s. The old single-screen movie houses could not compete with the multiscreen Charles Cinema located on Sale Street. The Pitt Theater was the last downtown theater to close its doors, and the building was demolished in 2004, two years after this photograph was taken.

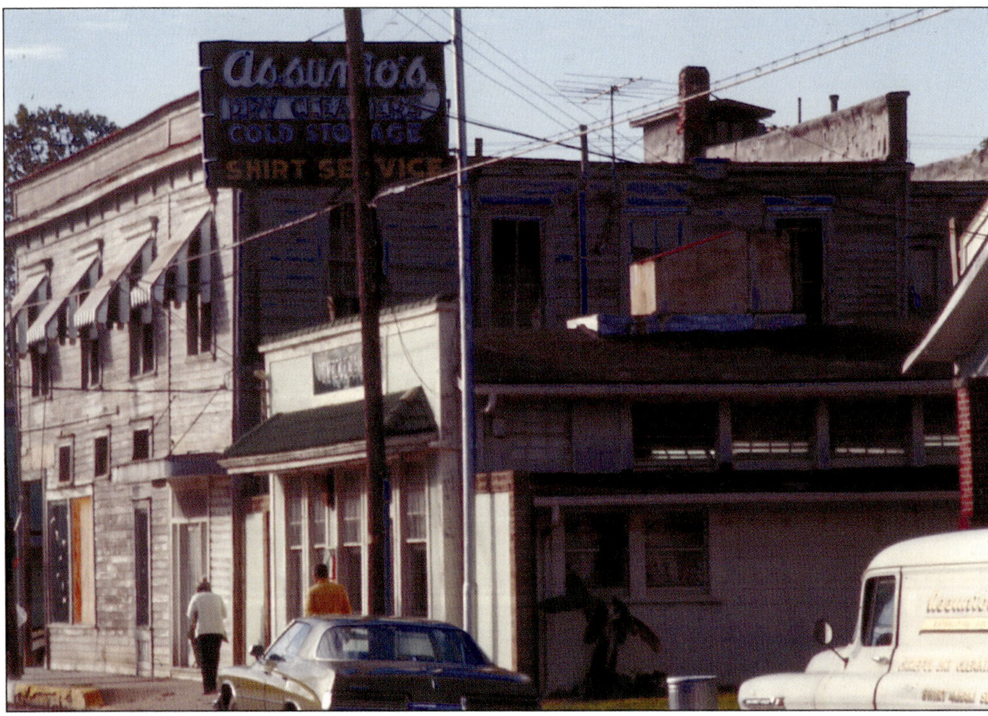

Assunto's Cleaners was owned and operated for decades by Jacinto Jay Assunto Sr. The Assuntos were an Italian family of merchants who arrived in Lake Charles in the early 20th century and were members of the Italo-American Progressive and Protective Club. This 1973 photograph of the intersection Lawrence and Ryan Streets shows buildings that were demolished in 1984.

During the 1970s, several blocks of downtown Lake Charles were renovated into a pedestrian mall. Streets were rerouted and blocked to create a safe walking area for shopping and recreation. Like similar projects in downtown areas across America that were created to address the flight of retail shopping to suburbs and shopping malls, this led to the eventual decay of the traditional city core.

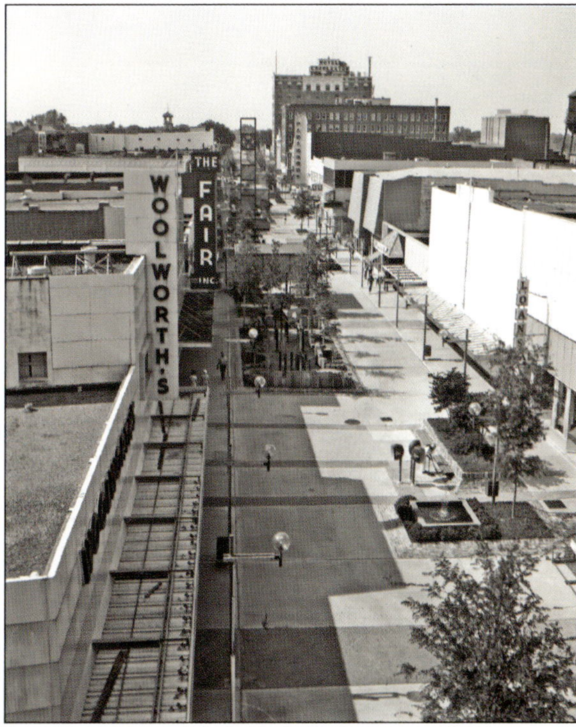

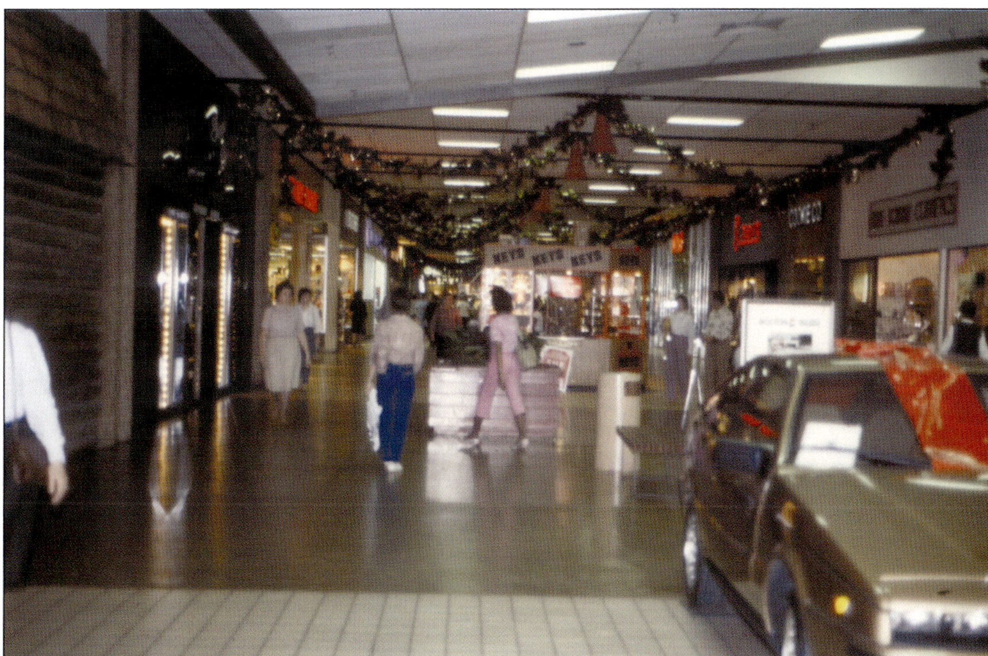

Prien Lake Mall opened in February 1972 with 18 stores, and the modern building boasted almost half a million square feet. The grand opening provided visitors with a shopping tour of the mall and a prize giveaway that included a 1972 automobile. Many Lake Charles retailers either opened branches in Prien Lake Mall or moved their operations entirely, leaving their previous downtown locations vacant.

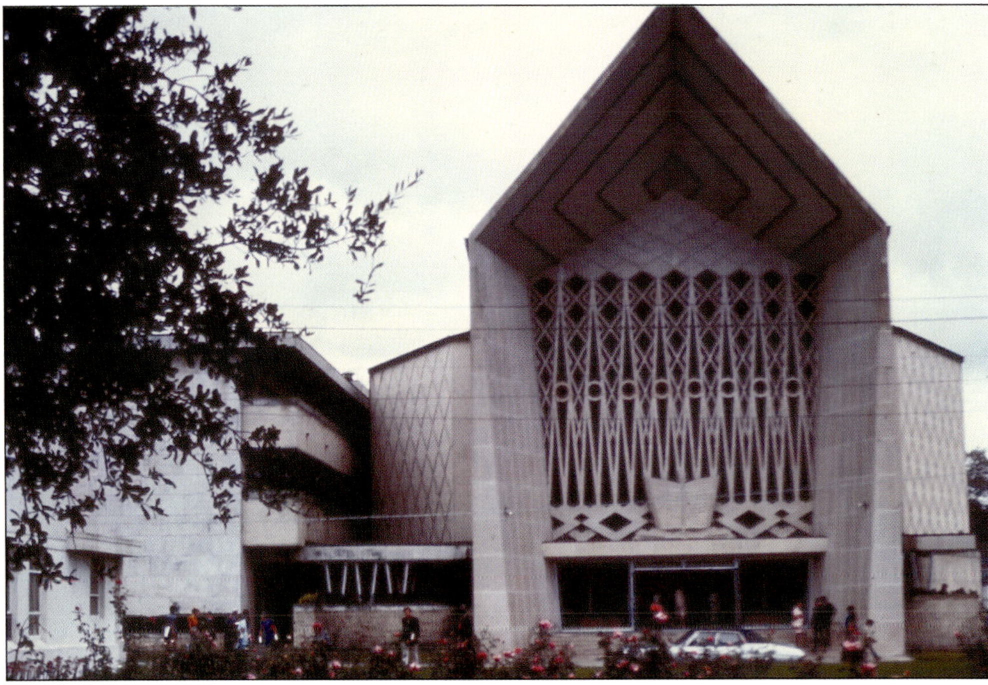

First Baptist Church formed in Lake Charles in 1880 with 18 charter members. The church grew steadily as Lake Charles grew, and it underwent several phases of construction. A 1957 formal dedication celebrated the church's new educational building and new sanctuary, both pictured here. Improvements in later years included a nursery education center in 1963 and family ministry center in 1997.

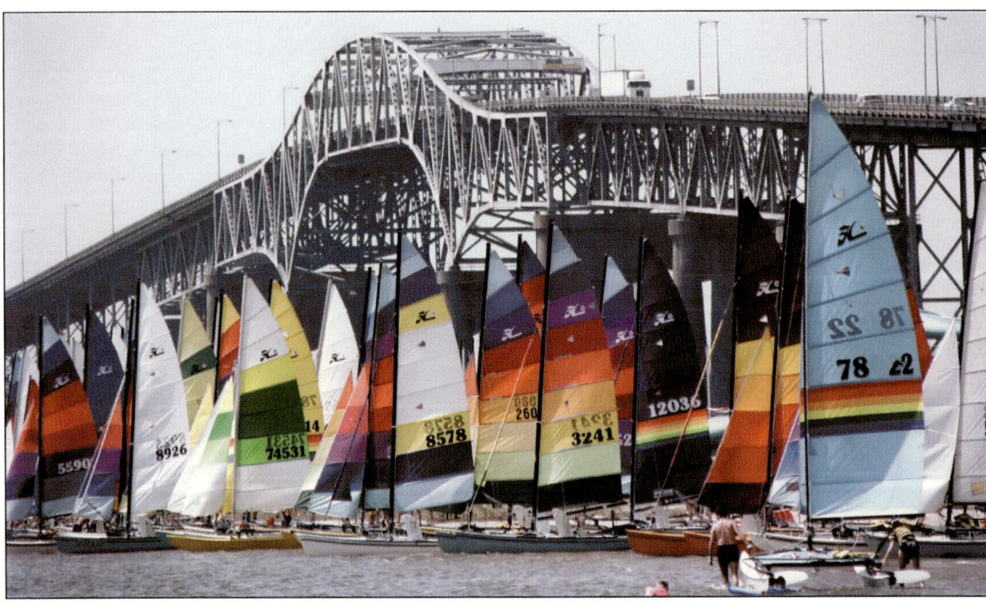

Construction on the Calcasieu River Bridge was completed in 1952. The bridge features wrought-iron crossed pistols, some of which have disappeared over the years. Before the construction of the bridge, drivers crossed the Calcasieu on a drawbridge between the current sites of the Bridge Point Yacht Club and the Port of Lake Charles. (Courtesy of www.monsoursphotography.net)

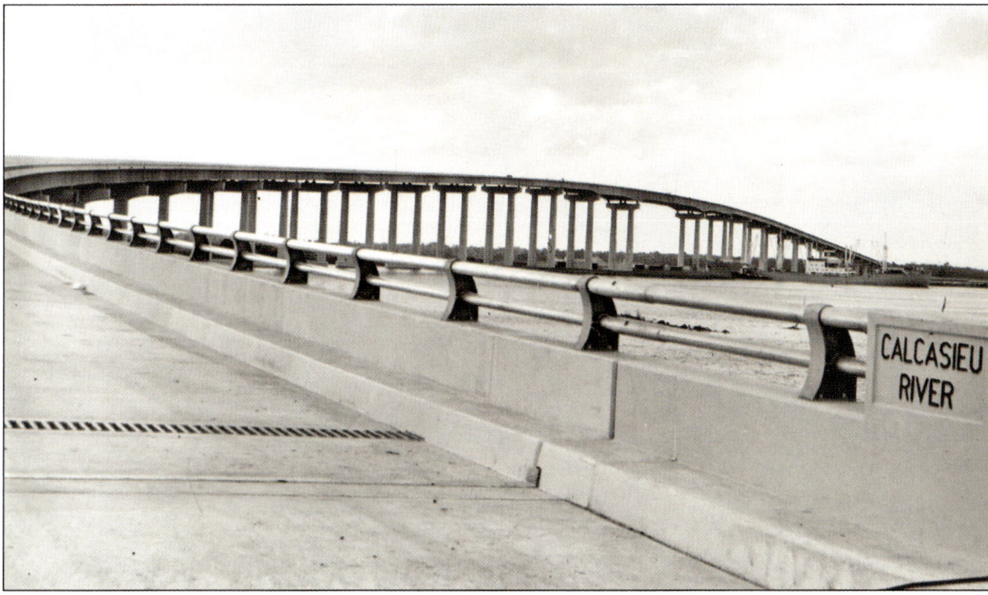

Israel LaFleur was a Lake Charles resident and Sulphur merchant who advocated for a new Calcasieu River Bridge to be constructed south of Lake Charles, arguing that the new bridge would open up new industrial possibilities south of the city. Construction was complete in 1964, and the bridge was dedicated to and named for LaFleur.

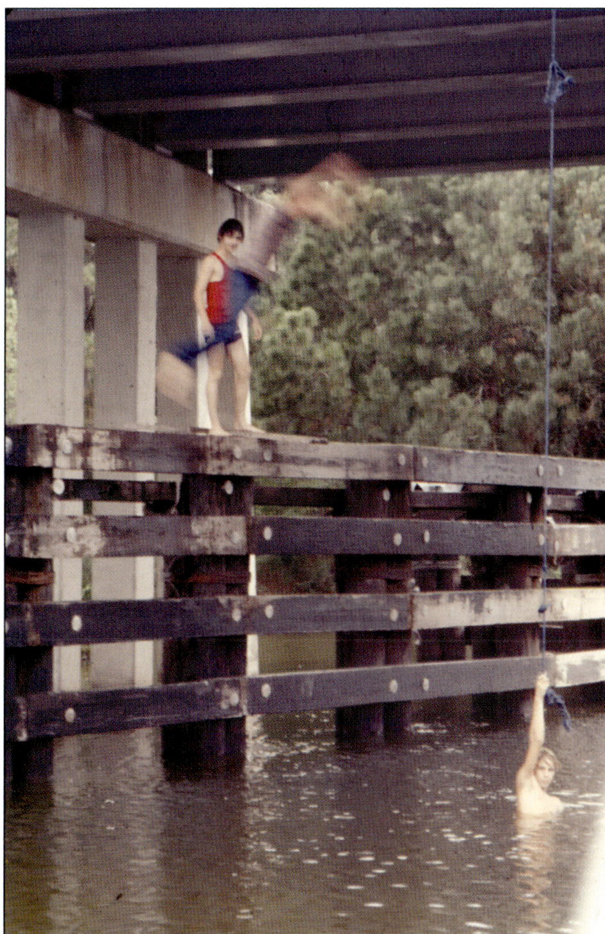

This 1983 photograph shows some swimmers in Contraband Bayou under the Prien Lake Road bridge. Construction on the steel structure began in 1960, about 40 feet south of the previous bridge over the bayou. Because Contraband Bayou is a popular waterway through the city, it was built tall enough for most pleasure boats to pass under.

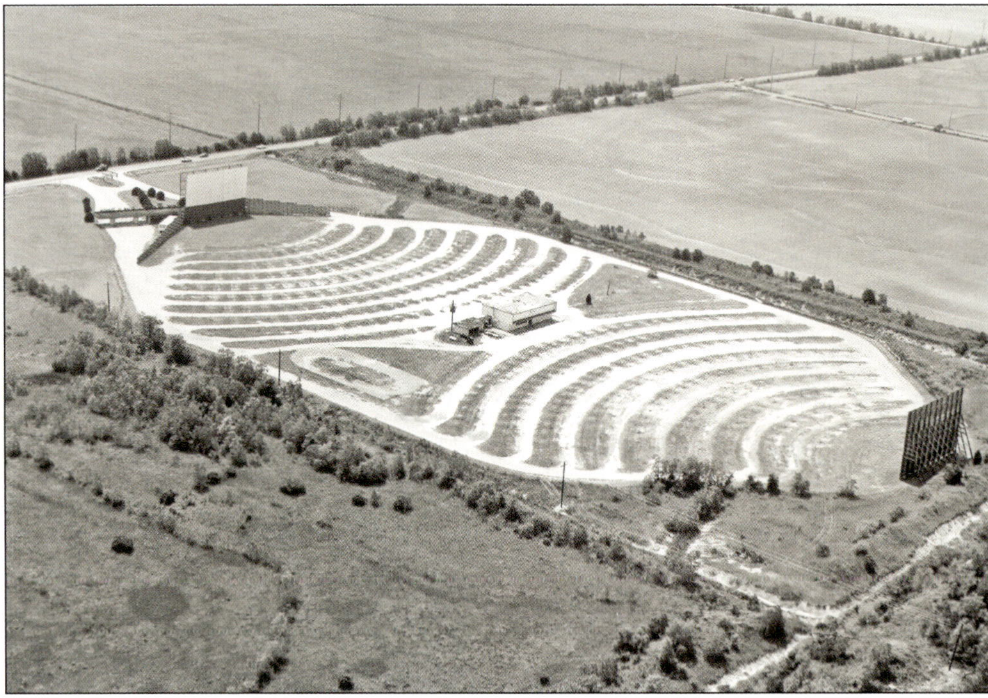

The New Moon Drive-In opened in 1954 on Highway 14, and it grew to include twin screens, capacity for 1,000 cars, an air-conditioned auditorium with 400 seats, an outdoor patio with 150 seats, concession stands, and a children's playground. It was the last of three Lake Charles drive-in theaters to close.

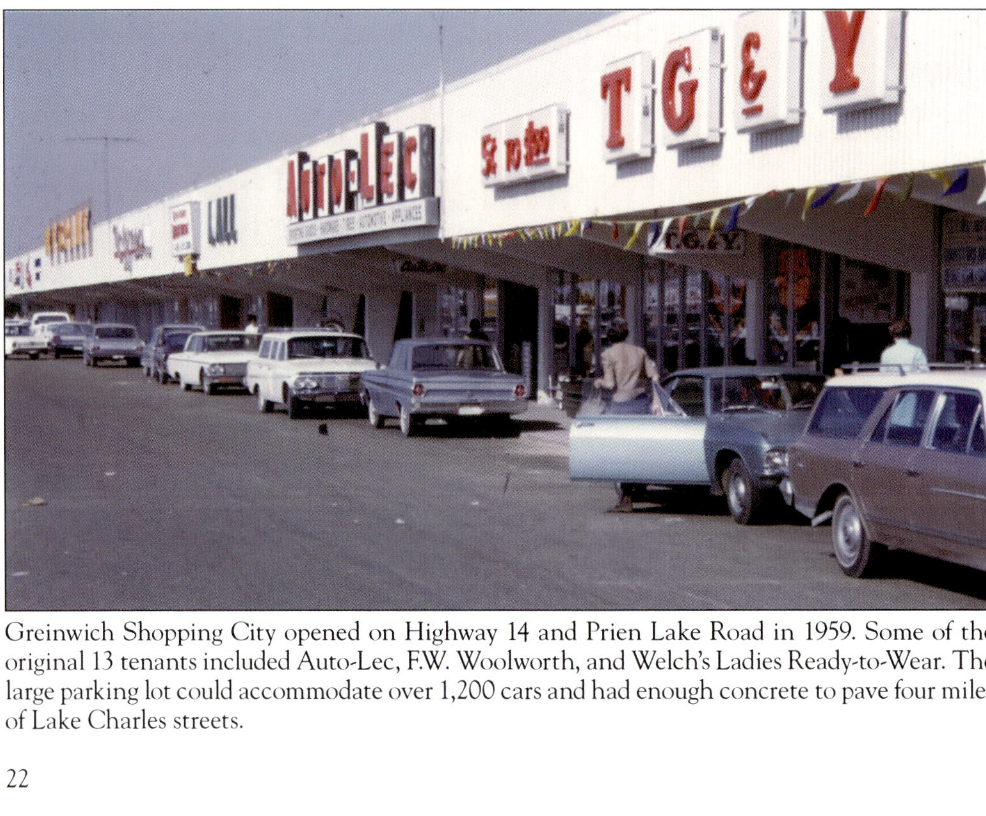

Greinwich Shopping City opened on Highway 14 and Prien Lake Road in 1959. Some of the original 13 tenants included Auto-Lec, F.W. Woolworth, and Welch's Ladies Ready-to-Wear. The large parking lot could accommodate over 1,200 cars and had enough concrete to pave four miles of Lake Charles streets.

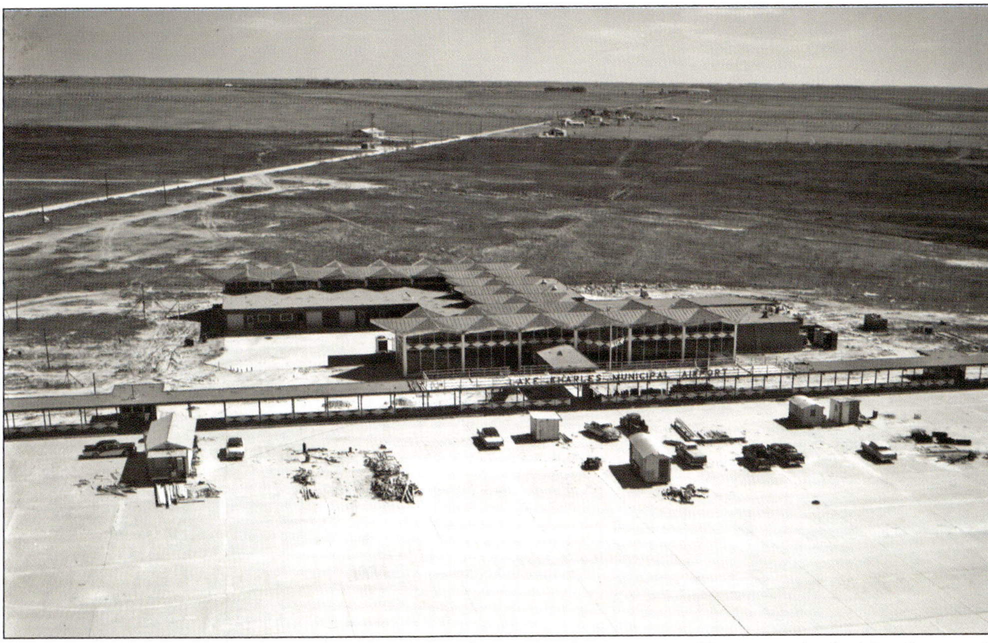

Construction on the Lake Charles Municipal Airport began in 1958 two and a half miles south of McNeese along Gulf Highway. Flights operated by Eastern Airlines began in December 1961. The March 1962 dedication included performances by the Blue Angels, the Fort Polk Parachute Team, and the McNeese State College Band. The airport's main terminal, pictured here, was destroyed during Hurricane Rita in 2005 along with some hangars and other airport facilities. After obtaining grant money from FEMA and other agencies, the new facility opened in 2009. United Airlines and American Airlines currently provide flights from Lake Charles to Houston and Dallas.

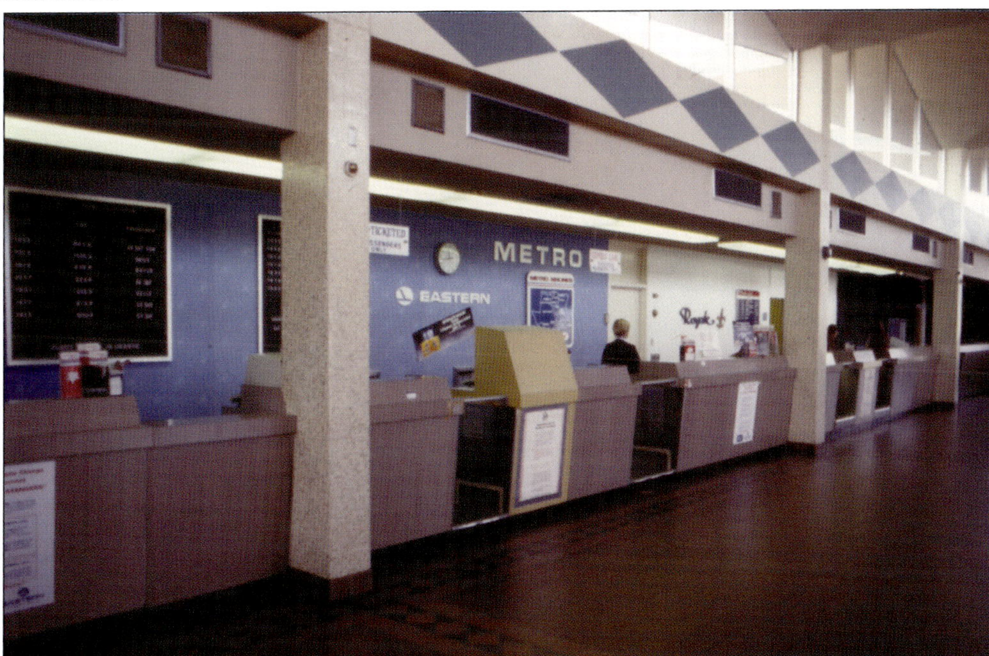

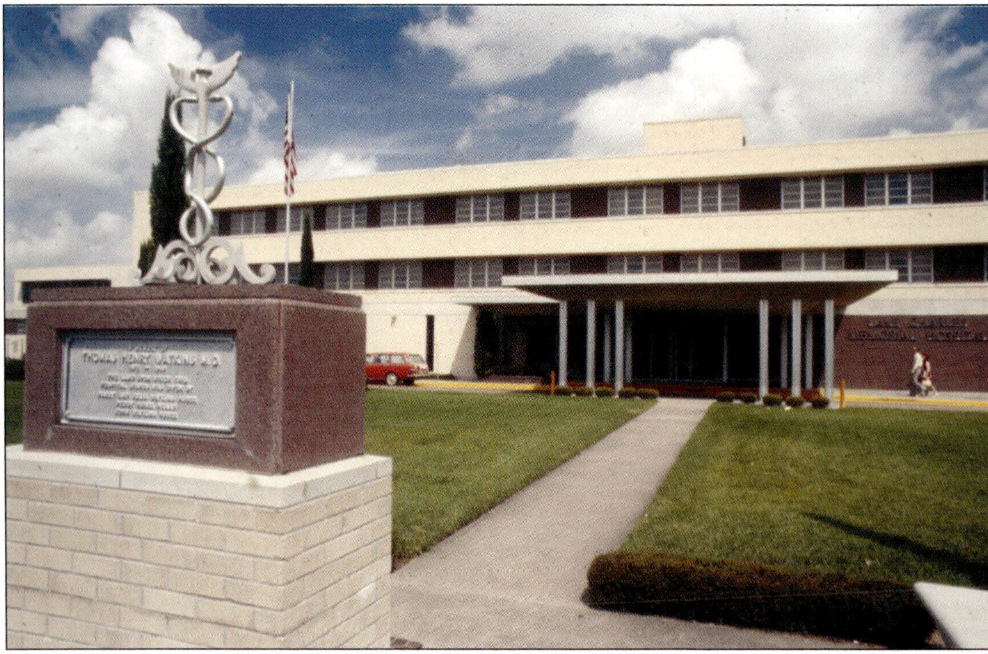

Lake Charles Memorial Hospital opened in 1952 on Oak Park Boulevard. Designed by local architects Dunn and Quinn, much of the funding was raised by the citizens of Lake Charles. A wing was added in 1958 to increase general patient and maternity rooms. A 1970 expansion included a larger emergency room, a new laboratory, and an intensive care unit.

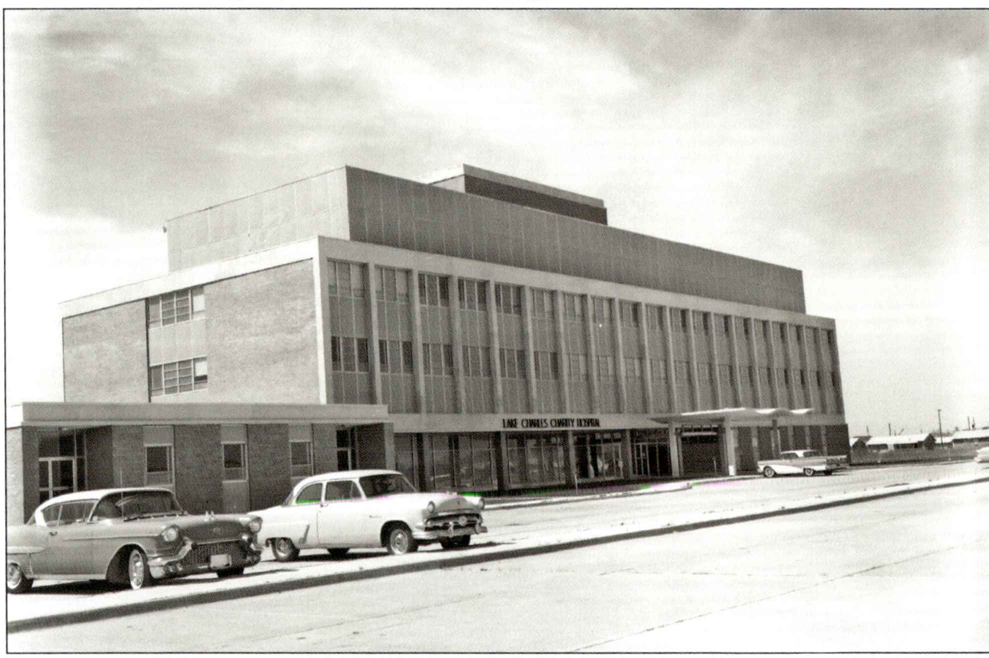

After heated debates over the hospital's location, construction on Lake Charles Charity Hospital began in June 1958. The Dunn and Quinn architectural firm designed the 164-bed building, which was rededicated as Olin Walter Moss Regional Hospital in 1979 as a tribute to the former chief of surgery at Lake Charles Charity Hospital.

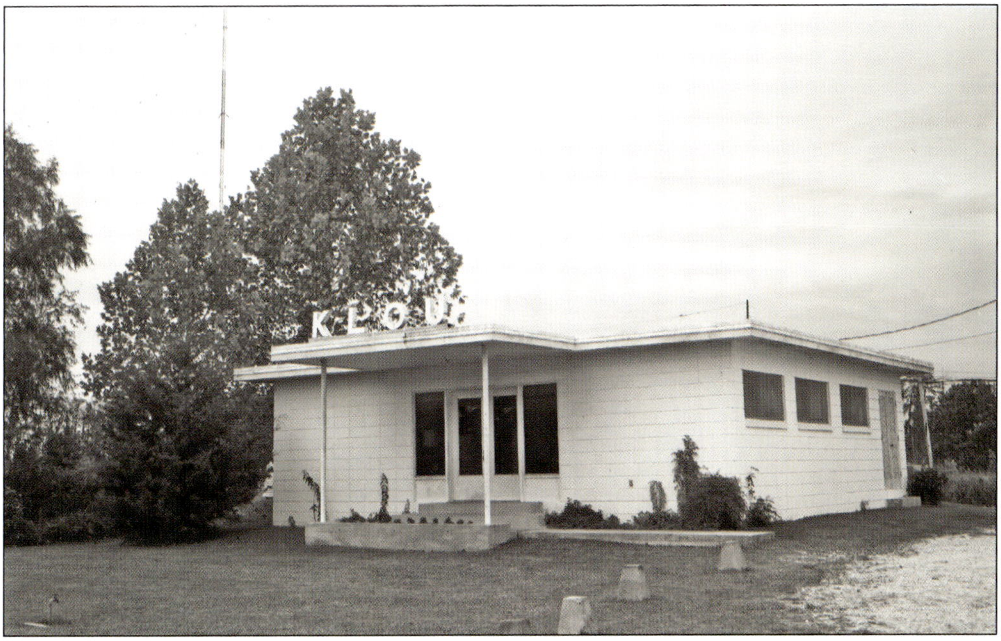

KLOU opened in 1947 on AM 1580. Its studio was in downtown Lake Charles, and its transmitter was on Harless Street. Pictured here is the Harless Street site, which housed operations after 1955. Albert and Dixie Johnson purchased KLOU in 1960 and adopted a Top 40 format. Johnny Janot, Rob Robin, and Ron Riley were KLOU personalities during the station's heyday.

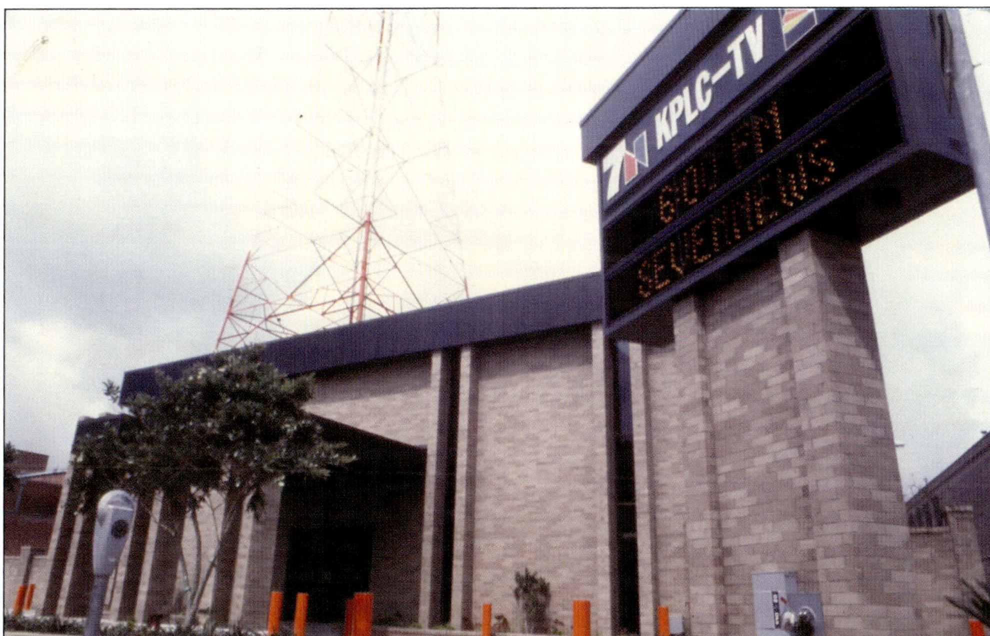

KPLC began as a radio station in 1935 and became an affiliate of the National Broadcast Corporation in 1944. In 1954, the station launched its television broadcast and moved into its current location at 320 Division Street. The station's original tower was 500 feet tall with a 74-foot antenna, which was replaced with a 1,500-foot tower in 1970.

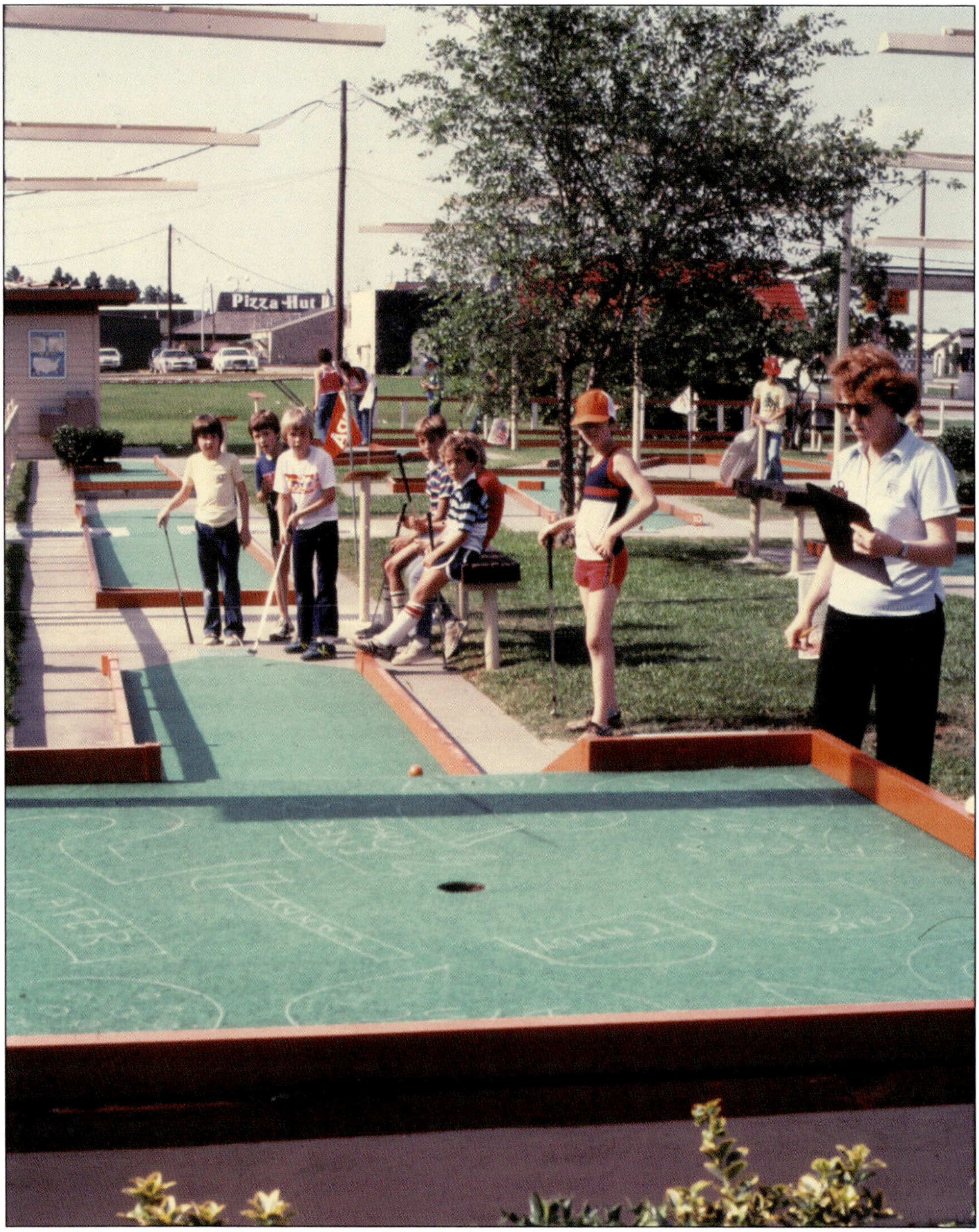

Al Kurtz opened Putt Putt Golf Course in 1958 at Oak Park Boulevard and Highway 14, near the Greinwich Bowling Center, which later became Bowlarama. Two years later, Kurtz sold his business to Al Simpson, an accomplished professional putter who was admitted into the Pro Putters Association Hall of Fame in 1998. The facility, pictured here, had two 18-hole miniature golf courses, and it regularly hosted tournaments where competitors could win hundreds of dollars. The business hosted several annual beauty pageants for Miss Putt Putt during the 1960s. The winner of the final pageant in 1967 was Nancy Ray, the baton twirler for the McNeese Cowboy Band. In 1996, Simpson passed the business to his son, Greg Simpson, who closed the Highway 14 location in 1998 and reopened at 620 Petro Point Drive in 2000. The updated facility features batting cages and a clubhouse for hosting parties.

Two

COMMERCE

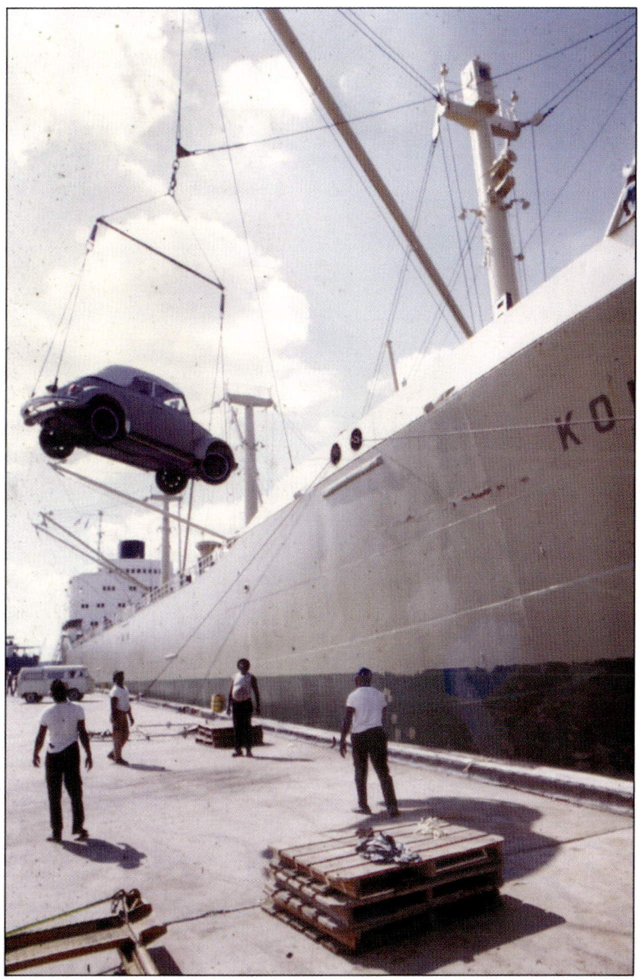

In the 1960s, the Port of Lake Charles had a storage lot for imported Volkswagens, and this photograph shows the first Volkswagen being lowered to the dock. The Port of Lake Charles opened in 1926, and the Calcasieu River Deep Waterway Project was completed in 1941. The port provides quick access to the Gulf of Mexico and railways leading to the nation's interior.

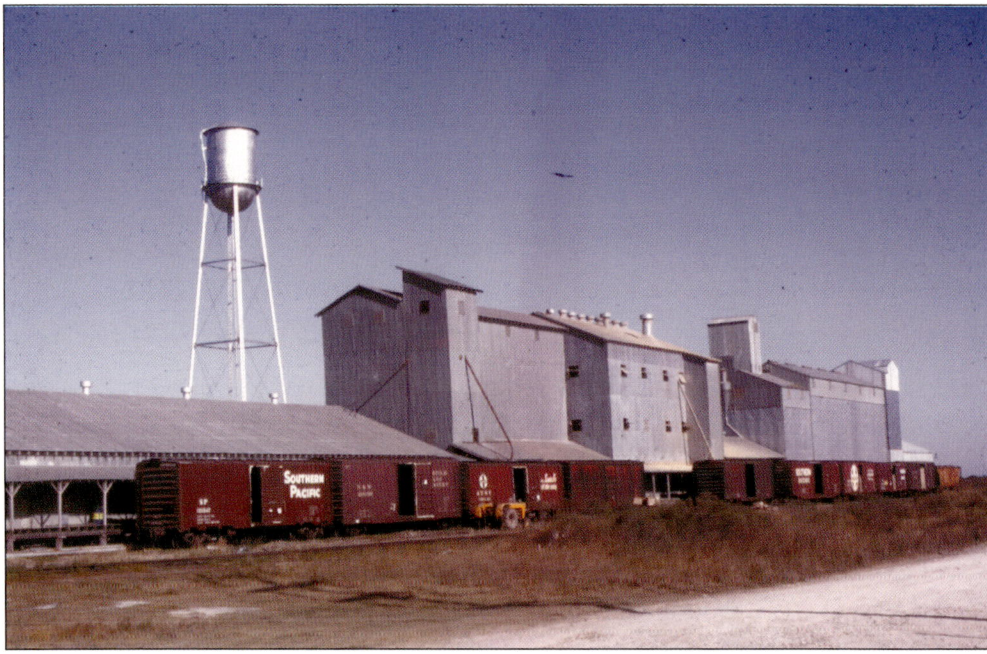

The rice industry has fueled the economy of Southwest Louisiana since the early 20th century. This 1964 photograph shows the Farmers Rice Milling Company, which opened in 1917. Now one of the largest mills in the world, it can process over 800 million pounds of rice per year.

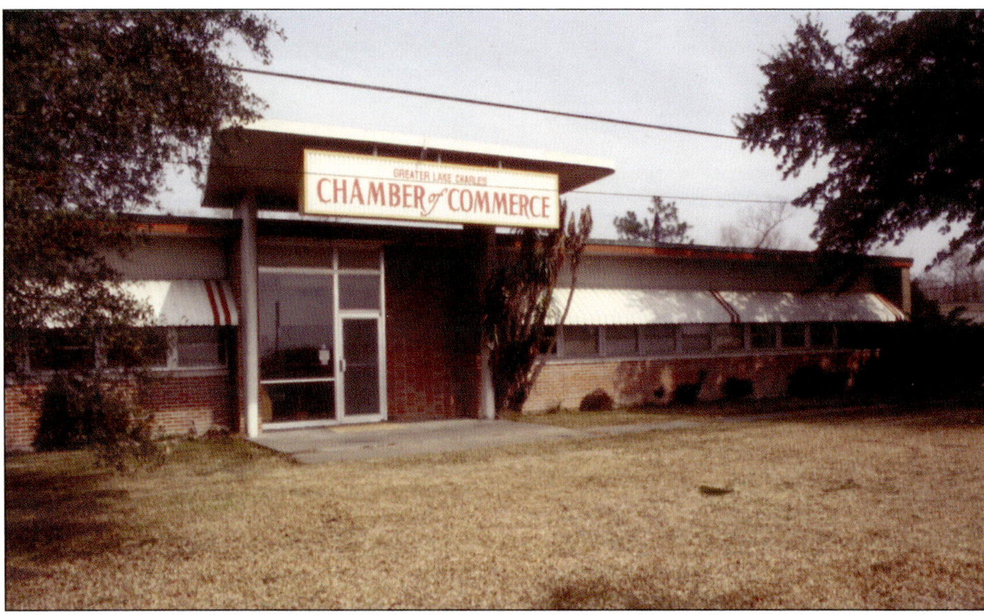

The offices of the Greater Lake Charles Chamber of Commerce were located at 900 North Lakeshore Drive in this 1983 photograph. The organization changed its name in 1984 to Chamber SWLA to more accurately identify its role in leading the commercial development of all of Southwest Louisiana. Chamber SWLA is now a part of the SWLA Economic Alliance whose offices are currently in the Southwest Louisiana Entrepreneurial and Economic Development (SEED) Center.

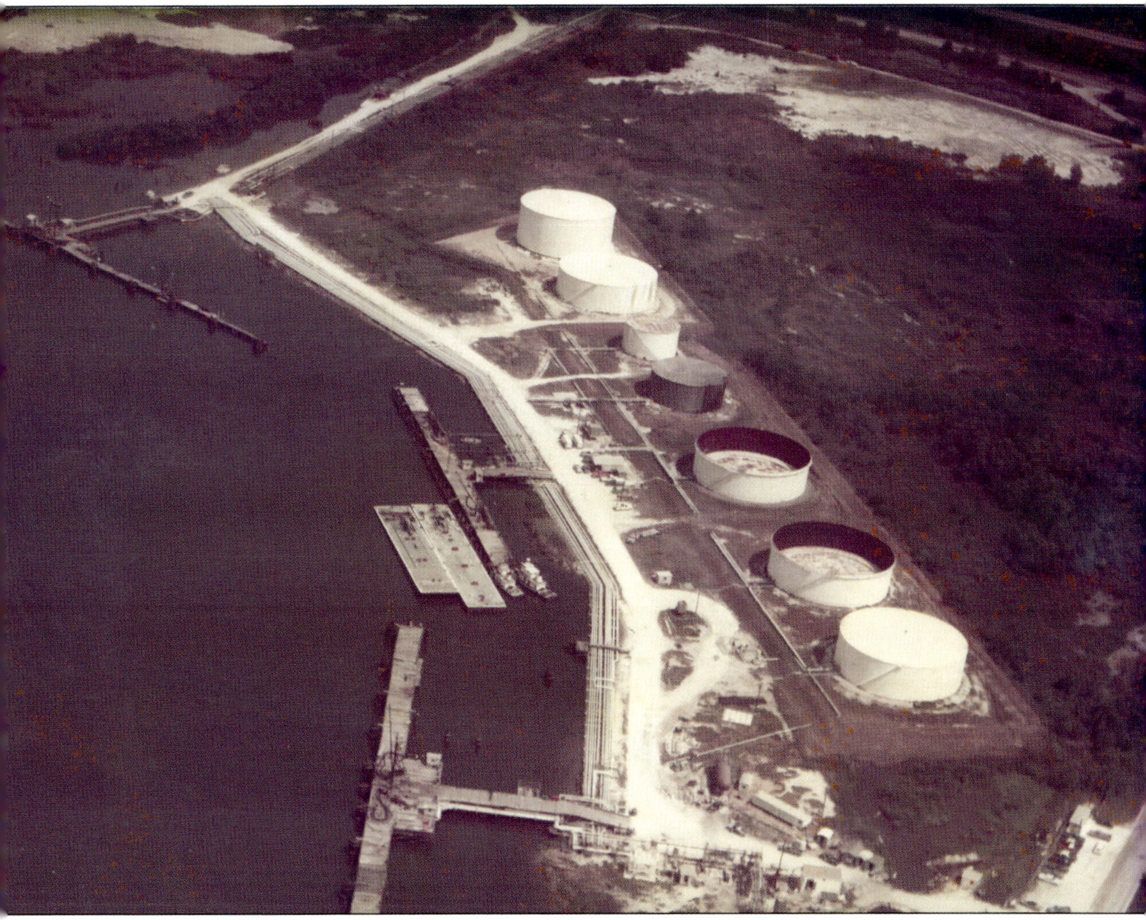

This photograph of the Conoco plant on the west bank of the Calcasieu River was taken in 1972. Built in 1941, it was the first of several petroleum products manufacturers in Calcasieu Parish. Renamed the Phillips 66 Lake Charles Refinery in 2012, the facility can process up to 239,000 barrels of crude oil daily. The city has a long history of petroleum and chemical manufacturing. Mathieson Alkali Works opened in 1933 and is considered to be the father of the local chemical industry. The petrochemical industry in Calcasieu Parish, much of which is located along the Calcasieu River near Lake Charles, employs thousands of workers and is considered to be one of the major centers of industry on the Gulf Coast. Other area petrochemical plants include Axiall, Citgo, PPG, and Sasol. (Courtesy of Lyn and Glenn Comeaux.)

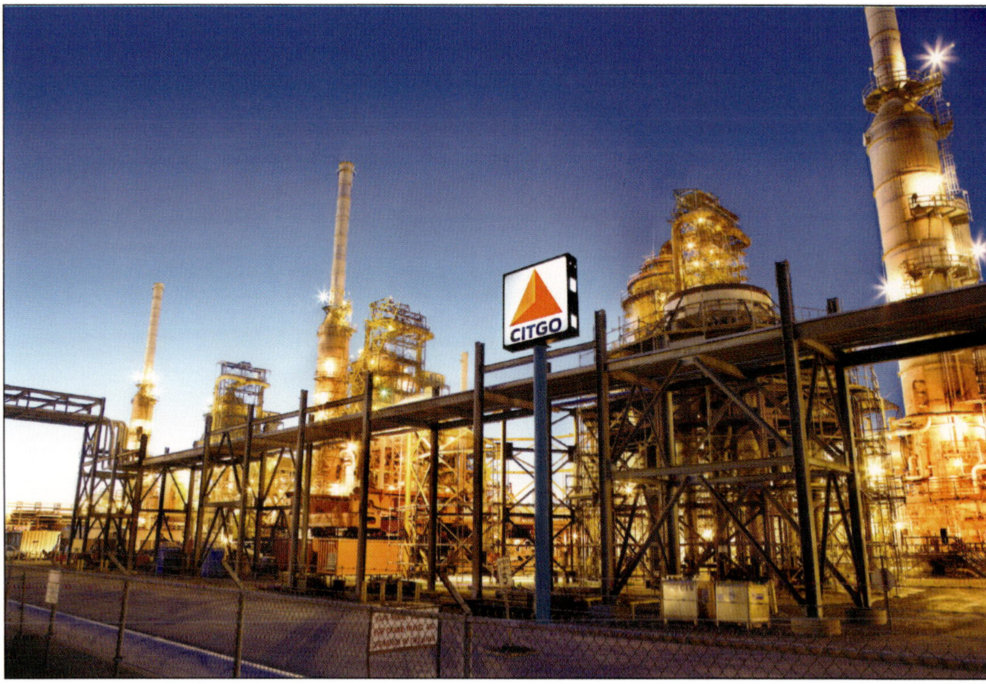

Citgo's Lake Charles Manufacturing Complex is the sixth-largest refining facility in the United States. The complex produces a variety of fuels and chemicals used in aviation, agriculture, and industry, as well as gasoline and propane for retail consumption. Located on the Calcasieu Ship Channel, Citgo employs over a 1,000 people in Southwest Louisiana. (Courtesy of Citgo.)

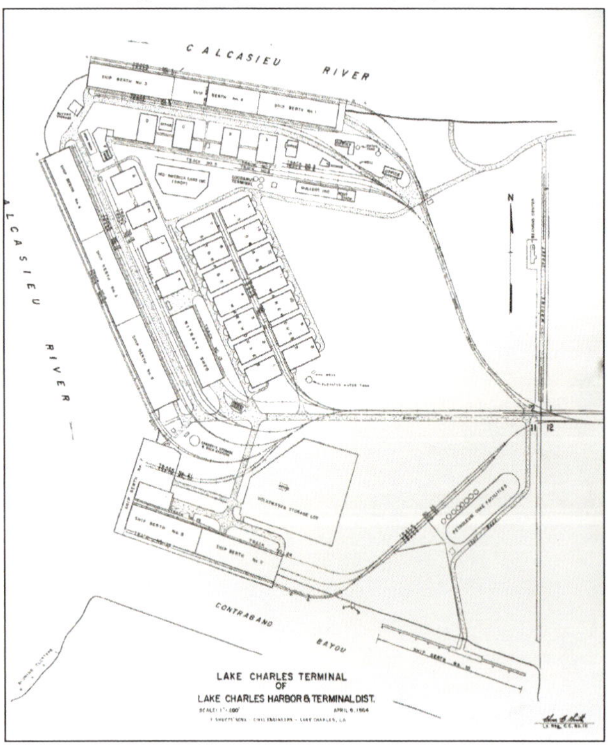

The Lake Charles Harbor and Terminal District was authorized by the Louisiana Legislature in 1924. The port operates two marine terminals and two industrial parks and manages the Calcasieu Ship Channel. The Port of Lake Charles is the 13th-busiest seaport in the United States and a fundamental part of the Southwest Louisiana economy.

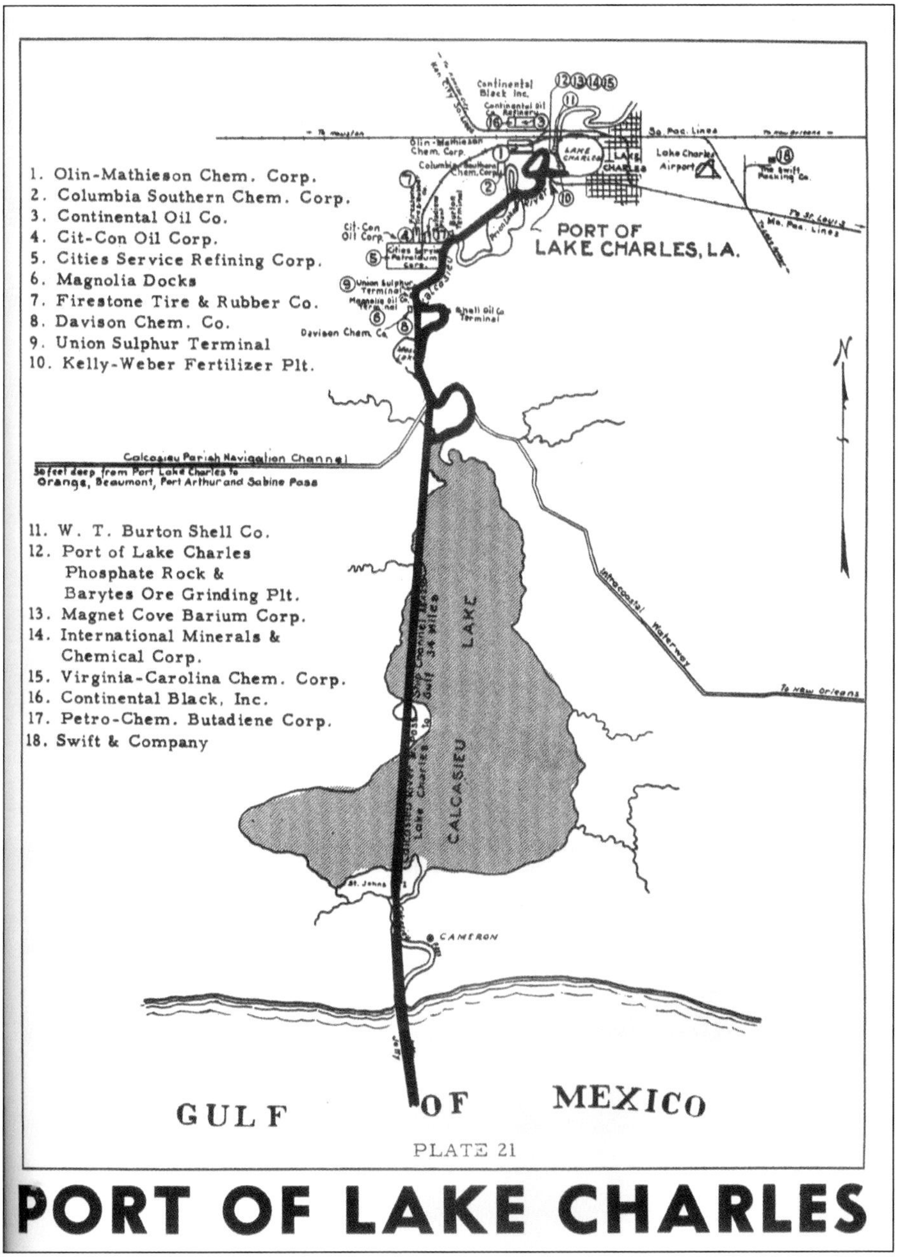

This 1955 map of the Calcasieu Ship Channel shows the 34-mile path of natural and manmade waterways leading from Lake Charles to the Gulf of Mexico. In 1922, parish voters approved a bond issue for the creation of a deepwater ship channel. Lake Charles and the Calcasieu River were dredged and widened southward to the Intracoastal Canal, where boats could navigate to the Sabine River and then to the Gulf. The route was a circuitous 75 miles. Pres. Franklin D. Roosevelt signed the Omnibus Rivers and Harbors Bill in 1938, which provided funds for the dredging of a straight channel to the Gulf of Mexico from Lake Charles. The original channel was 33 feet deep, and its bottom was 250 feet wide. The channel has been widened and re-dredged several times over the years, and it is now 40 feet deep and 400 feet wide. The Calcasieu Ship Channel is crucial to Southwest Louisiana's huge industrial complex.

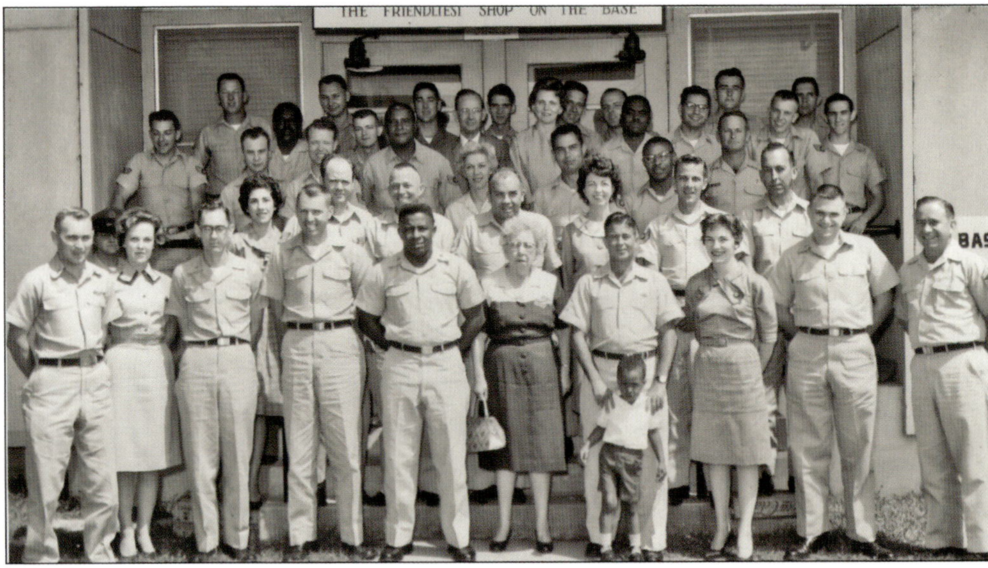

In 1951, the Lake Charles Air Force Base was part of the Strategic Air Command during the Cold War. It was renamed Chennault Air Force Base in 1958, not long before the Air Force modernized its fleet and began phasing out operations at Chennault. Soon after this photograph of these Chennault employees was taken, the base closed permanently in 1963.

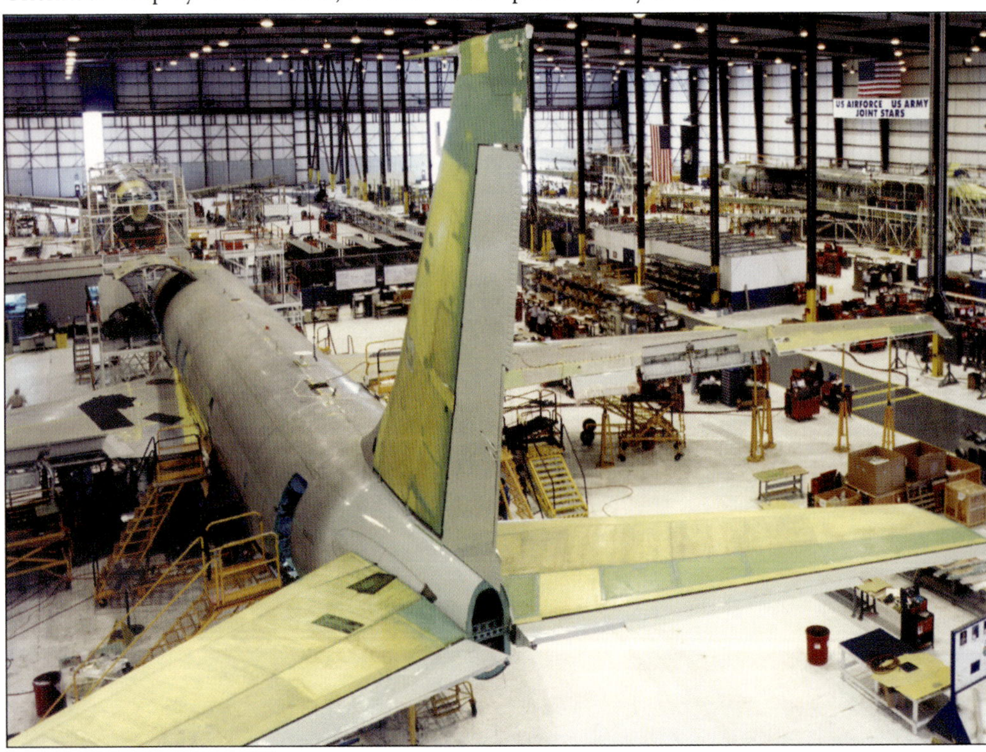

In 1991, Grumman Corporation opened operations at the Chennault Airport as a base to manufacture J-STARS or Joint Surveillance Target Attack Radar System airplanes. Now called the Northrop Grumman Maintenance and Modification Center, it maintains, modifies, and upgrades J-STARS airplanes as well as KC-10 Extenders, which are used for aerial refueling.

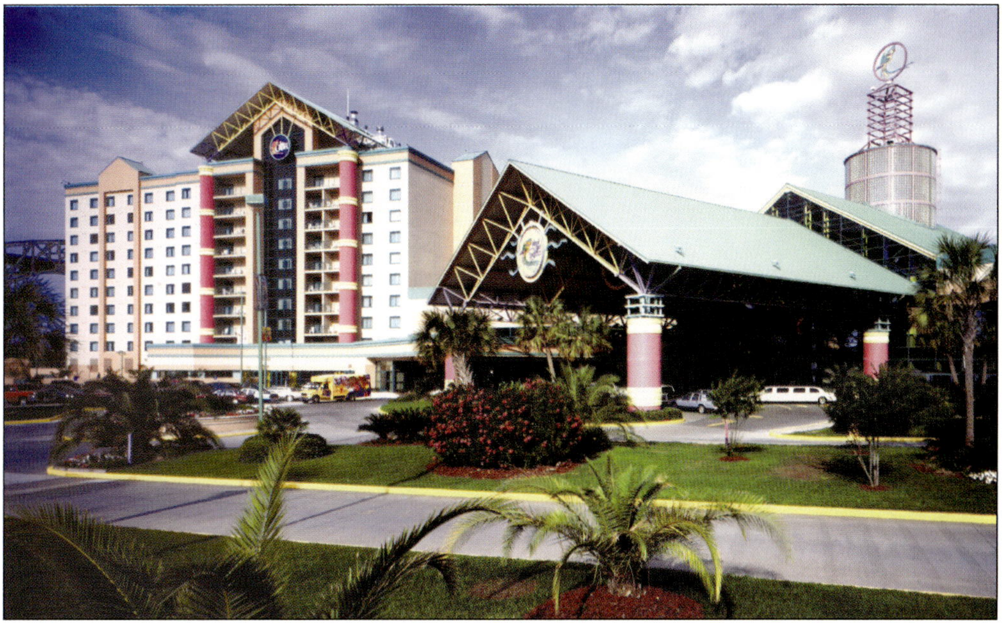

In 1995, the Isle of Capri Casino on Lake Charles opened across the Calcasieu River in Westlake. The Crown Riverboat was the area's third riverboat casino after Players Riverboat Casino and Star Casino, and a year later, the Isle of Capri added the Grand Palais Riverboat. (Courtesy of www.visitlakecharles.org.)

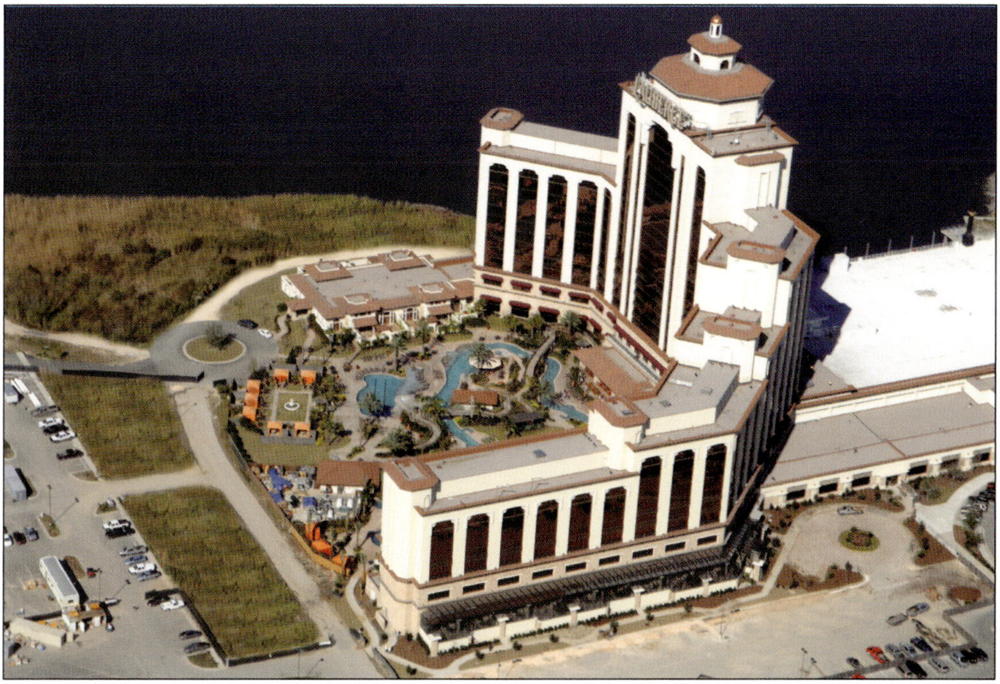

L'Auberge du Lac Casino and Resort opened in May 2005, shortly before Hurricane Rita caused some damage to the facility and destroyed the nearby Harrah's Casino. The resort includes a spa, a swimming pool with a lazy river, several upscale restaurants and retail stores, and over 1,000 rooms.

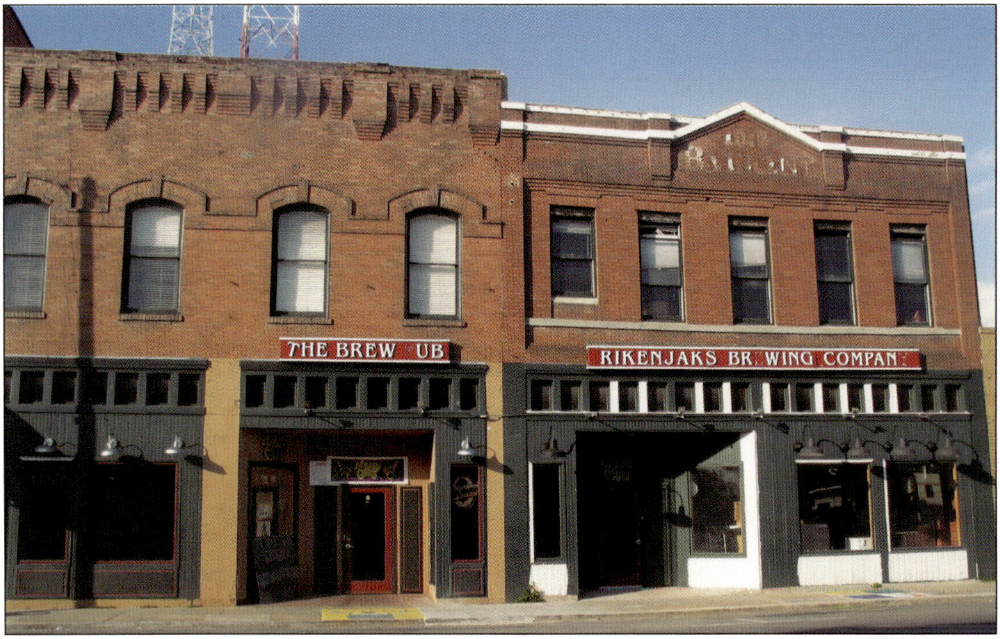

Rikenjaks Brewing Company moved its operations from Jackson, Louisiana, to downtown Lake Charles on Broad Street in 1998. The original owners were McNeese State University alumni Steve Cannon and Pat Stutes, and their famous brews included Old Hard Head, Lafitte Wheat, and Contraband Brown Ale. The business changed ownership several times before closing permanently in 2008.

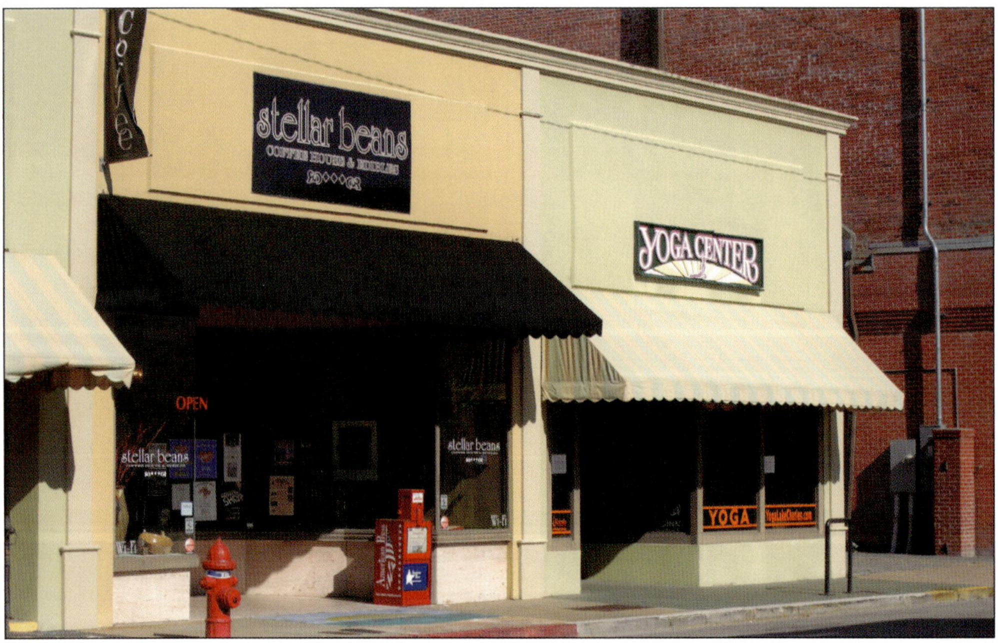

The Yoga Center of Lake Charles opened in 1998 and Stellar Beans in 2009. These locally owned and operated businesses on Broad Street represent the grassroots revitalization of the older downtown areas of Lake Charles. These businesses often participate in downtown events and festivals. (Courtesy of www.visitlakecharles.org.)

Three

City Leadership

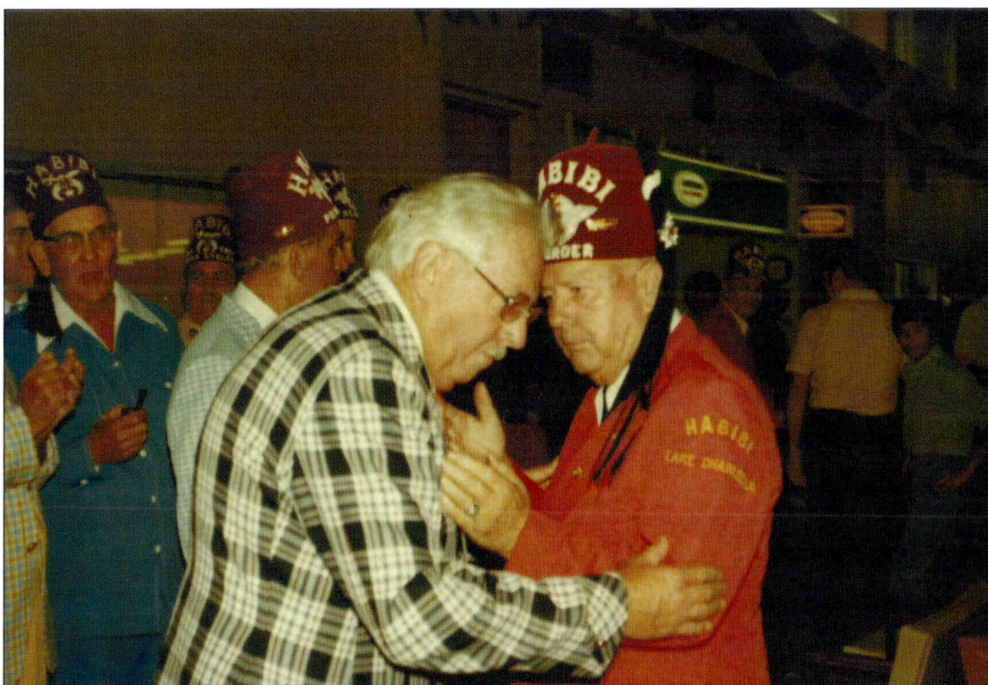

Voris King was a leader in the Lake Charles civic and business communities during the mid-20th century. King was a 33rd-degree Scottish Rite Mason, as well a member of the Elks Lodge, the Coastal Club, the Rotary Club, and many other local organizations. He received many honors, including the title of honorary Louisiana state senator.

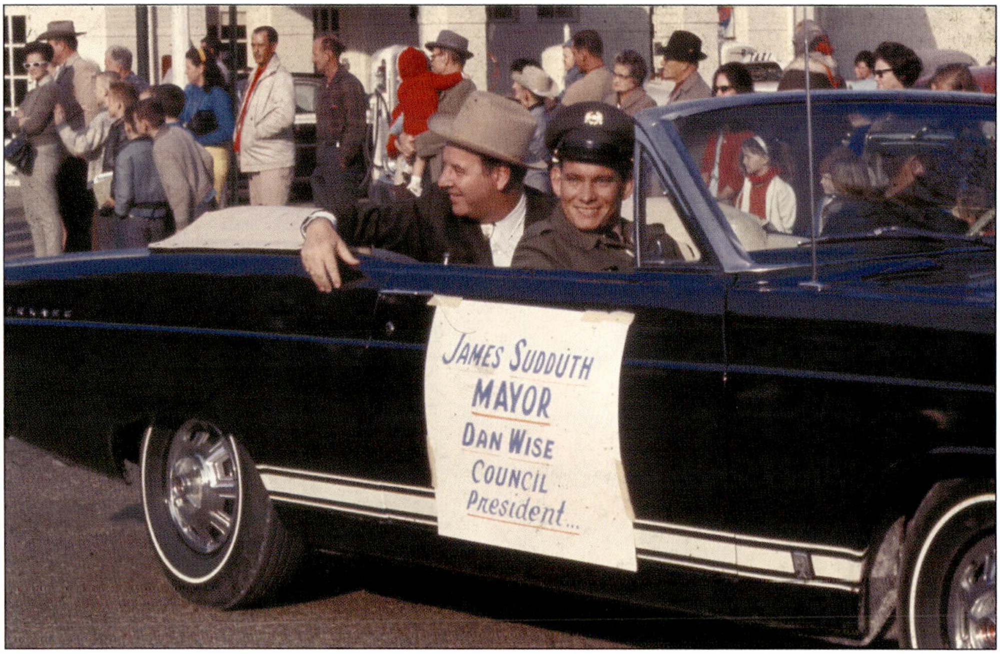

Lake Charles mayor James E. Sudduth (back seat) served from 1965 to 1973 and 1989 to 1993. Besides mayor, Sudduth was also city finance director and director of the Port of Lake Charles during his 40-year public service career. The Lake Charles Civic Center was one of his projects, and the Sudduth Coliseum inside is named for him.

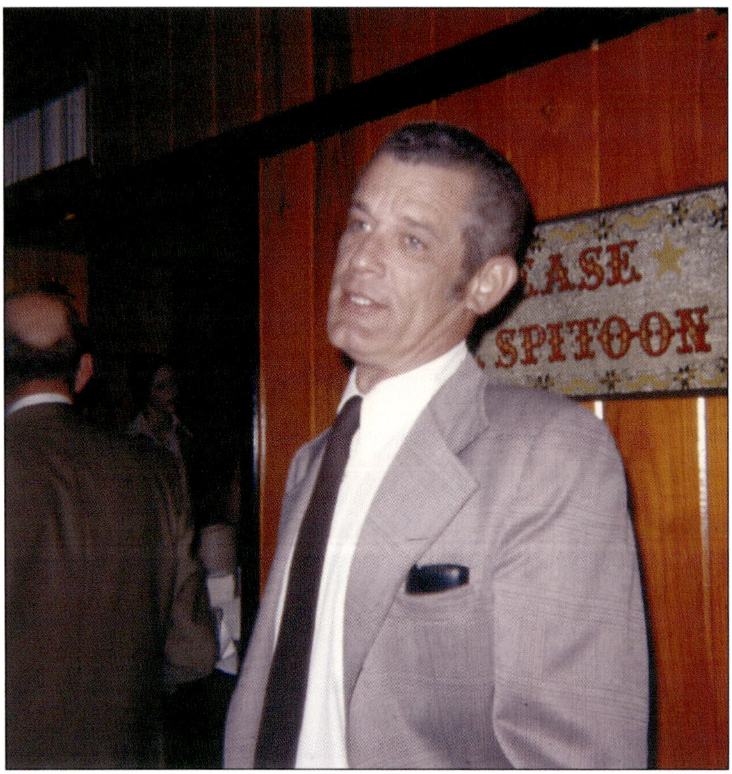

This 1973 photograph shows Mayor William "Bill" Boyer, the mayor of Lake Charles from 1974 to 1981. In 1977, under his leadership, the city paid $1.25 million for the Pioneer Building as a new location for city hall. Boyer later became executive director of the Lake Charles Housing Authority, and he oversaw the several housing developments for elderly residents, including Chateau du Lac.

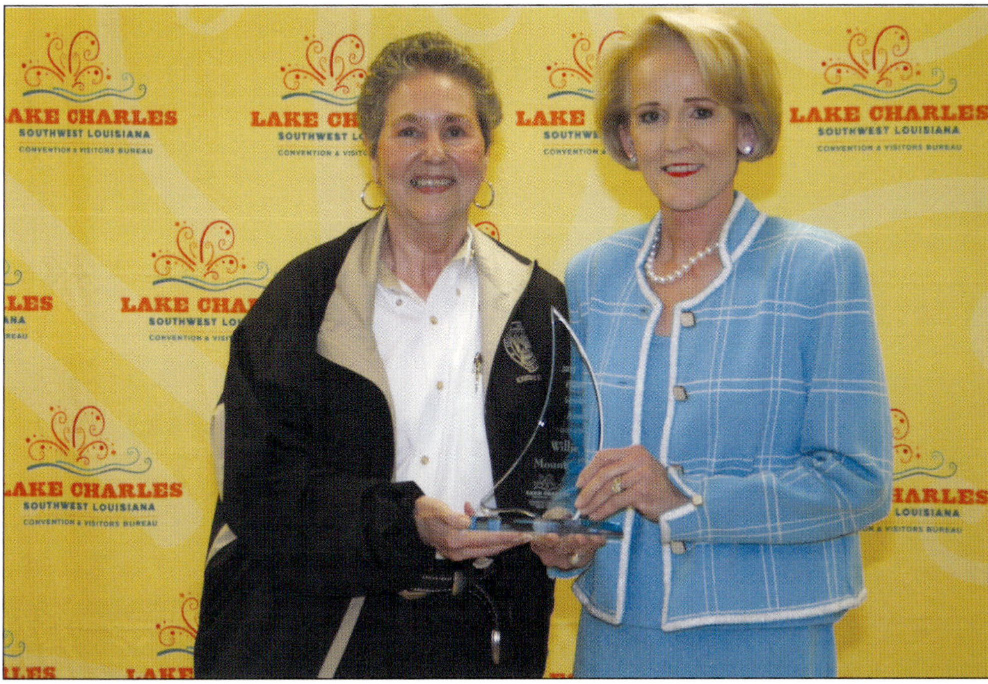

Willie Landry Mount, right, served as the mayor of Lake Charles from 1993 until 1999, when she resigned to serve in the Louisiana Senate for the next 12 years. She was the city's first female mayor and District 27's first female senator. She stands with Sandy Treme, Calcasieu Parish police juror from DeQuincy. (Courtesy of www.visitlakecharles.org)

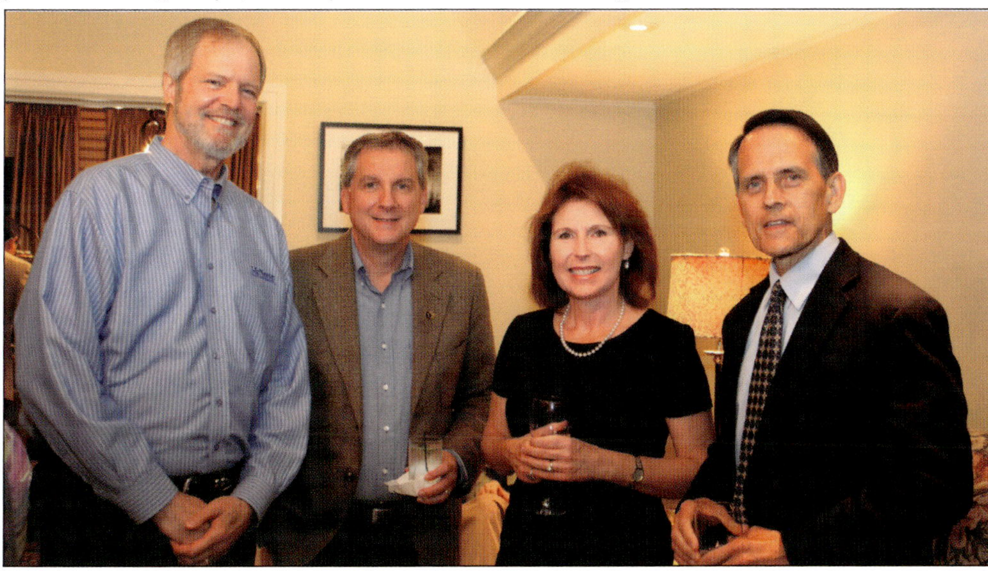

Randy Roach has been the city's mayor since 2000. His administration has completed many bond projects, including road improvements and expansions, park improvements, and lakefront and downtown refurbishment projects. His careful leadership during and after Hurricane Rita fostered pride in the city during a tumultuous time. This 2014 photograph shows, from left to right, McNeese president Dr. Phillip Williams, Dr. Ray Miles and his wife, Tanya Emmer Miles, and Mayor Roach. (Courtesy of Banners Arts and Humanities Series.)

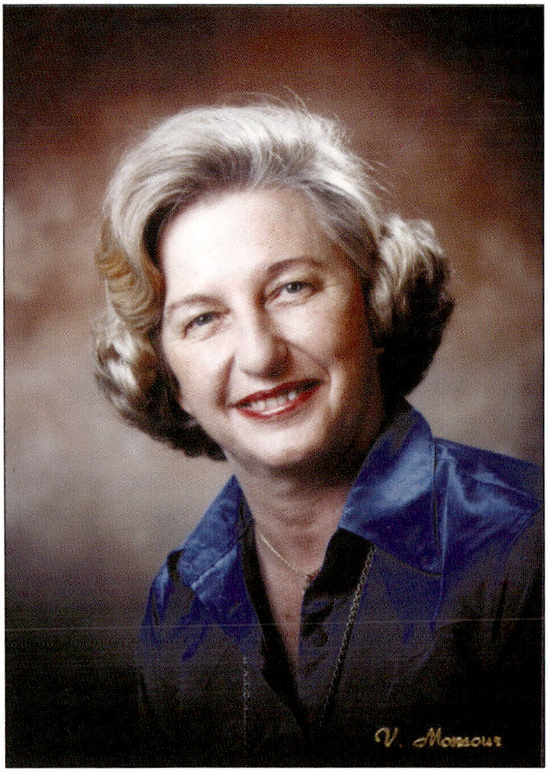

Margaret Lowenthal served two terms as representative for House Districts 35 and 36, and she was the first female legislator from Calcasieu Parish. Previously, Lowenthal was one of the first women to serve on the Calcasieu Parish Police Jury. She received several honors throughout her career, including the Legislator of the Year from the Louisiana State Arts Council in 1983.

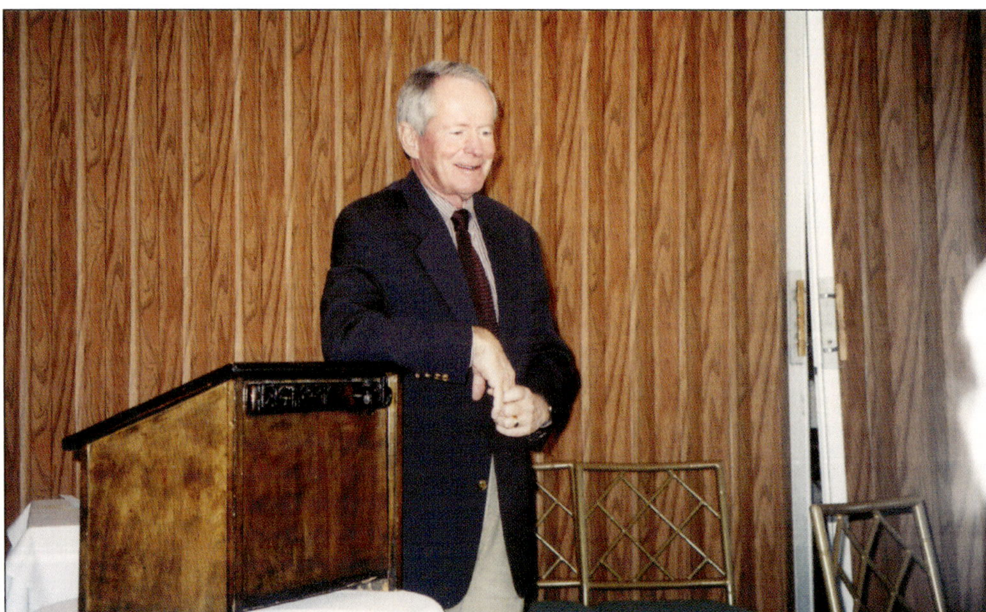

Vic Stelly succeeded Margaret Lowenthal as the representative for House District 35, serving from 1988 until 2004. Known primarily for the Stelly Plan, he wrote tax reform legislation, passed in 2002, that increased income taxes while lowering sales taxes on food and utilities. Stelly was appointed to the Louisiana Board of Regents by Gov. Kathleen Blanco and served from 2007 to 2011.

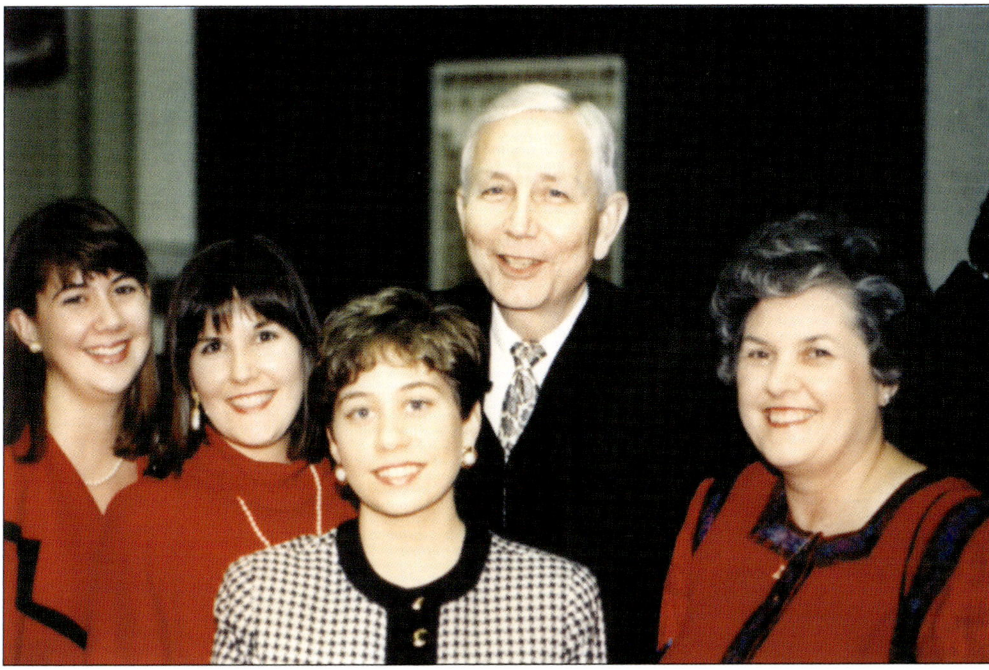

William Lasater "Bill" McLeod represented this region in the state house for eight years and state senate for 15 years. Many knew him for his "personal legislative visits" at grocery stores in his district. This 1991 photograph shows him with his wife, Lady Marilyn "Cissie" Qualls McLeod, and their three daughters, from left to right, Sara, Martha, and Ruth.

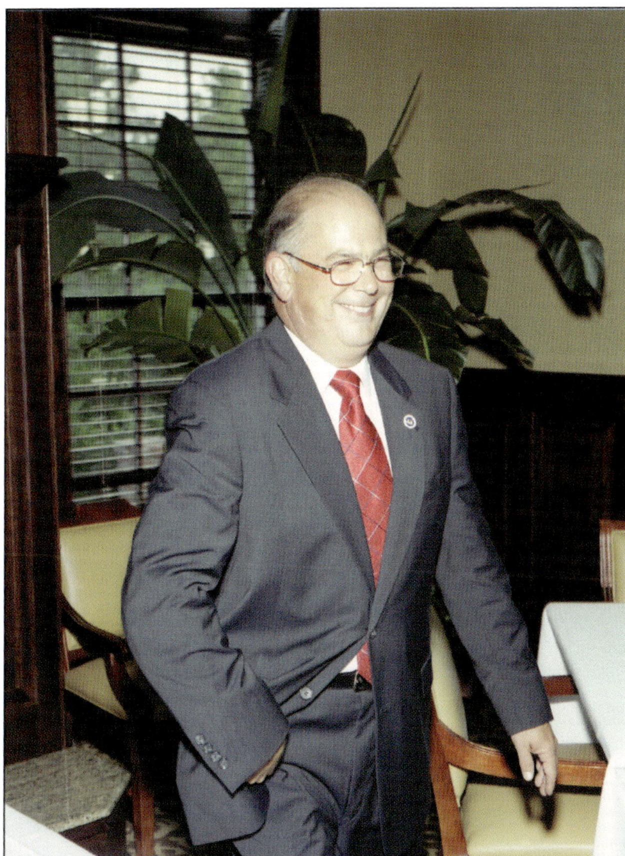

A graduate of Barbe High School and McNeese State University, Dan Flavin served as the representative for House District 36 from 1996 until 2005. During his tenure, he showed support for McNeese and local education, and he worked on several road expansion projects in the city. Flavin is also a prominent realtor in Lake Charles.

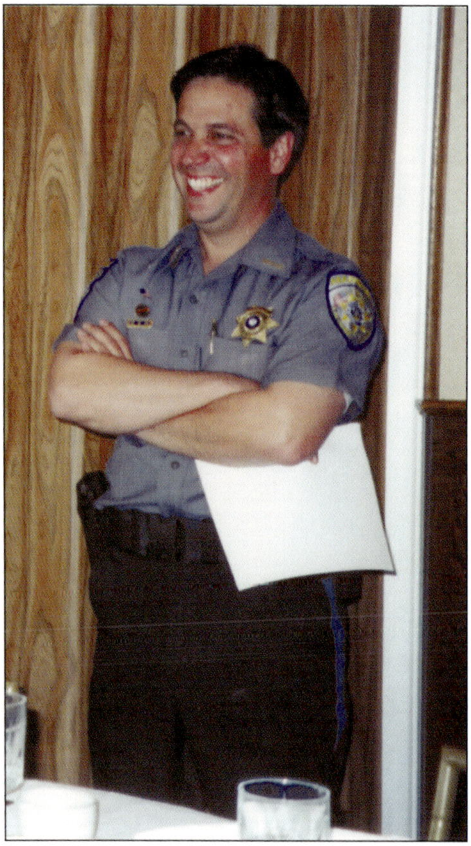

Tony Mancuso began his career in law enforcement at the Calcasieu Parish Sheriff's Department in 1984 as a deputy. He served as Ward 3 city marshal from 1997 to 2003 until he was elected sheriff of Calcasieu Parish. His popularity as sheriff led to unopposed reelections in 2007 and 2011. Mancuso's leadership brought cooperation to the Southwest Louisiana law enforcement community.

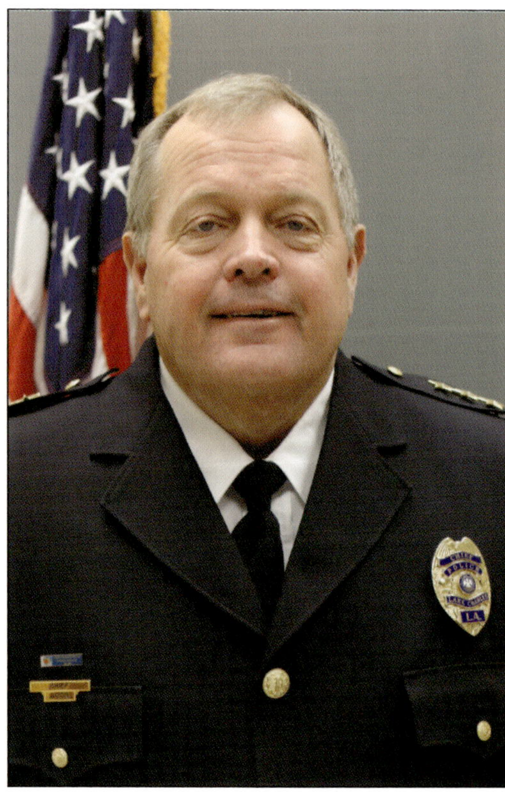

Donald Dixon has been the chief of the Lake Charles Police Department since his initial appointment by the Lake Charles City Council in 2002. Prior to serving as police chief, Dixon was the senior resident agent of the Lake Charles division of the Federal Bureau of Investigation. Dixon has worked to raise salaries, provide additional training, and increase the professionalism of the city's police force. (Courtesy of the Lake Charles Police Department.)

Thomas Broadus Shearman purchased the *American Press* during World War II, and it continues to be a family-owned newspaper that serves Southwest Louisiana. Shearman passed in 1988, and three years later, McNeese renamed its fine arts center in honor of him and his wife, Flora.

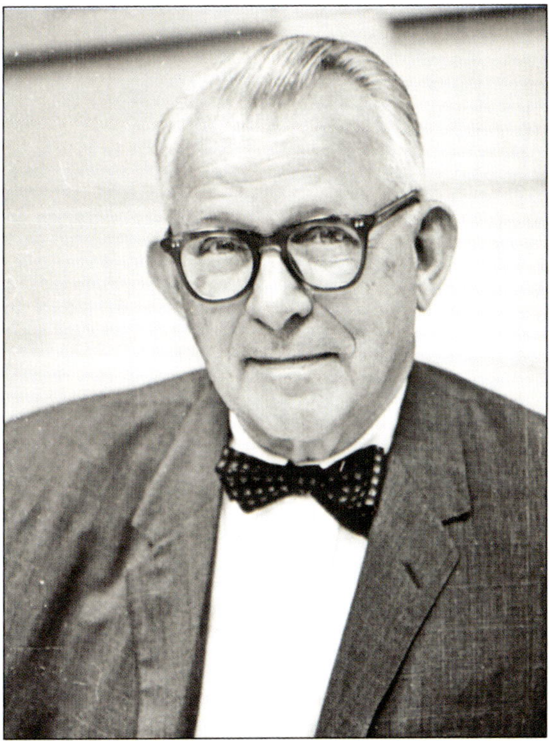

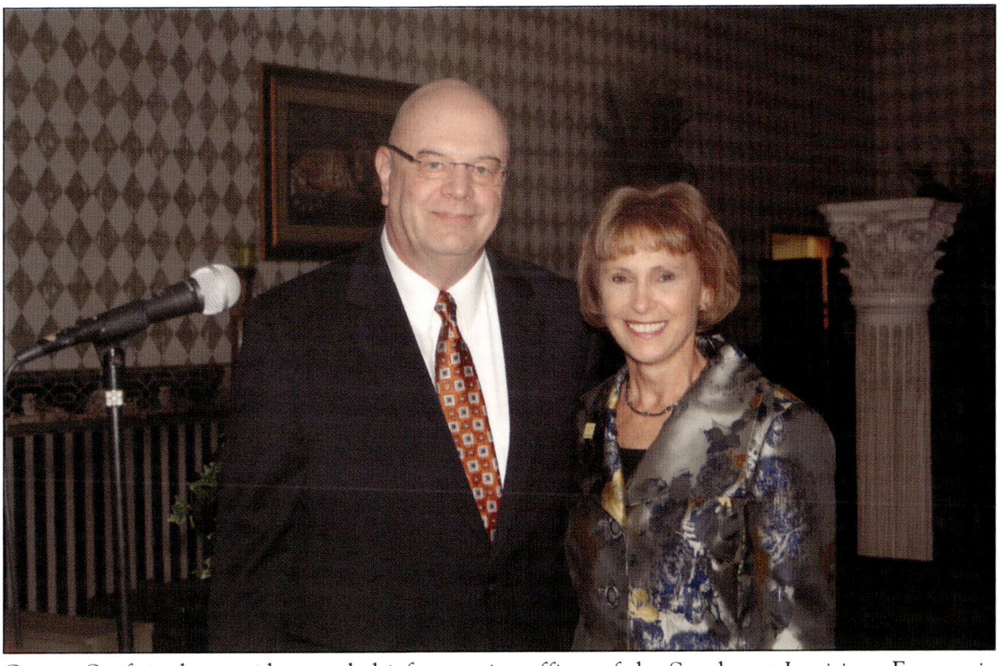

George Swift is the president and chief executive officer of the Southwest Louisiana Economic Development Alliance, which is an umbrella organization for several regional economic development associations that work to recruit and retain businesses in Southwest Louisiana. He stands with Marianne White, who works as the coordinator of planned giving at McNeese. (Courtesy of McNeese State University.)

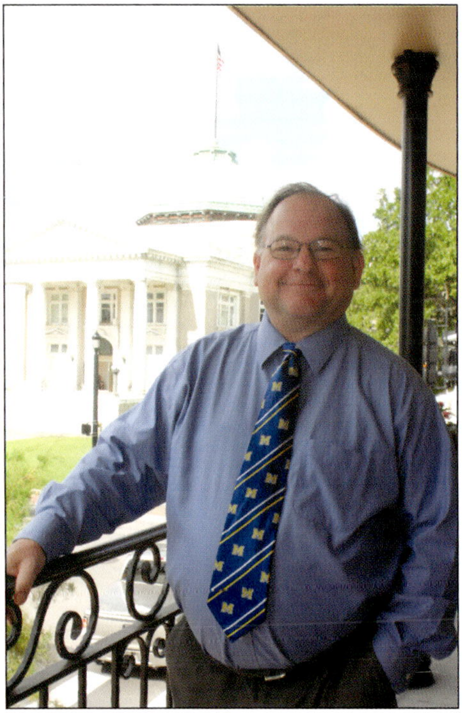

Rick Richard is president of Empire of the Seed, an organization that pursues diverse projects including the preservation and reuse of historic buildings, coastal plains conservancy, and other projects related to energy and business development. He is a former chairman of the Lake Charles Downtown Development Authority, which works with businesses to plan growth in the downtown historic district. (Courtesy of McNeese State University.)

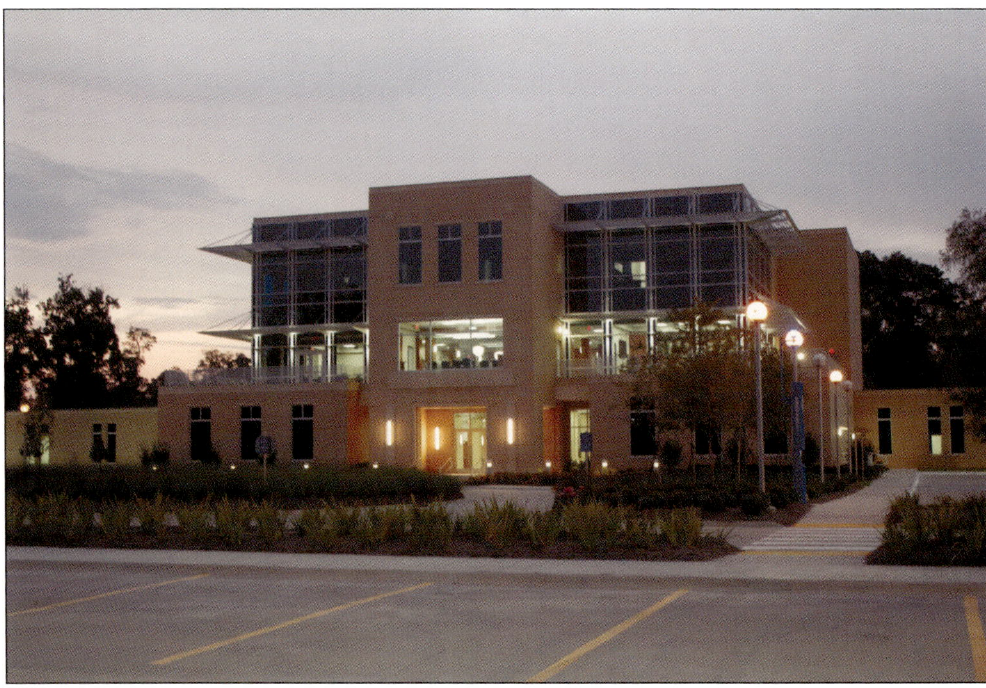

The Southwest Louisiana Entrepreneurial and Economic Development Center, or SEED Center, opened in 2013 as a cooperative effort between the Calcasieu Parish Police Jury, the City of Lake Charles, McNeese State University, and the Southwest Louisiana Alliance. It fosters economic development by providing a business incubator, an innovation center, and other resources for McNeese students and regional entrepreneurs. (Courtesy of McNeese State University.)

Four

Education

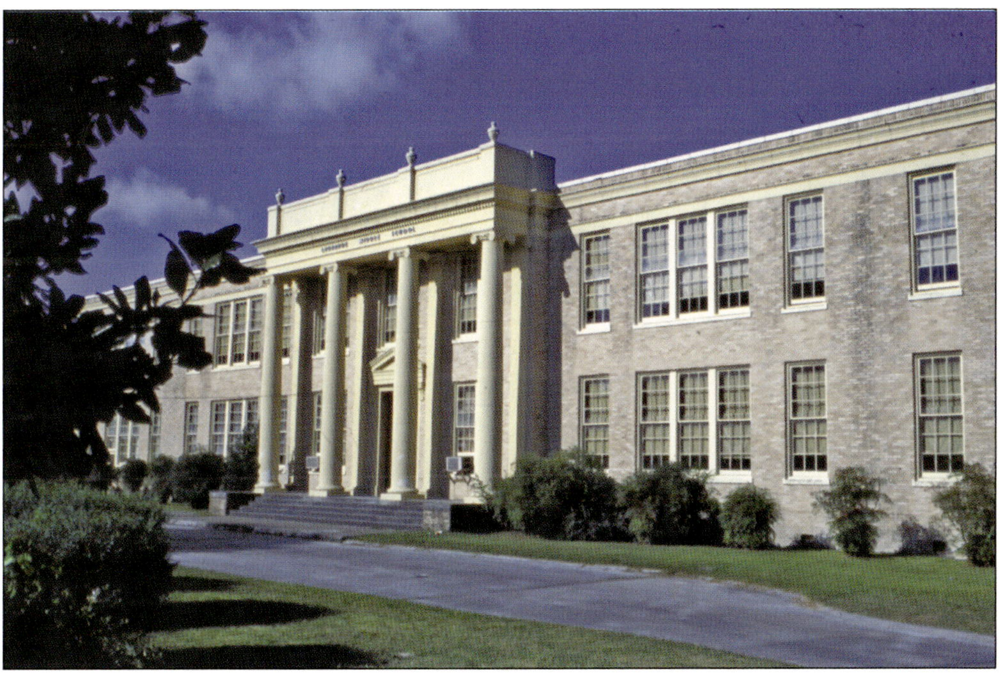

The original location of LaGrange School was on Ryan Street between School and LaGrange Streets. This building became LaGrange Middle School in 1954, when the new LaGrange Senior High opened on College Street. The school had been closed for several years in 1989 when the school board voted to demolish the building.

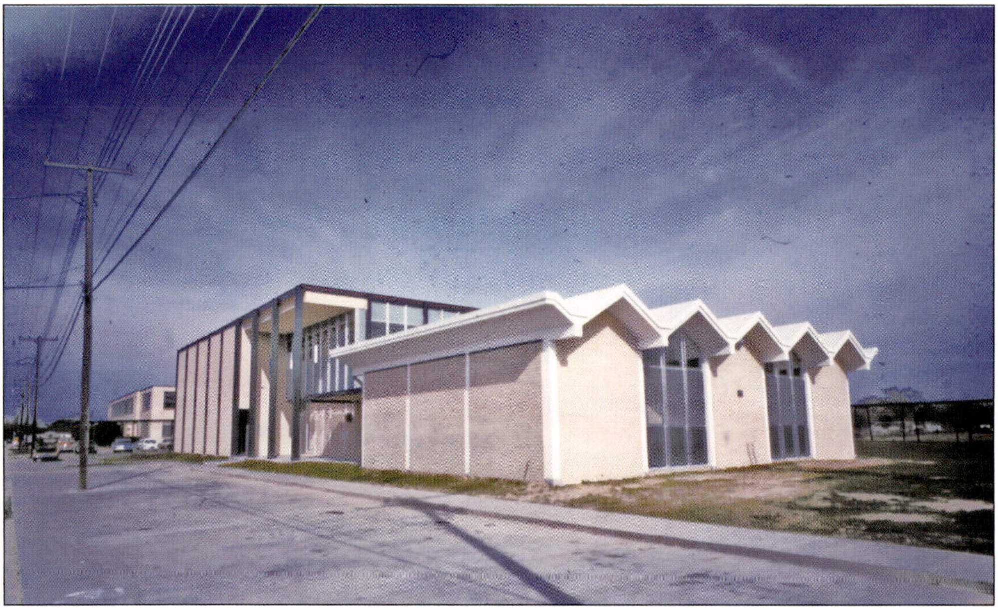

The Second Ward Colored School, which had served the community since the late 19th century, changed its name to W.O. Boston High School in 1949. Eugenia K. Reynaud Junior High, pictured here, opened in 1963 next to Boston High School. Reynaud Junior High was the second completely air-conditioned school building in the city and one of the few in the state.

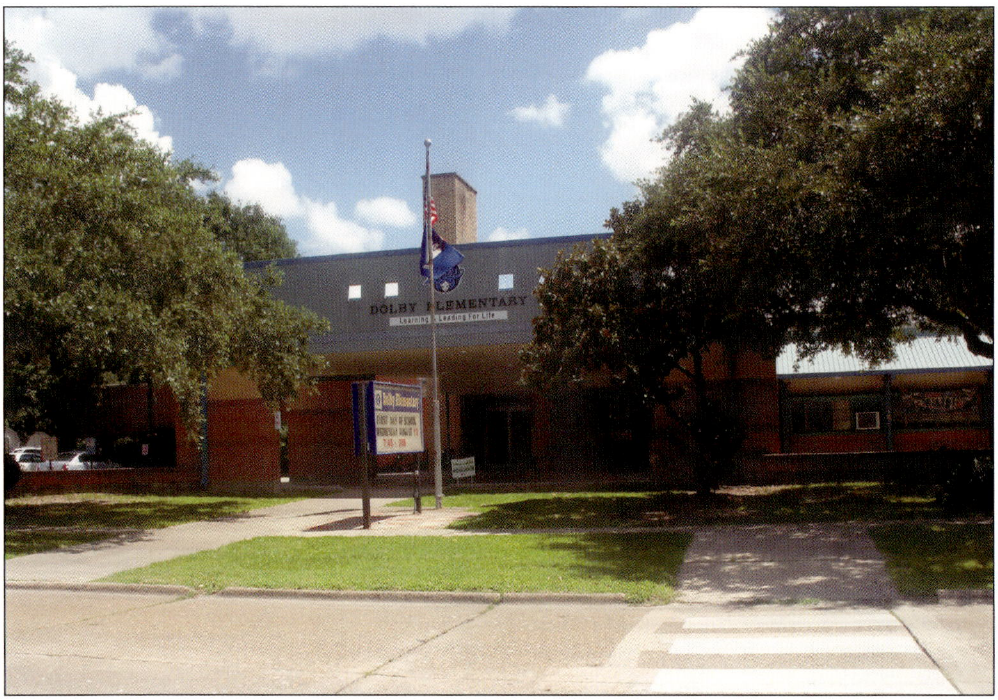

The Lake Charles City School Board did not adjust its 1906 boundaries as the city's population grew. As a result, Calcasieu Parish School Board was educating many of the city's students at LaGrange Senior High and at many new elementary schools built during the 1950s and 1960s, including Dolby Elementary, pictured here, which opened in 1953.

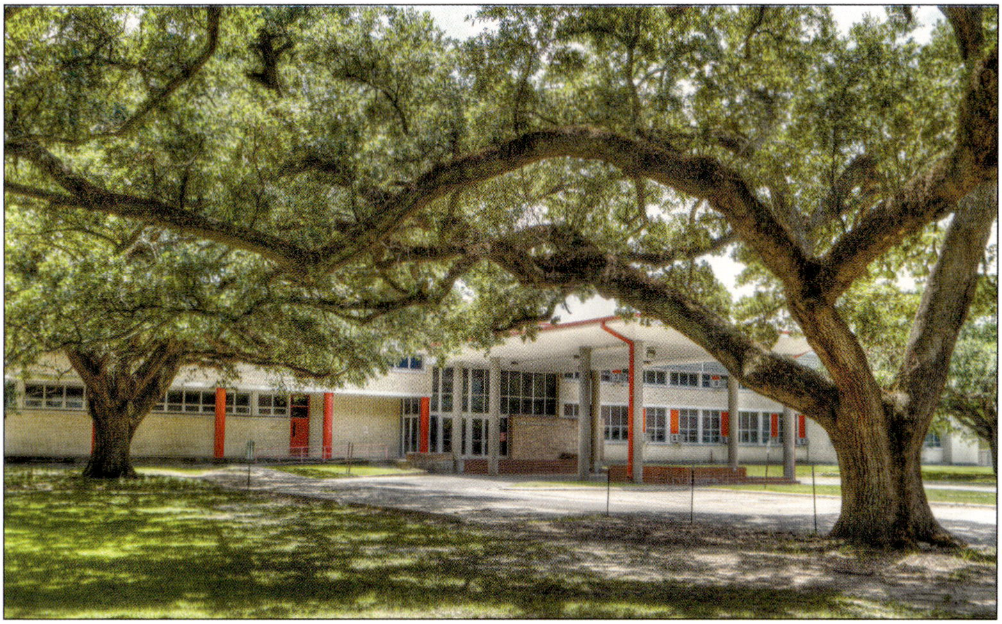

W.O. Boston High School merged with Lake Charles High School in 1984 to create Lake Charles–Boston. The school began its transition to Lake Charles Boston Academy of Learning in 2007, an institution providing career and technical classes, fine arts classes, distance education services, and advanced studies for all Calcasieu Parish students.

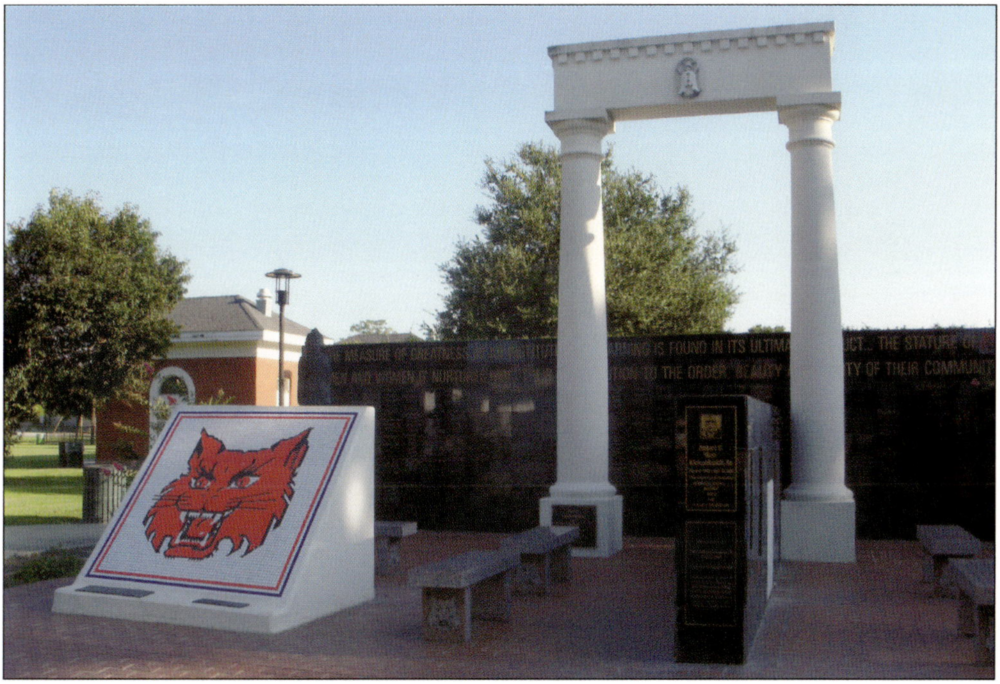

The Lake Charles High School Memorial at Lock Park was created by many alumni who raised funds to memorialize the school after its change to Lake Charles–Boston. It includes a Wildcat mosaic and columns that replicate those on the original Lake Charles High School building. There is also a statue representing the Kilties, an all-female marching and drumming corps.

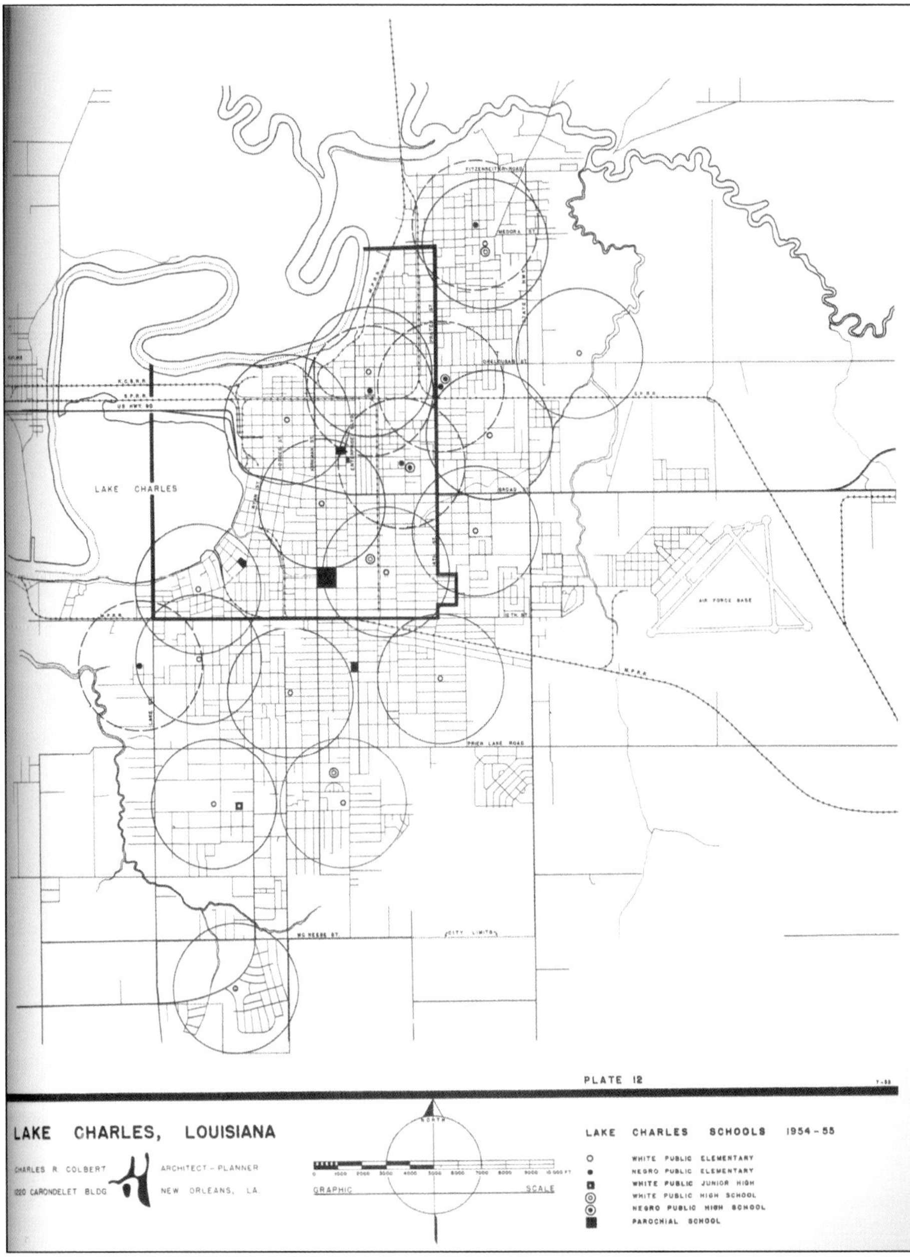

This 1955 map depicts the original boundaries of the Lake Charles City School Board prior to its merger with the Calcasieu Parish School Board, which operated the rest of the public schools in the city. Authorized by the Lake Charles School Board and chaired by George Deer, professor of education at Louisiana State University, a committee of outsiders conducted a study in 1964 that examined local enrollment and population trends, financial and legal statuses of each district, attitudes of all stakeholders, and benefits for the teachers. The committee finally determined that while there was no crisis or emergency creating an immediate need to consolidate the two systems, the population trends indicated that it would be advantageous for those in the city system to be a part of a larger, unrestricted parish unit. This merger required a constitutional amendment, which was passed by the 1966 Louisiana Legislature. It officially took place on July 1, 1967.

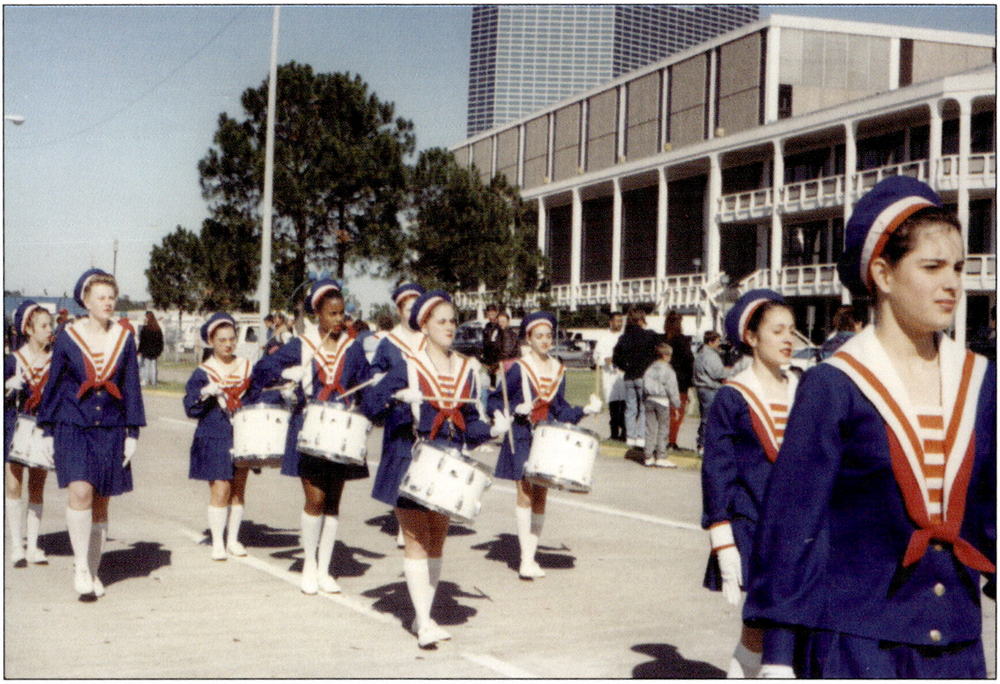

The all-male St. Landry High School and the all-female St. Charles Academy merged in 1970 to become St. Louis Catholic High School. The Tigerettes, a marching squad from St. Charles Academy, changed their name to the St. Louis Blues that year. This photograph shows the Marching Blues in a parade on Lakeshore Drive in 1984.

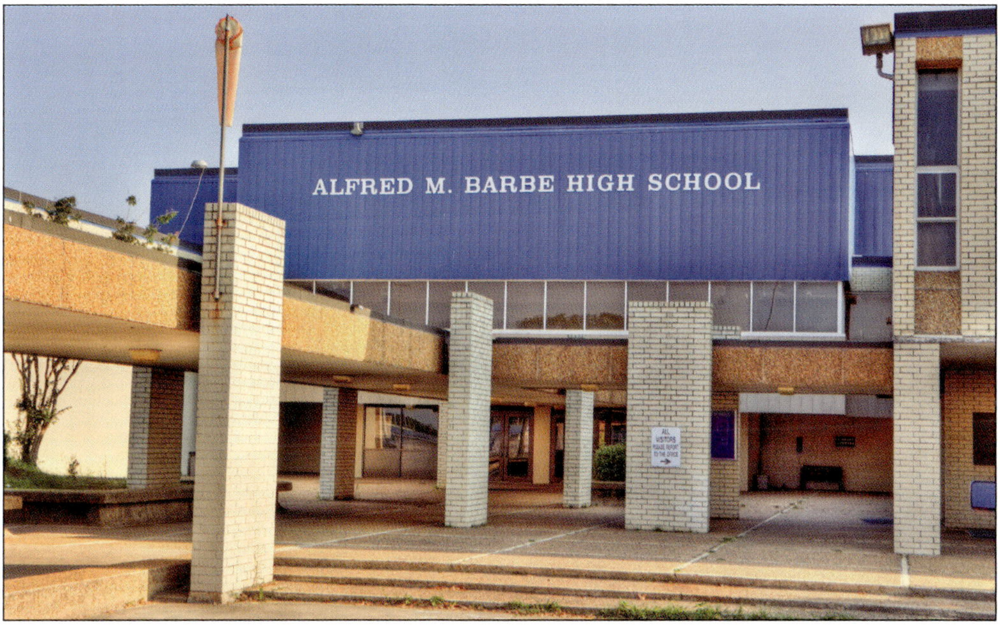

Built in response to the southward expansion of the city, Barbe High School held its first classes in the fall of 1971. Among the school's original 12-building layout was a vocational training school. Funding for the facilities came from the Drew Estate Fund, for which Judge Alfred Michael Barbe was a trustee. (Courtesy of Dennis Thibodeaux.)

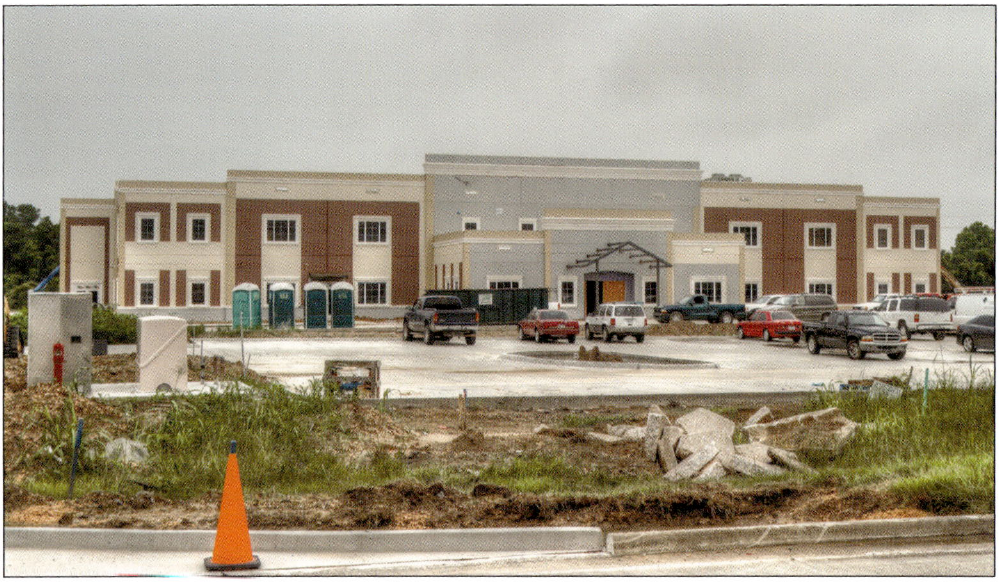

The Southwest Louisiana Charter Academy is the second charter school to open in Lake Charles as a tuition-free school available to all kindergarten though eighth-grade students in Calcasieu Parish. The Louisiana Legislature passed the Charter School Law in 1995, and now Louisiana leads the nation in using charter schools to educate over 60,000 students in the state. (Courtesy of Dennis Thibodeaux.)

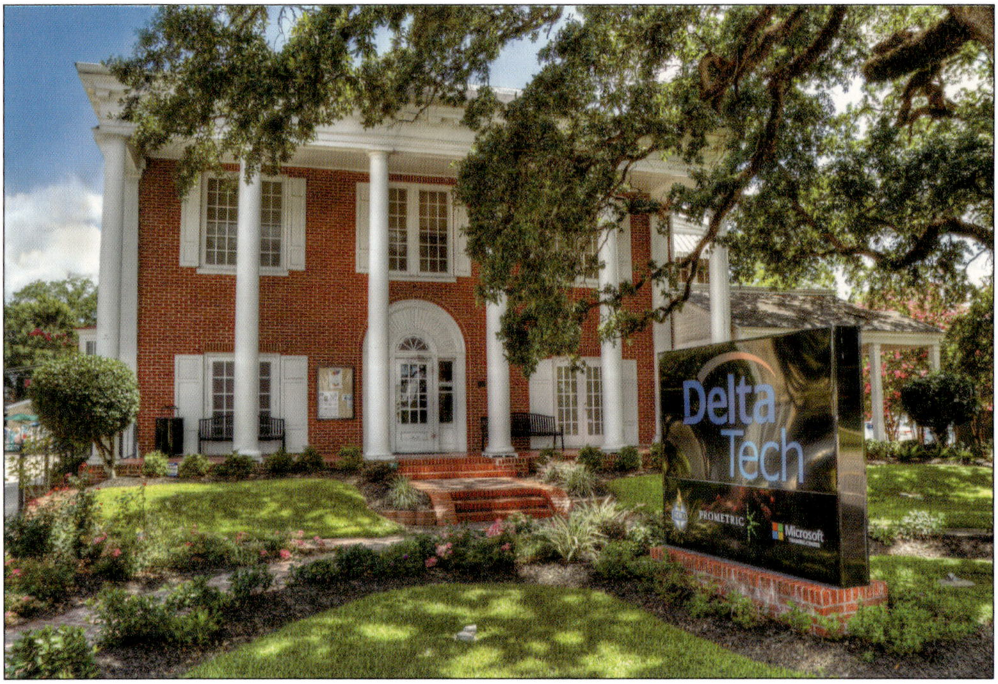

Delta School of Business opened in 1970 in the Gayle Building on Broad Street and expanded to include this historic home in 1977. Original courses included keypunch, speedwriting, and drafting. Renamed Delta School of Business and Technology in 1987, its programs now include training for jobs in medical and technical fields. (Courtesy of Dennis Thibodeaux.)

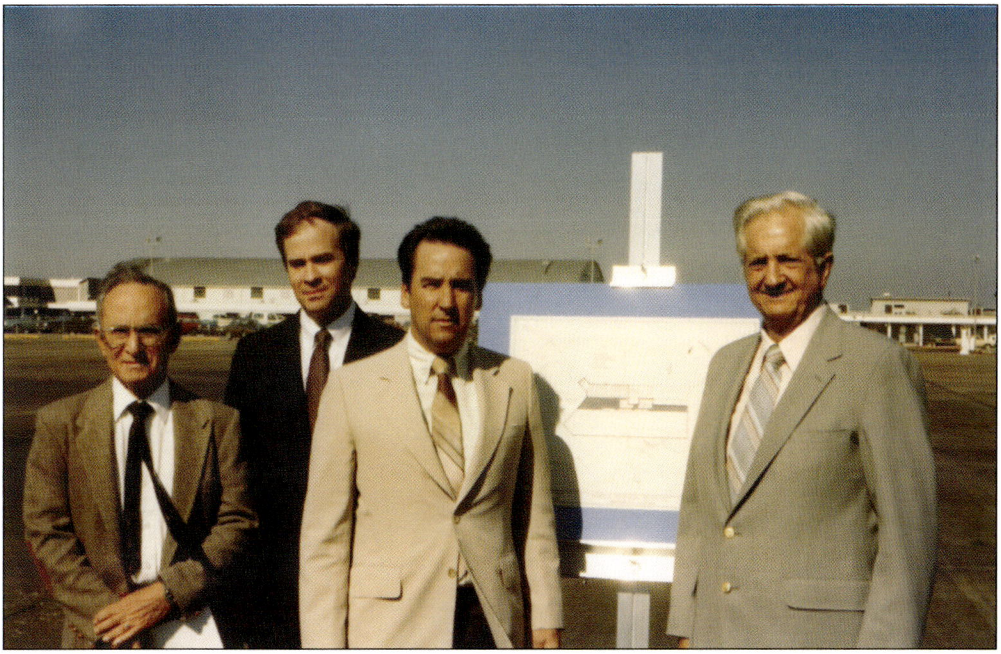

Originally located on the corner of Kirkman and Mill Streets, the Southwest Louisiana Trade School began offering classes in 1940. The school expanded to the former post office on Broad Street in 1962. The lands and facilities at the former Chennault Air Force Base were redistributed in 1973, and SOWELA's five-building complex opened there in 1980. The photograph above depicts the early stages of planning for SOWELA's Chennault expansion, and the 1980 entrance is pictured below. SOWELA offers programs that prepare students to work in industries including health care, aviation, culinary arts, and petrochemicals.

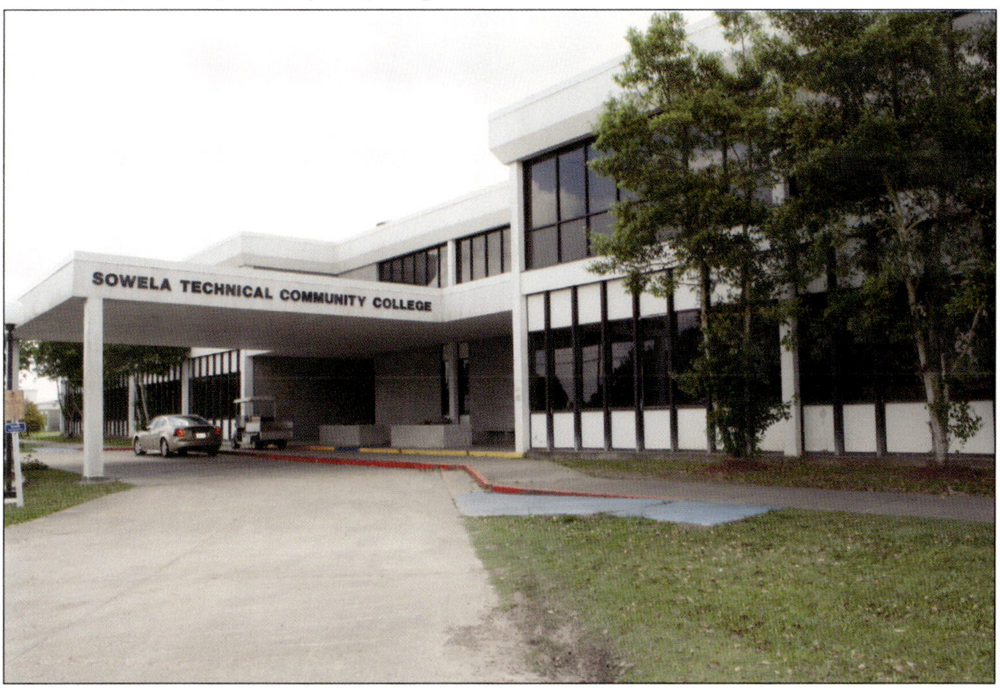

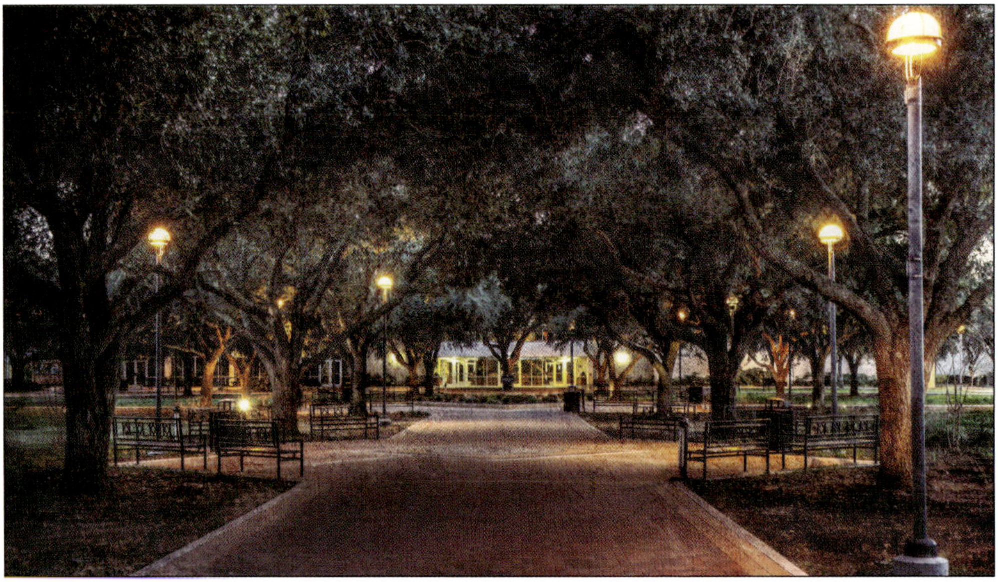

Founded in 1939 as Lake Charles Junior College, McNeese State University has an annual enrollment of over 8,000 students from around the world. Pictured here is the New Ranch of the Holbrook Student Union at the south end of the McNeese Quad. The quad was refurbished in 2010 using student fees for campus development. (Courtesy of Dennis Thibodeaux.)

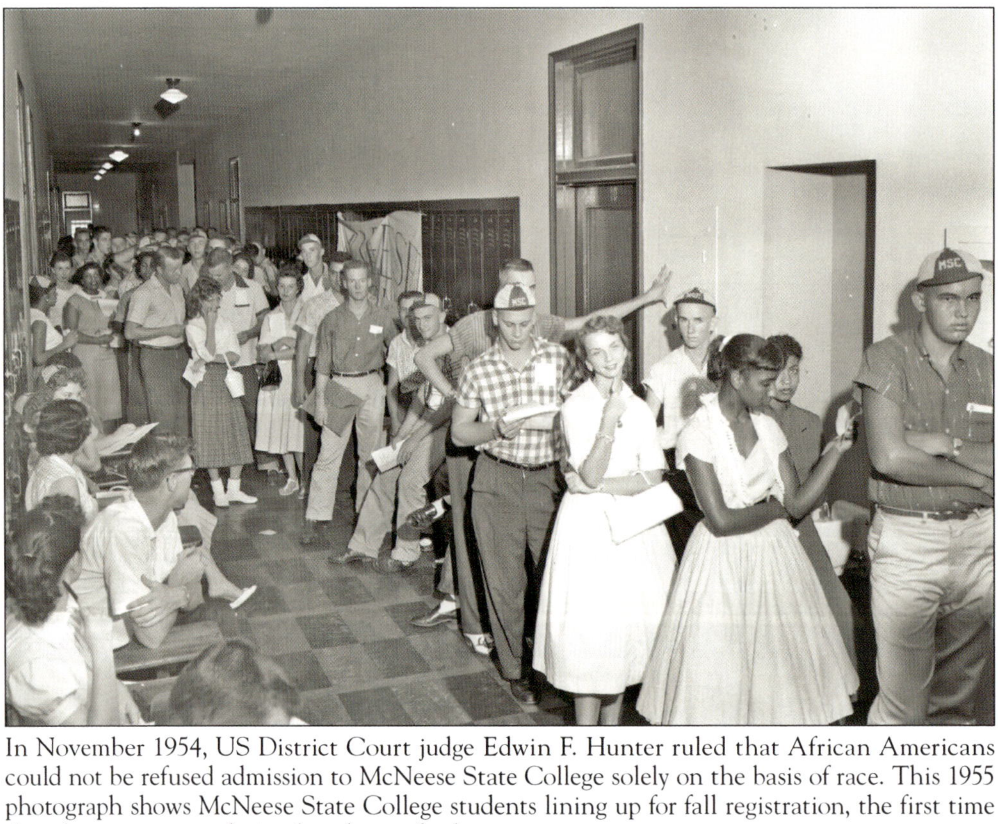

In November 1954, US District Court judge Edwin F. Hunter ruled that African Americans could not be refused admission to McNeese State College solely on the basis of race. This 1955 photograph shows McNeese State College students lining up for fall registration, the first time that the institution admitted students of color.

Lake Charles Junior College, later named McNeese, was built on the local poor farm in 1939, and one of the original buildings was used for a rodeo arena. The school's mascot is the cowboy in honor of the area's rodeo heritage. Rowdy the Cowboy was born in 1982, named for Clint Eastwood's character on the television show *Rawhide*.

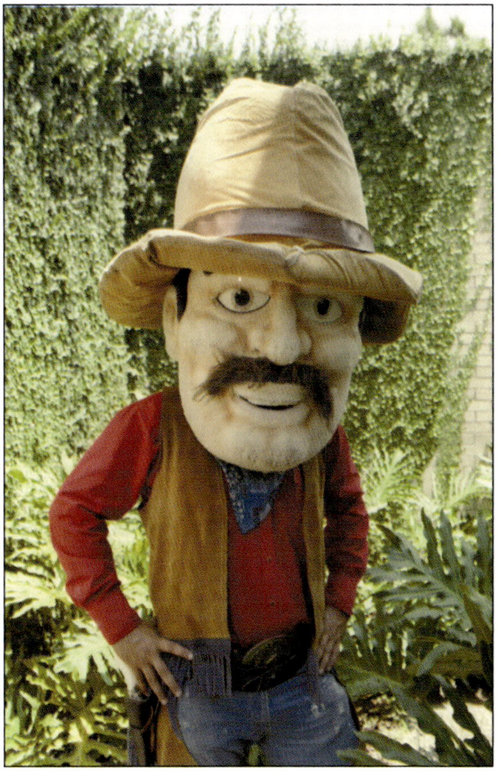

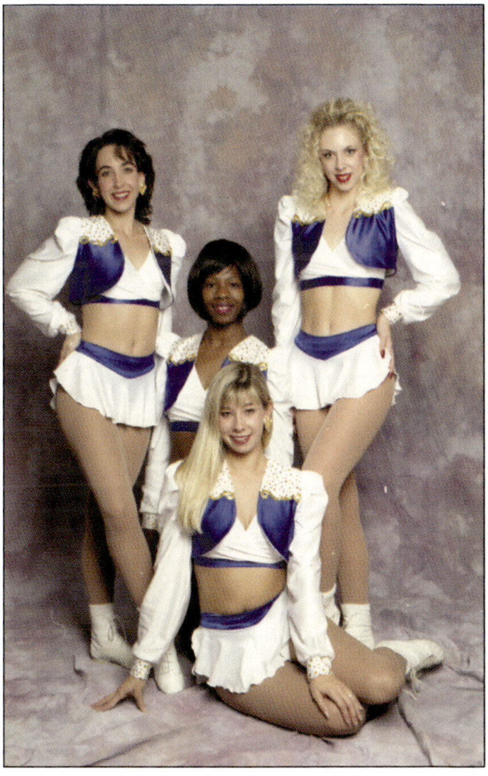

This photograph from 1990 shows some of the members of the McNeese State University Cowgirl Kickers. The Kickers is a dance team that performs at home football games, men's and women's basketball games, and various university and community events. Kickers receive scholarships each semester and must demonstrate academic achievement, advanced dance skills, and a positive university image.

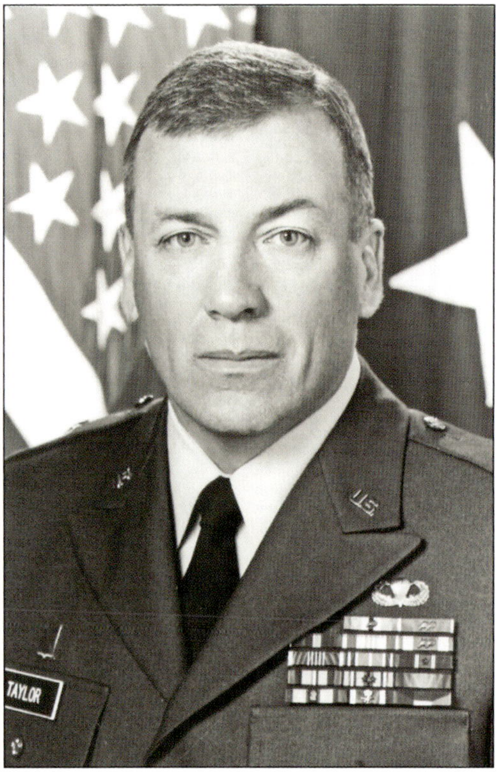

After his Air Force service during World War II and earning his education, Joe Gray Taylor became a professor of history in Louisiana, arriving at McNeese State University in 1963. He chaired the McNeese history department from 1968 until 1983, when he became dean of the College of Liberal Arts. He wrote many books and journal articles on Air Force, Louisiana, and Southern history. (Courtesy of McNeese State University.)

Dr. John Wood (right) founded the Master of Fine Arts Creative Writing program at McNeese State University in 1981. He is pictured here with Dr. Robert Olen Butler, who taught creative writing at McNeese from 1985 to 2000. Butler won the Pulitzer Prize in 1993 for his collection of short stories *A Good Scent from a Strange Mountain*.

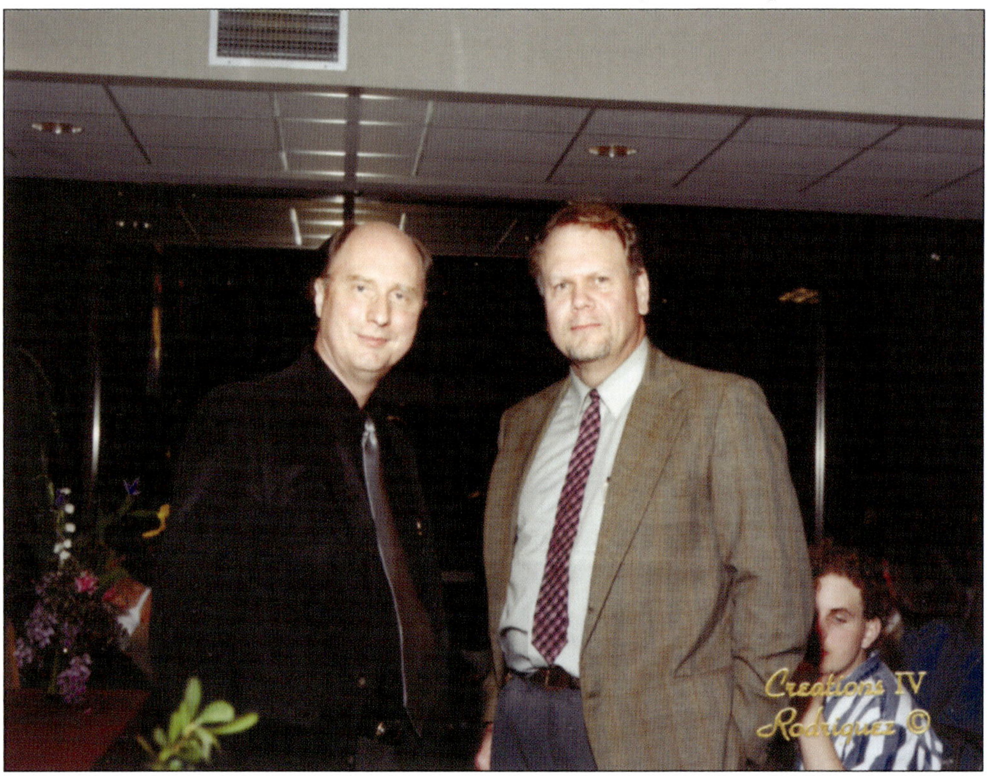

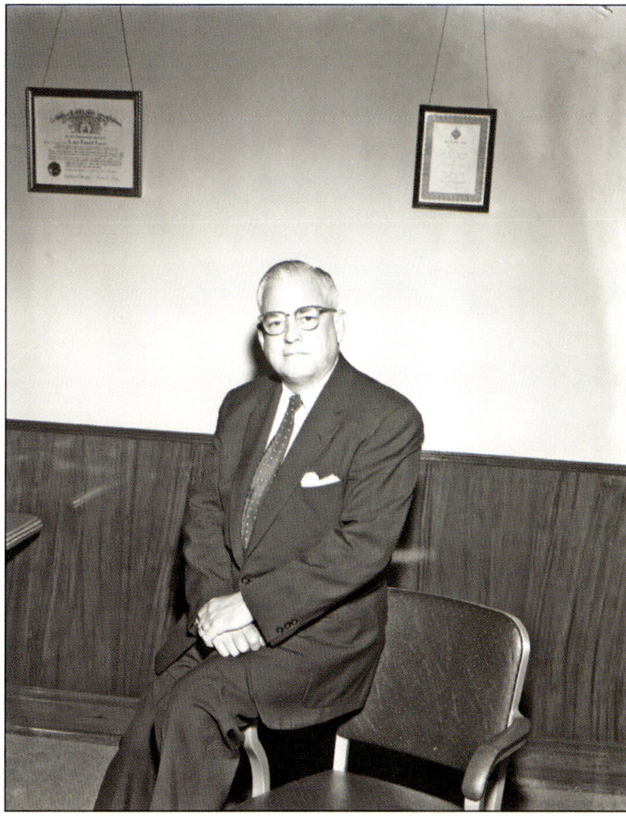

Frazar Memorial Library at McNeese State University was named for the institution's fourth president, Lether Frazar, pictured here. Frazar's presidency lasted from 1944 to 1955, when he left to serve as Louisiana's lieutenant governor under Gov. Earl Kemp Long. The library opened in 1961 between Beauregard Drive and the Contraband Bayou, and it was remodeled with a four-story addition in 1974. The library features an extensive archive with materials documenting the history of Southwest Louisiana. The card catalog pictured here has been replaced with an online catalog and over 100 information databases that support the university's curriculum.

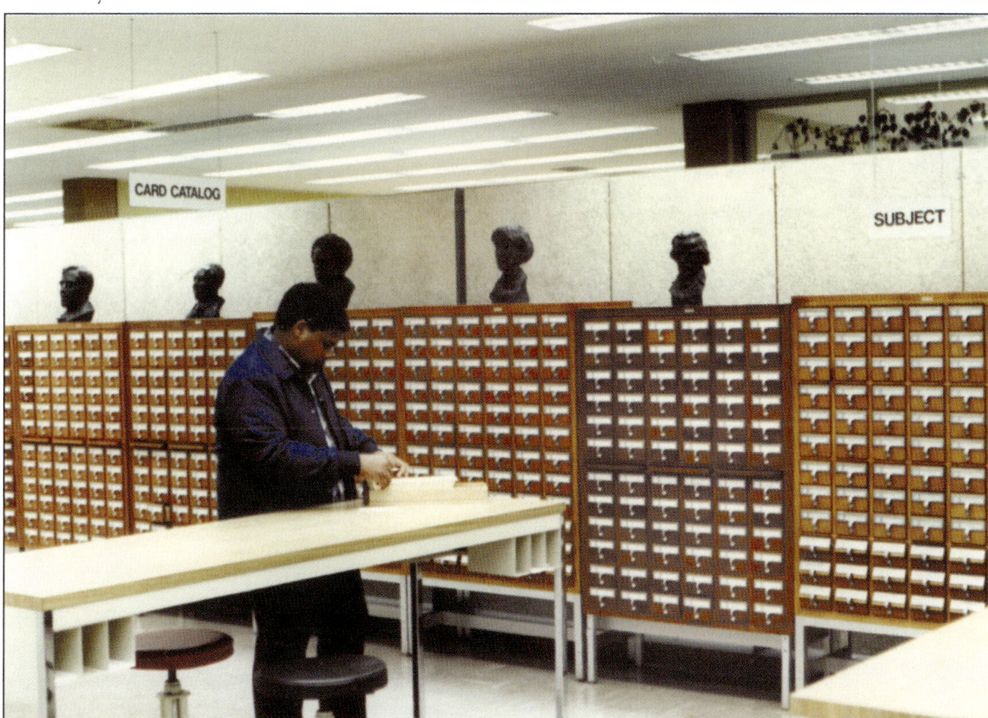

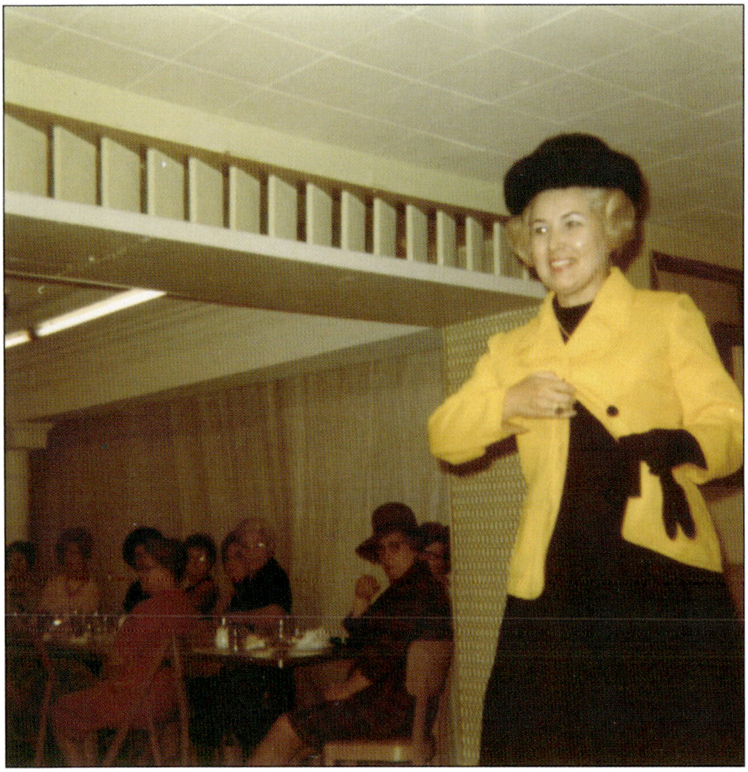

Norma Tornabene was the dean of women at McNeese State University beginning in 1970 after receiving her master's of education in administration and supervision from McNeese. In 1973, she was elected vice president of the Louisiana Region of the American Association of University Women and appointed by Gov. Edwin Edwards to the Commission on Status for Women.

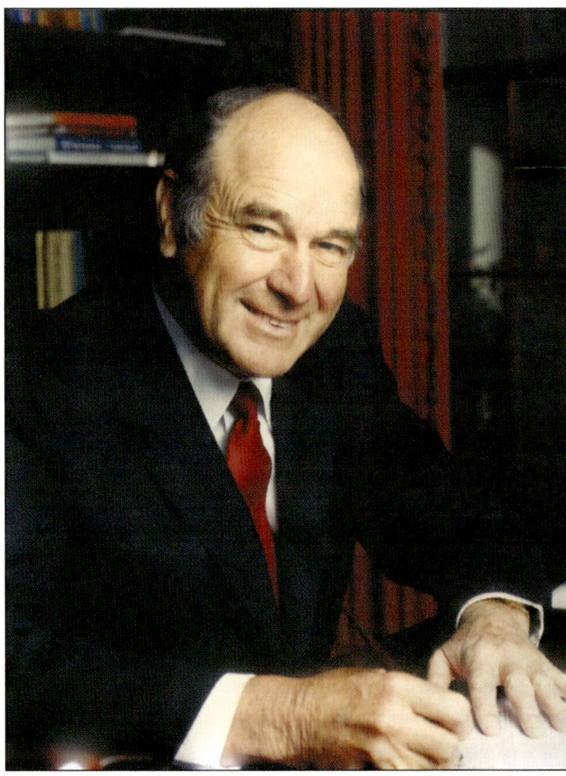

Dr. Jack Doland played football and basketball as a student at McNeese Junior College, and he later served as head football coach, athletic director, and then president of McNeese State University from 1980 to 1986. He resigned his presidency to serve in the Louisiana Senate until his death in 1991. The Jack V. Doland Field House at McNeese was named in his honor.

Five

Arts and Recreation

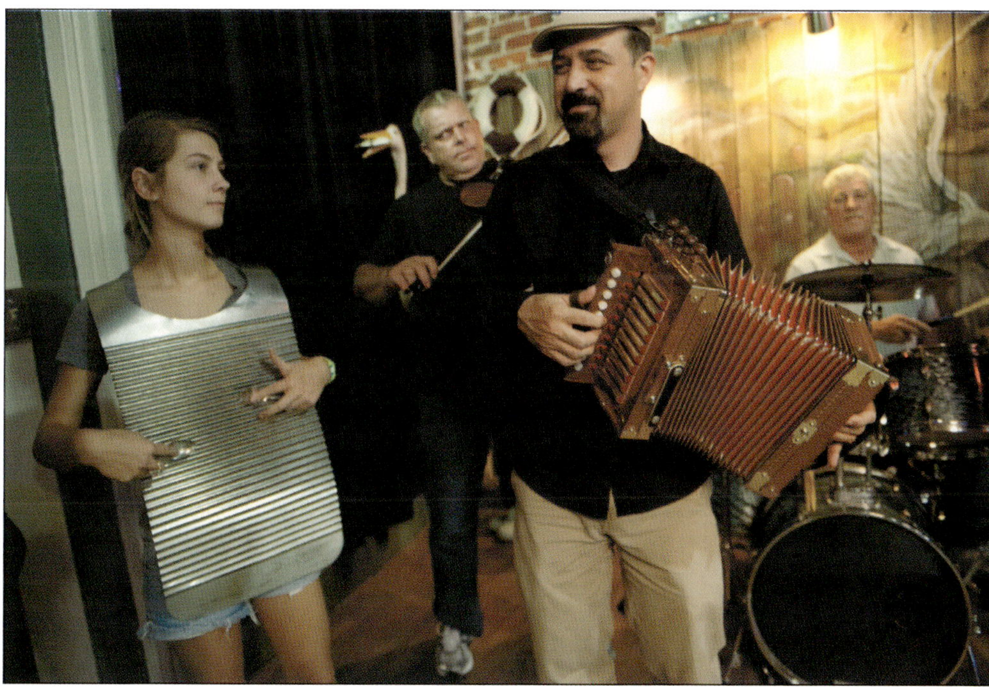

McNeese alumnus Chris Miller is a talented accordion player who formerly led the local band Kingfish and now plays with Bayou Roots. He serves as the chorale director at Barbe High School and at First Presbyterian in Lake Charles. Miller is pictured here with his daughter, Candace, Danny Peet on drums, and Chad Cormier on fiddle. (Courtesy of www.visitlakecharles.org.)

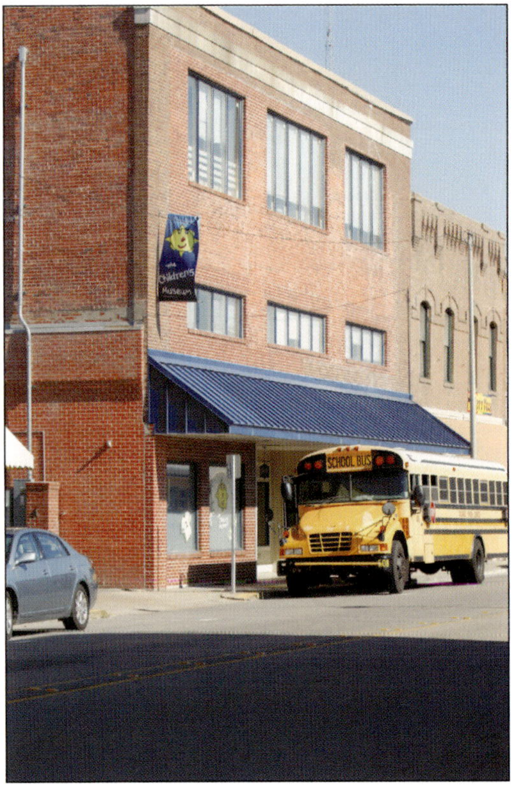

The Children's Museum opened in 1988, providing hands-on programs and exhibits for families. The museum is part of the United Way organization and supported by local organizations and businesses. Now located on Broad Street in downtown Lake Charles, the museum bounced back quickly after suffering fire damage in 2009. (Courtesy of www.visitlakecharles.org.)

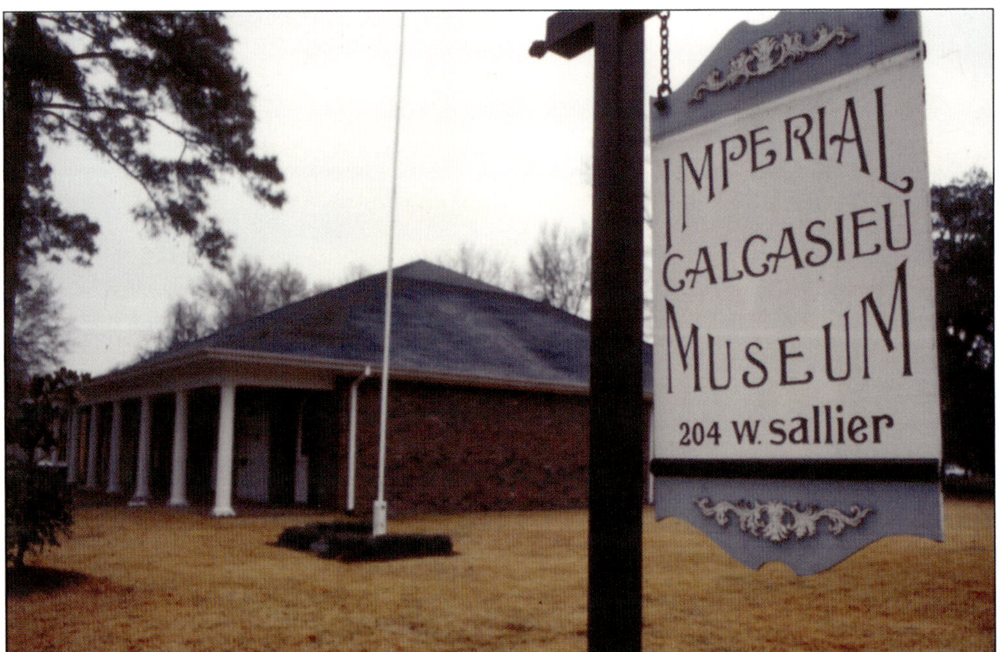

Imperial Calcasieu Museum began in 1963 as a room in city hall, thanks to the efforts of the Junior Welfare League. Later that year, it moved to an old stable at the intersection of Clarence and Front Streets. The museum moved to its current location near the Sallier Oak in 1971.

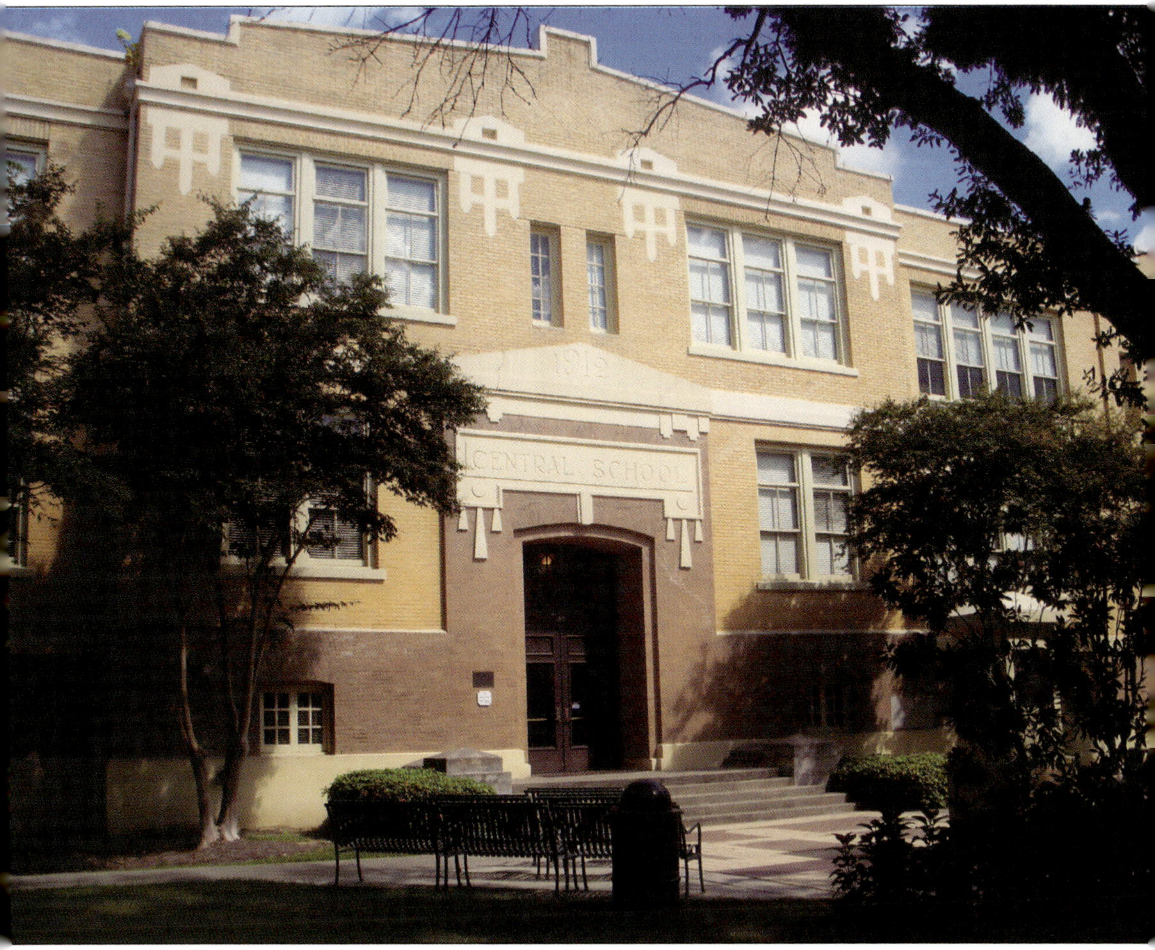

Central School, located in the heart of the Charpentier Historic District on Kirby Street, was originally part of the Lake Charles City School Board system. It was annexed into the Calcasieu Parish School Board system in 1966, and it operated as an elementary school until 1976. The Calcasieu Arts and Humanities Council, now the Arts and Humanities Council of Southwest Louisiana, began using the building in 1986. In 1993, the community passed a six-month quarter-cent sales tax to restore the deteriorating school, which now houses galleries, studios, performance spaces, and offices. The Arts and Humanities Council of Southwest Louisiana allocates grant money to artists and arts organizations in Southwest Louisiana, and it organizes festivals and events to encourage a thriving arts community and bolster tourism. Popular events include Live at the Lakefront and the Gallery Promenade.

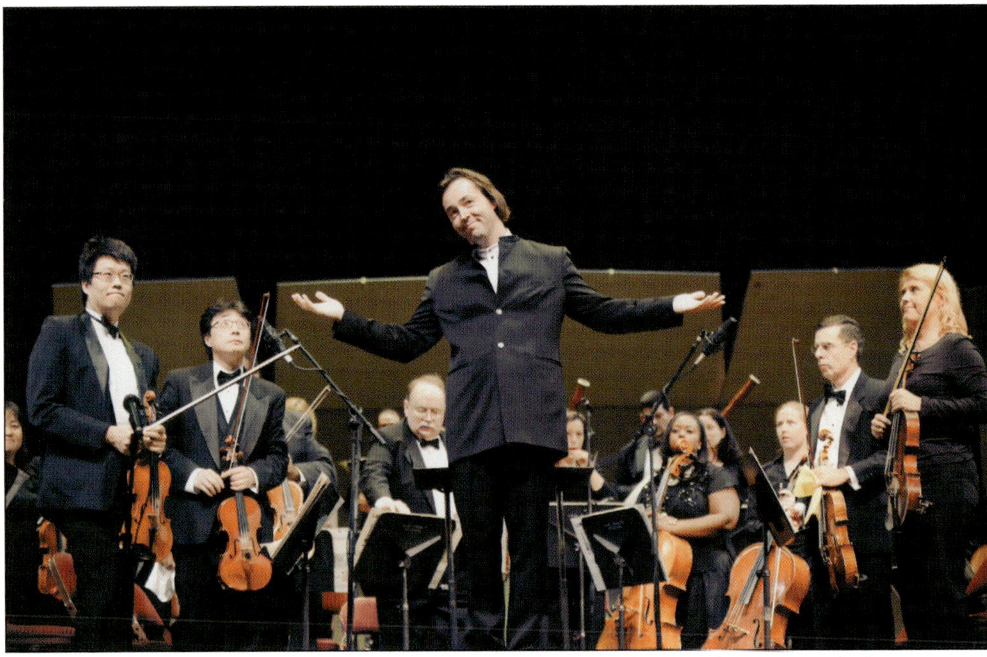

Originally formed in 1938, the Lake Charles Symphony was reorganized in 1958 with the assistance of the Lake Charles Junior Welfare League. Bohuslav Rattay, a native of Bohemia and pictured here, took over the directorship of the Lake Charles Symphony in 2010 after the passing of longtime conductor William Kushner. (Courtesy of Lindsey Janies.)

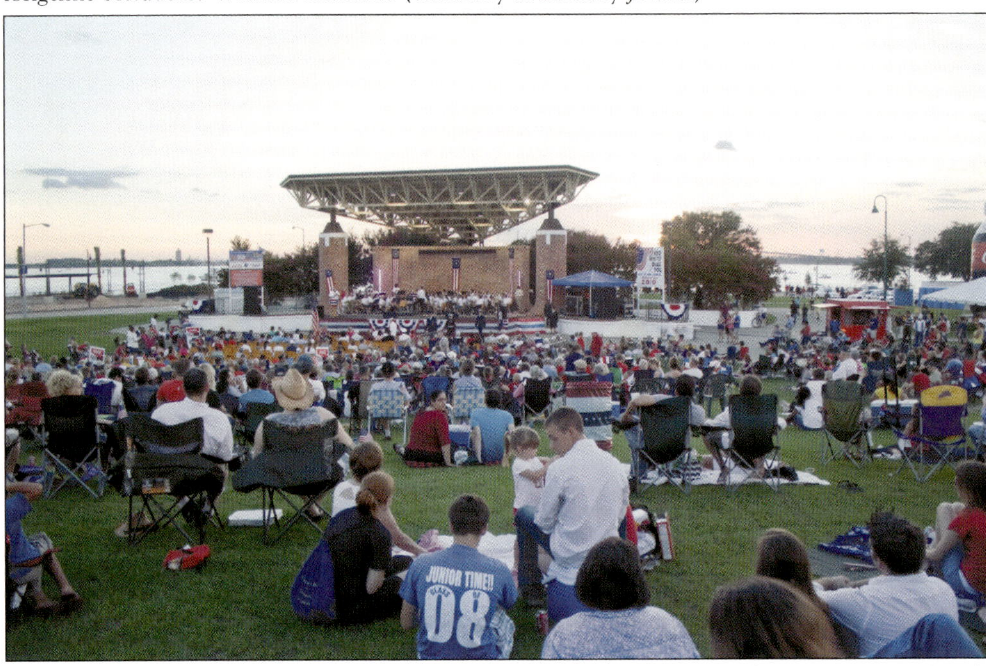

The Lake Charles Community Band was formally organized in 1988 by Dr. Norman Smith. Participants are volunteer musicians who come from all over Southwest Louisiana. The band plays several shows throughout the year, and performances are held at the Arcade amphitheater near the Lake Charles Civic Center and lakefront. (Courtesy of Dennis Thibodeaux.)

Chester Daigle II (left) is pictured with his wife, Pat Daigle, and Mayor Randy Roach at the Mayor's Art Awards ceremony where he was named 2012 Artist of the Year. Daigle is a member of the local band City Heat, which he formed in 1995 to be a house band for the Isle of Capri Casino. (Courtesy of Parker Brand Creative.)

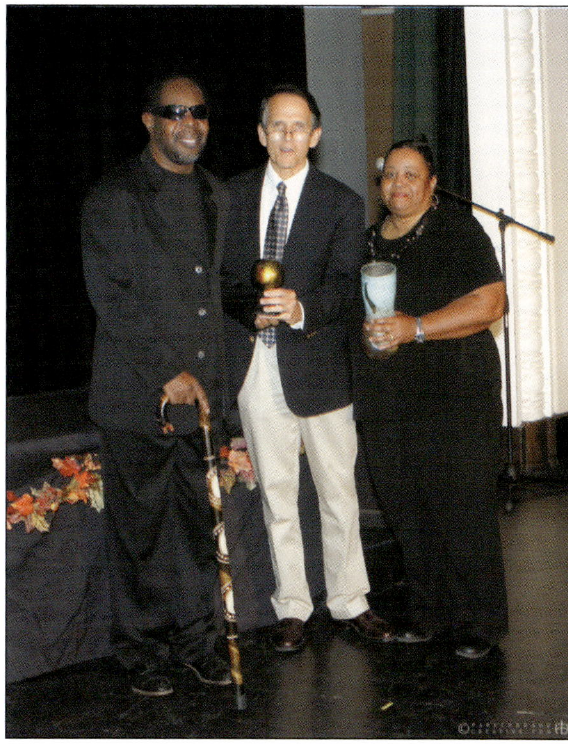

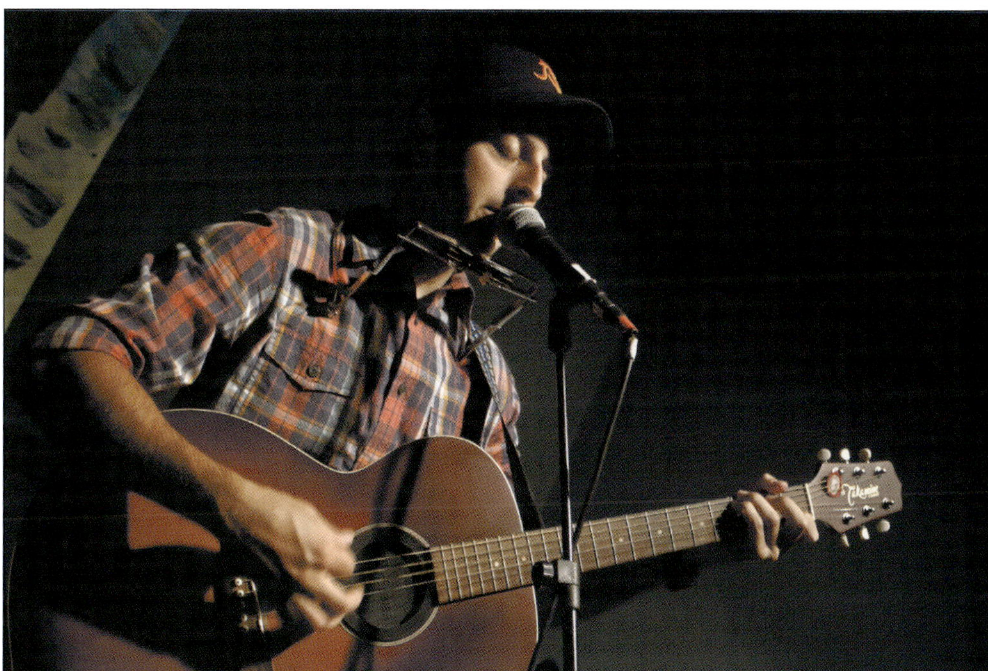

Local musician Paul Gonsoulin graduated from St. Louis High School in 2002. He has been a member of several local bands, including Bobcat, the Magic Tones, and the Yams, and he was a founding member of the Flamethrowers. He released his first studio album in 2013, *House Fire*. (Courtesy of Daniel Castro Photography.)

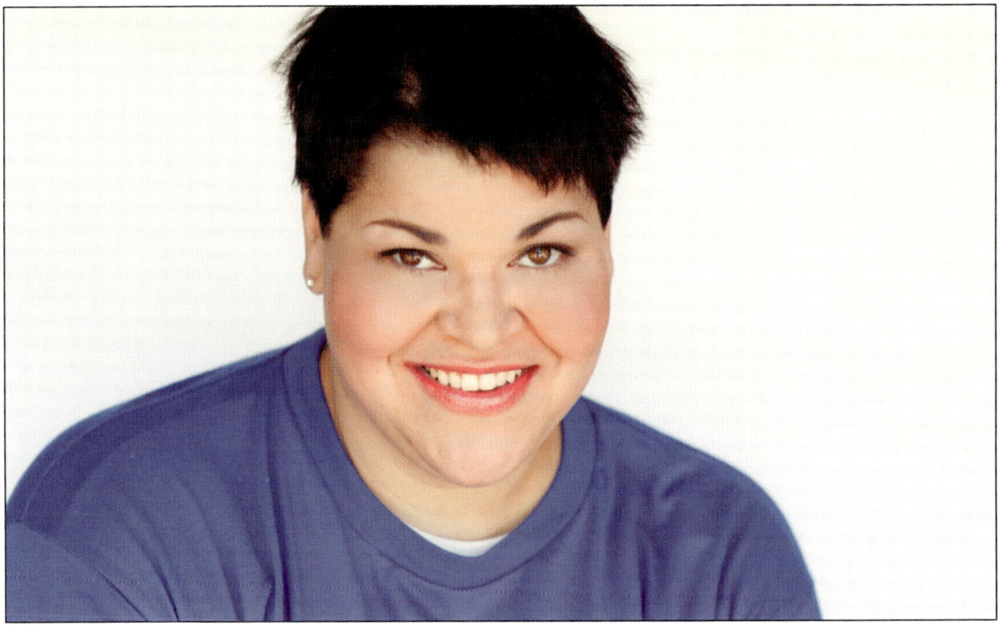

Jen Kober graduated from Barbe High School in 1991. She attended school in Chicago and performed with the Second City improvisational troupe before returning to Lake Charles to attend McNeese, where she was a member of the award-winning McNeese Forensics Team. She is a popular live performer and talented actress with roles in various productions, including HBO's *Treme*. (Courtesy of Jen Kober.)

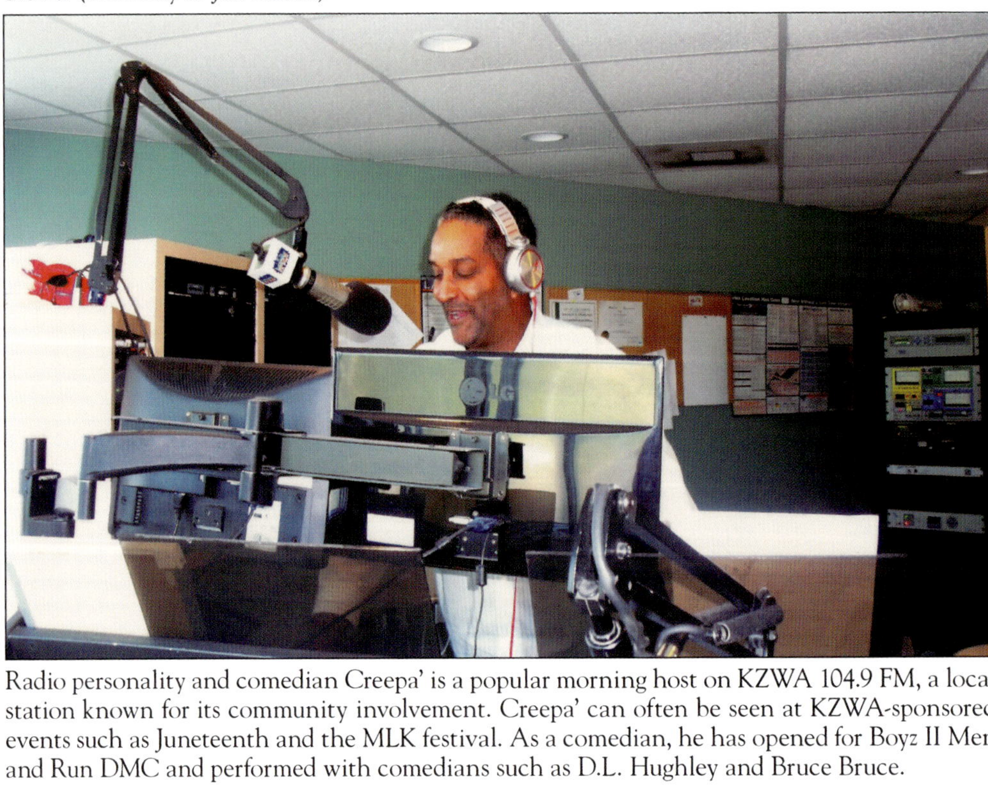

Radio personality and comedian Creepa' is a popular morning host on KZWA 104.9 FM, a local station known for its community involvement. Creepa' can often be seen at KZWA-sponsored events such as Juneteenth and the MLK festival. As a comedian, he has opened for Boyz II Men and Run DMC and performed with comedians such as D.L. Hughley and Bruce Bruce.

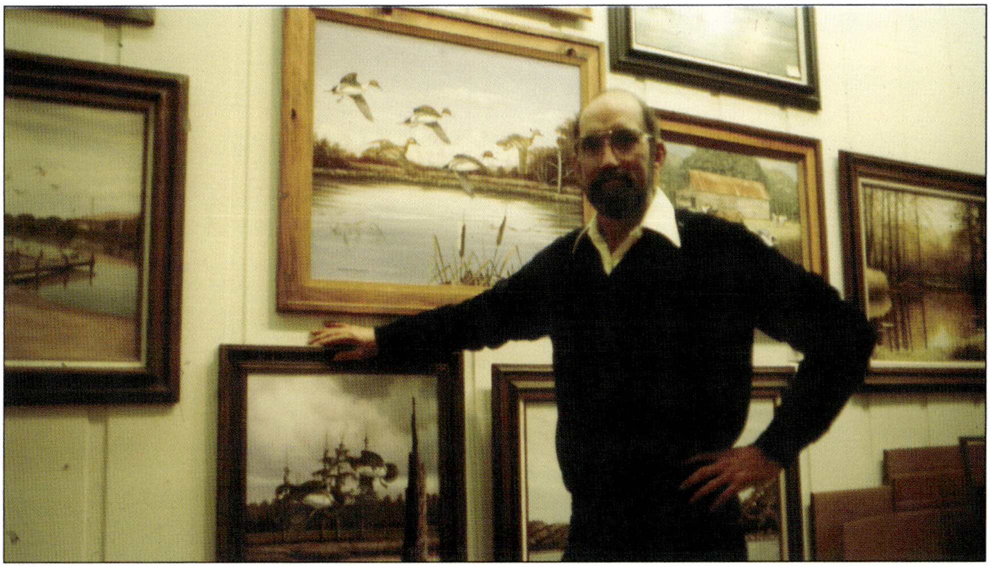

Elton Louviere is known for his paintings depicting landscapes in Southwest Louisiana. He began his career as an illustrator painting billboards for Lamar Advertising, and he opened Louviere Sign Company, an outdoor sign business, in Lake Charles in 1968. He and his wife later moved to Moss Bluff and opened Louviere Fine Arts in 1976.

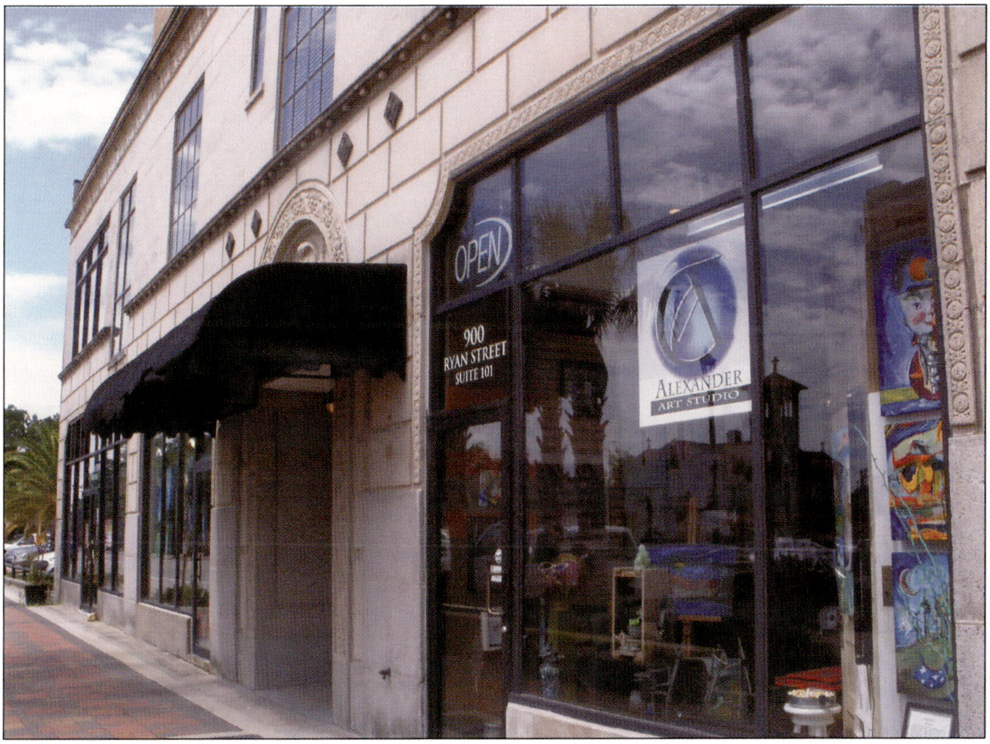

Candace Alexander founded her studio in Central School in 2002, soon after graduating from McNeese with a visual arts degree. In 2012, she moved to her current studio, a large space on the first floor of the Charleston Hotel. Alexander's work, including her popular Fleur de lis–Worlds Within series, has led to her being voted the best artist in Lake Charles four times.

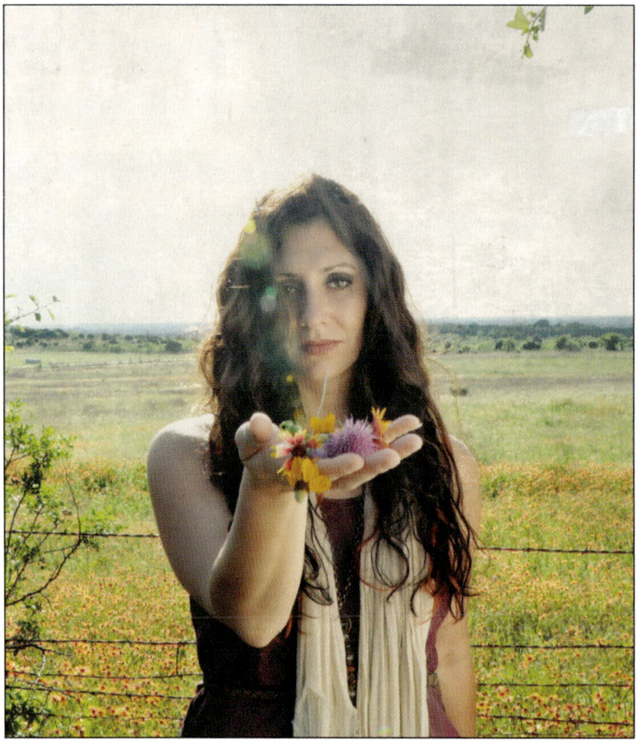

Many area musicians find opportunities in Austin, Texas, including Wendy Colonna, a singer-songwriter who graduated in 1995 from Barbe High School, where she studied under choral director Chris Miller. Wendy performed during Sunday Brunch at Pujo Street Café, and she continues to perform at venues around the city, in addition to touring nationally and internationally. (Courtesy of Steve Alcala and Wendy Colonna.)

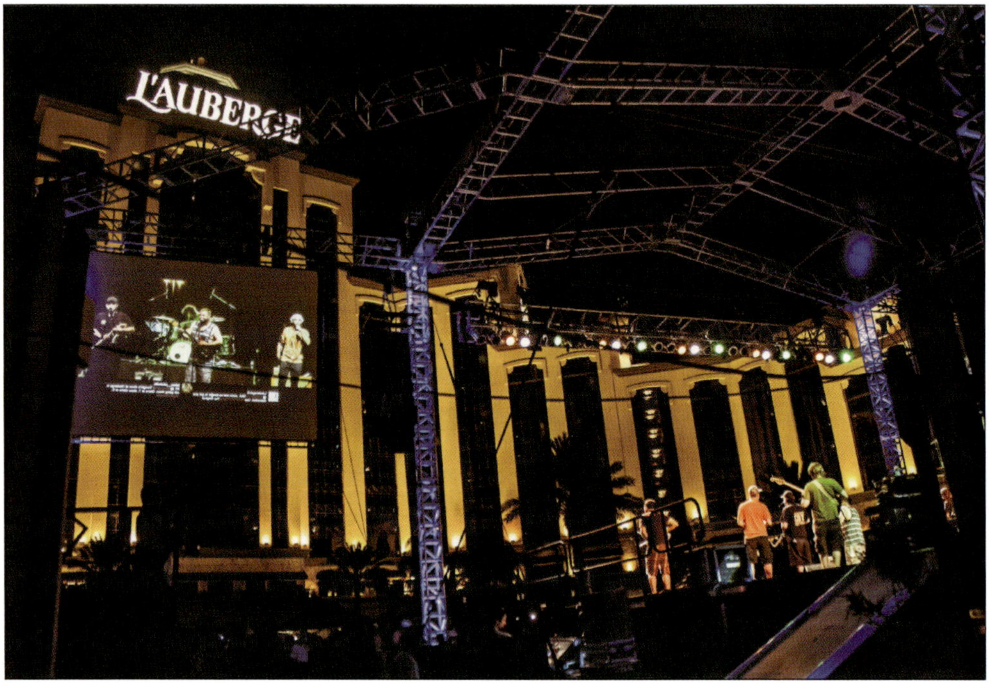

Ashes of Babylon also furthered their career by moving to Austin, and this 2012 photograph shows a performance at L'Auberge du Lac's Liquid Society, an annual series of concerts by the resort's pool. Formed in 2006, the band's Louisiana-infused reggae music has received acclaim from music critics and reggae fans. (Courtesy of Daniel Castro Photography.)

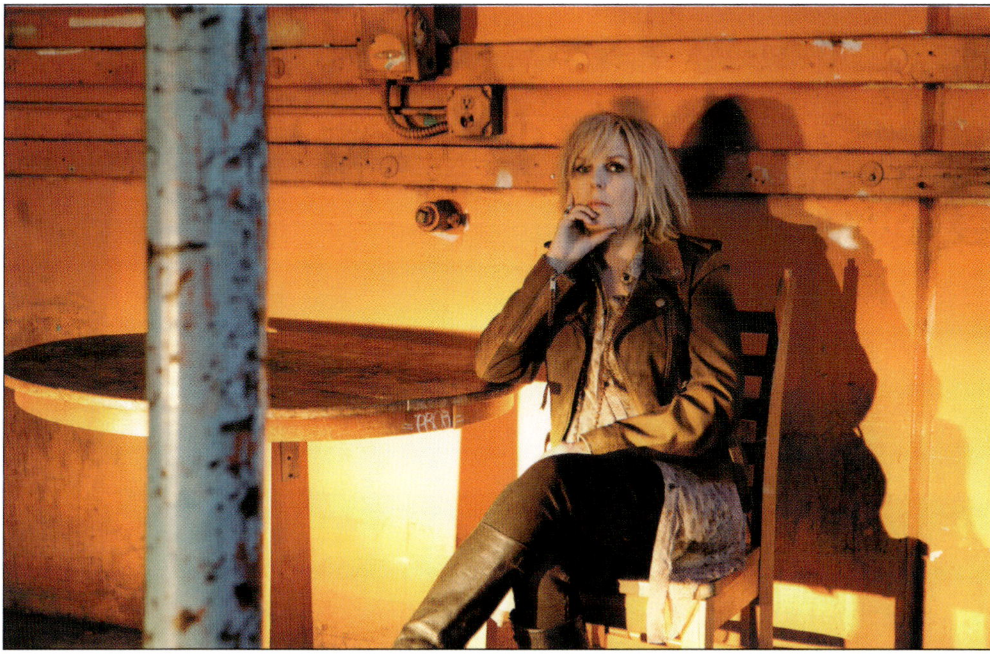

Lucinda Williams is a renowned singer-songwriter from Lake Charles whose music has been characterized as blues, rock, country, and folk. Her father, Miller Williams, was a poet and literature professor at McNeese. Lucinda Williams won a songwriting Grammy in 1994 for "Passionate Kisses," performed by Mary Chapin Carpenter. She won a Grammy in 1998 for her album *Car Wheels on a Gravel Road*, which went gold and included the locally beloved song "Lake Charles." (Courtesy of Michael Wilson.)

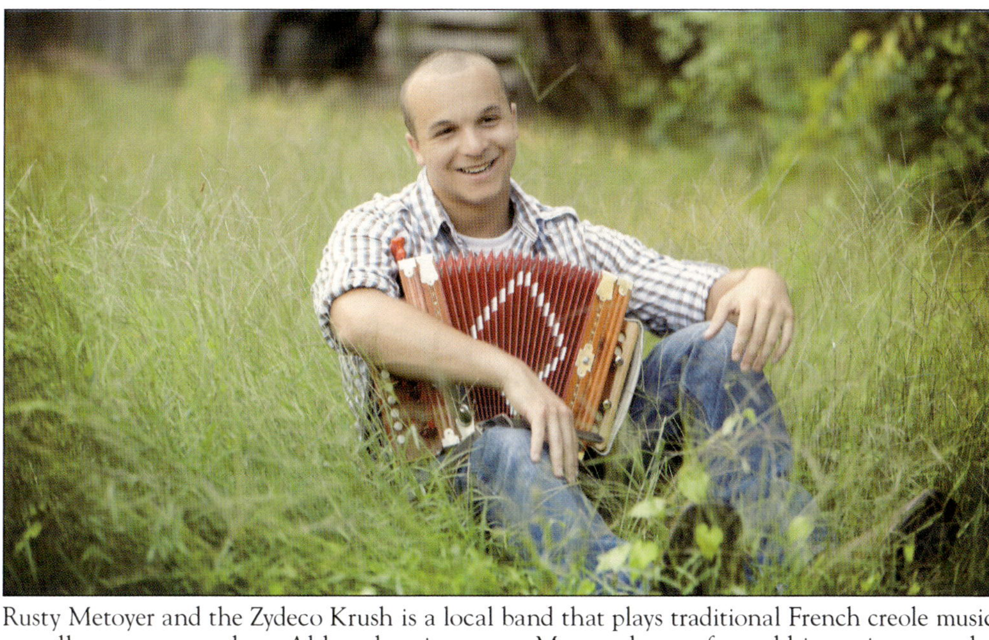

Rusty Metoyer and the Zydeco Krush is a local band that plays traditional French creole music as well as nouveau zydeco. Although quite young, Metoyer has performed his music across the United States and in France. He and the Zydeco Krush perform regularly at venues along the Gulf Coast. (Courtesy of Rusty Metoyer.)

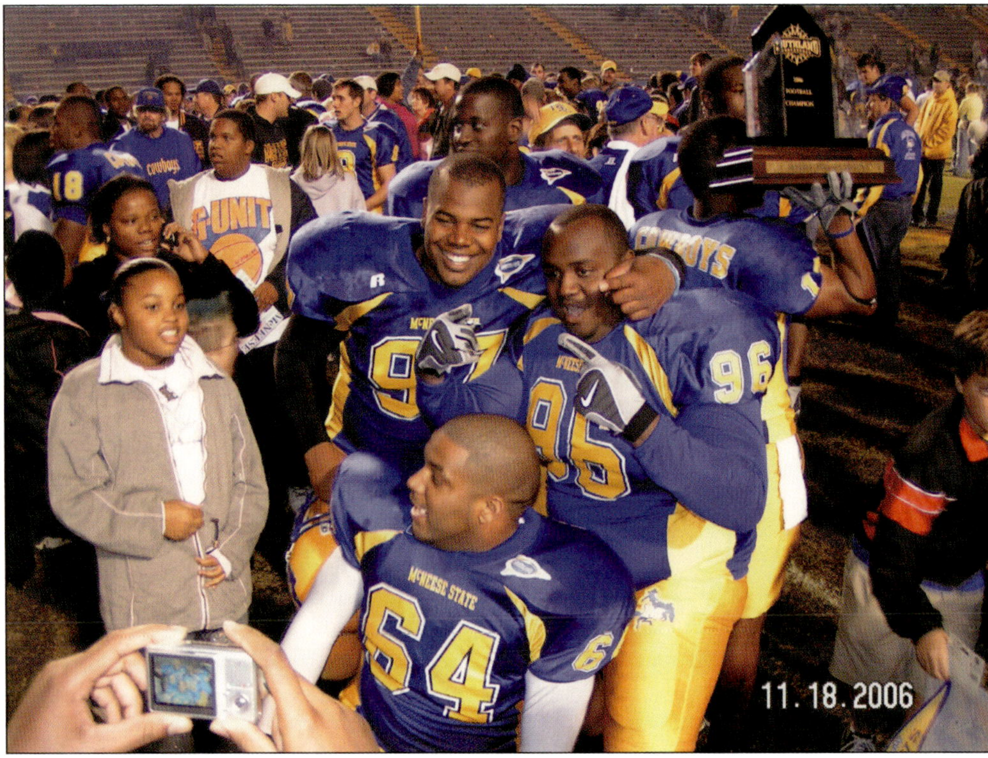

McNeese football players pose for photographs after defeating Nichols State University to clinch the Southland Conference Championship title in 2006. It was a dramatic year that saw Hurricane Rita recovery efforts and the changing of coaching leadership mid-season. Pictured are No. 97 Jerrell White, No. 96 Ken Jones, and No. 64 Brandon Toullier. (Courtesy of Dennis Thibodeaux.)

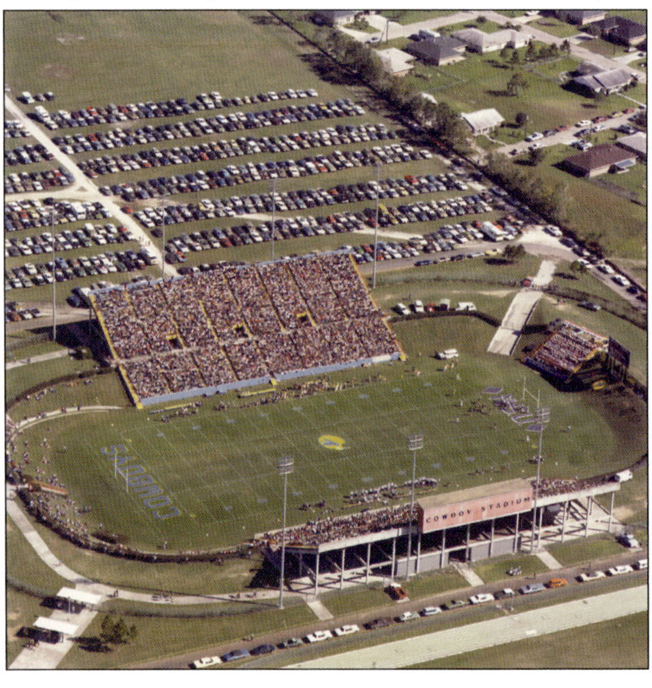

This aerial photograph shows Cowboy Stadium, home of the McNeese State University Cowboy football team. Originally constructed in 1965, it underwent an expansion in 1975 to accommodate over 17,000 fans. The Noland SkyRanch was added in 1998, and the Jack V. Doland Field House was added in 2011.

McNeese women's basketball enjoyed a banner year in 2011, when the team won the first of two back-to-back Southland Conference Championships and attended the NCAA Tournament for the first time since the program's inception in 1976. Cowgirl guard Ne'Aisha Anderson shoots a three-pointer in this 2011 photograph. (Courtesy of Dennis Thibodeaux.)

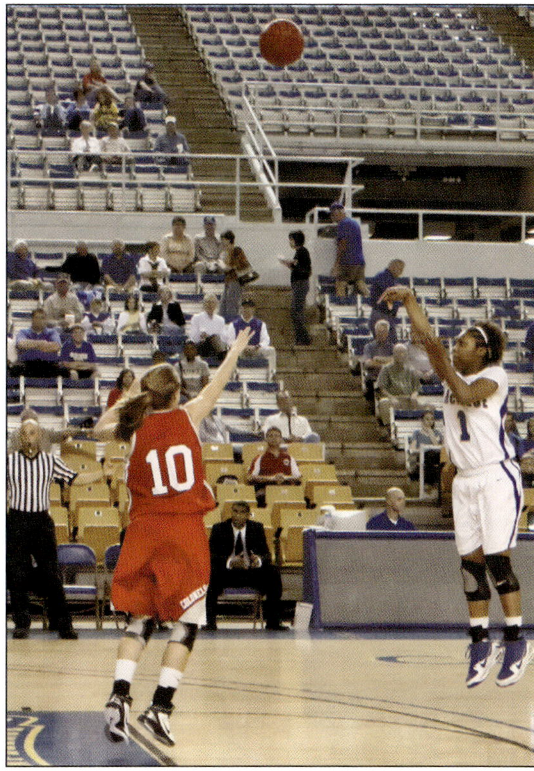

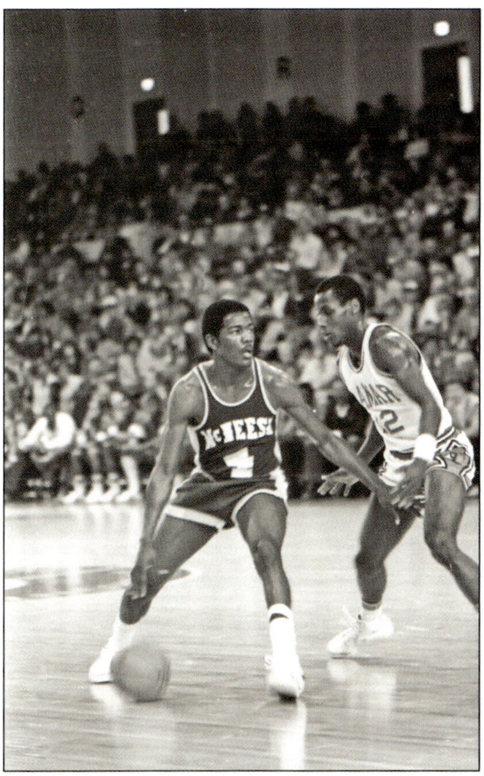

Joe Dumars is a former McNeese State University basketball player who was the 11th-leading scorer in NCAA history when he graduated in 1985. That year, Dumars began his 14-year career with the Detroit Pistons, including two championships. He was the inaugural recipient of the National Basketball Association's Sportsmanship Award in 1996 and is the namesake of the Dumars Trophy. (Courtesy of McNeese State University.)

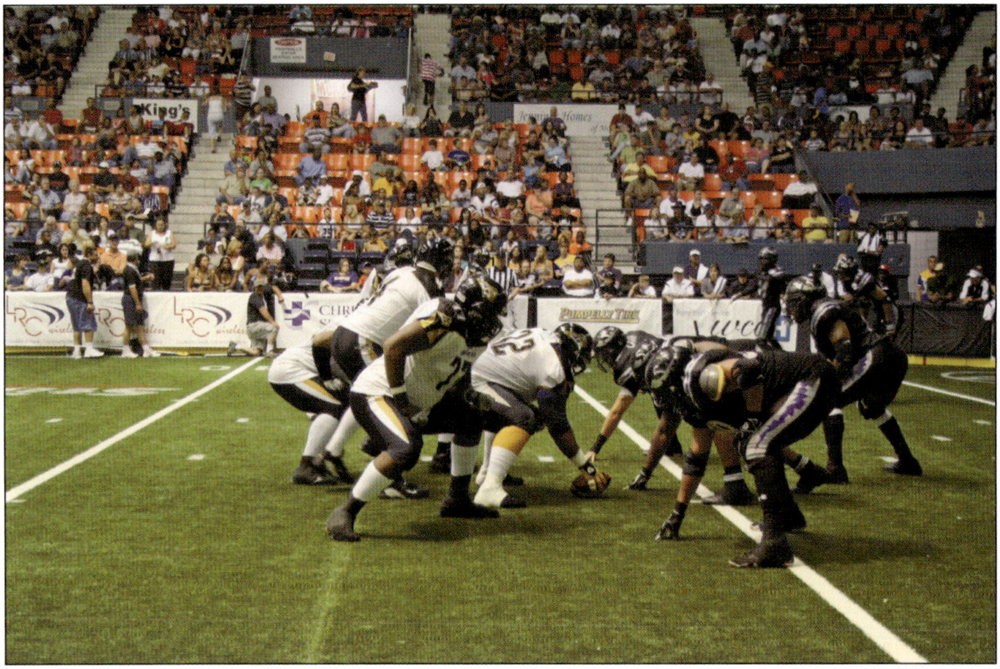

The Louisiana Swashbucklers (previously known as the Landsharks) began as a Lake Charles–based indoor football franchise that lasted from 2001 until its dissolution in 2013. Games were held in the Sudduth Coliseum at the Lake Charles Civic Center. This photograph depicts a playoff game in 2007 against the Odessa Roughnecks. (Courtesy of Dennis Thibodeaux.)

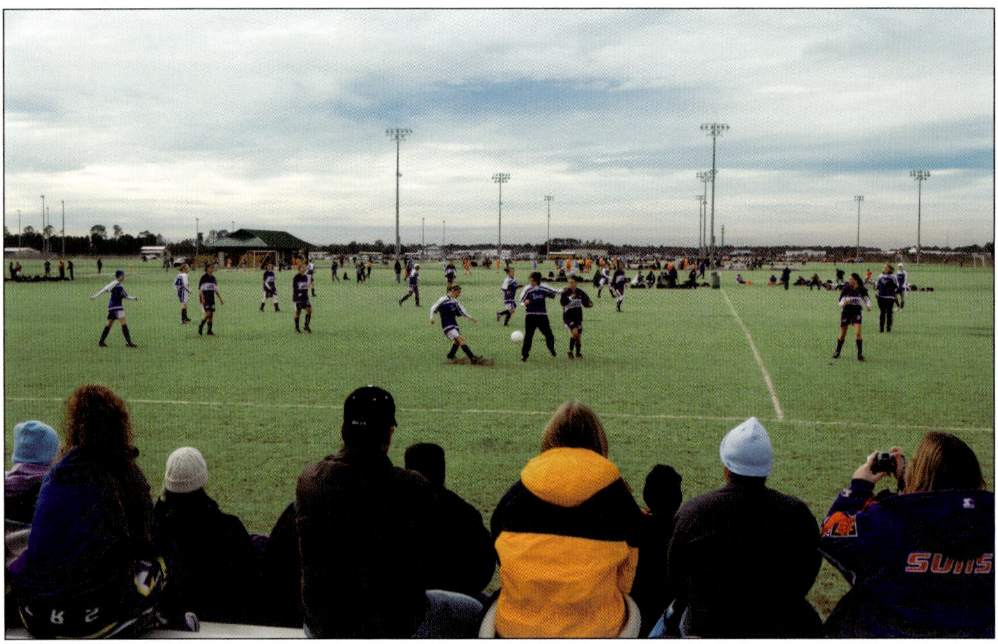

The Calcasieu Soccer Club organizes soccer leagues for different ages and competition levels, including the Screamin' Eagles Under 4 Soccer League. Games are held at the LaGrange Soccer Complex on School Street and at the Multi-Sports Complex at the Lake Charles Power Center. (Courtesy of www.monsoursphotography.net.)

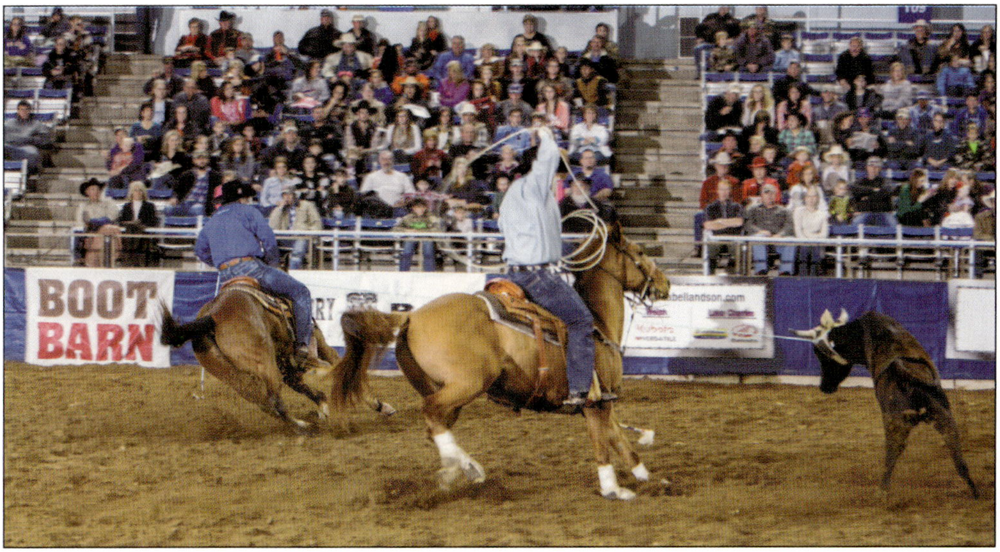

Rodeo is a long-standing tradition in Southwest Louisiana, and this photograph was taken at the Southwest District Livestock Show and Rodeo at Burton Coliseum. This major event features professional rodeo competitors and a livestock exhibit that awards over $50,000 in scholarships to winners. (Courtesy of www.monsoursphotography.net.)

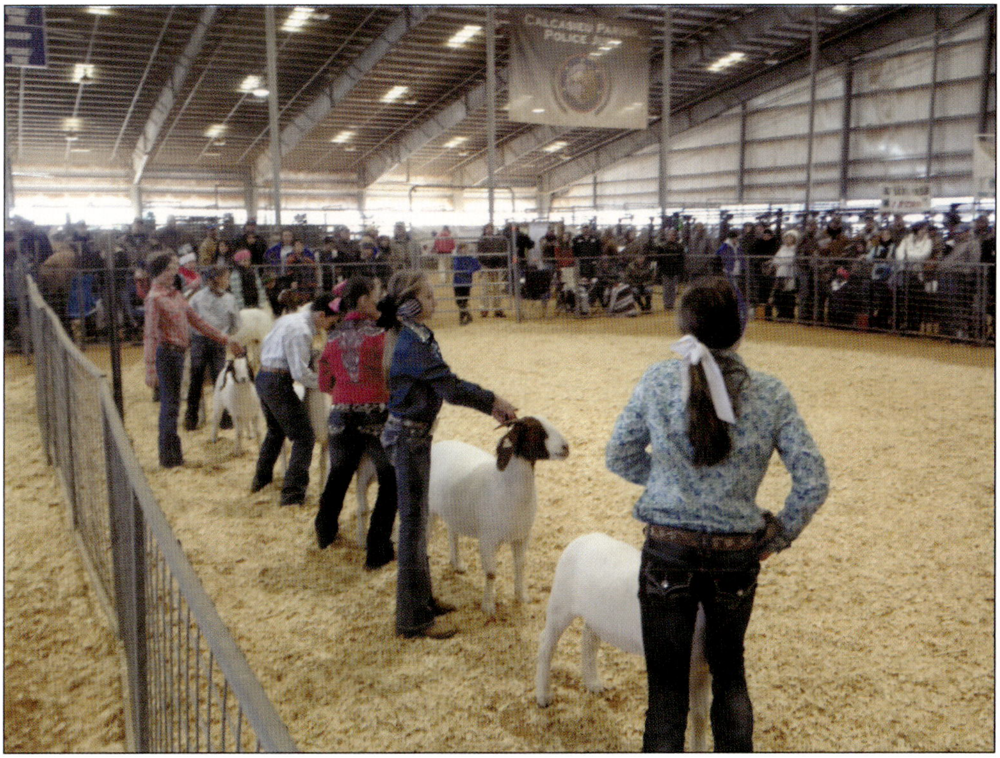

Seaman Knapp, father of the Southwest Louisiana rice industry, was hired in 1902 by the US Department of Agriculture, which created the 4-H youth program. The Calcasieu Parish has one of the oldest 4-H clubs, which is now operated by the LSU AgCenter. This photograph shows a 4-H livestock show at the Burton Complex on Common Street. (Courtesy of the LSU AgCenter.)

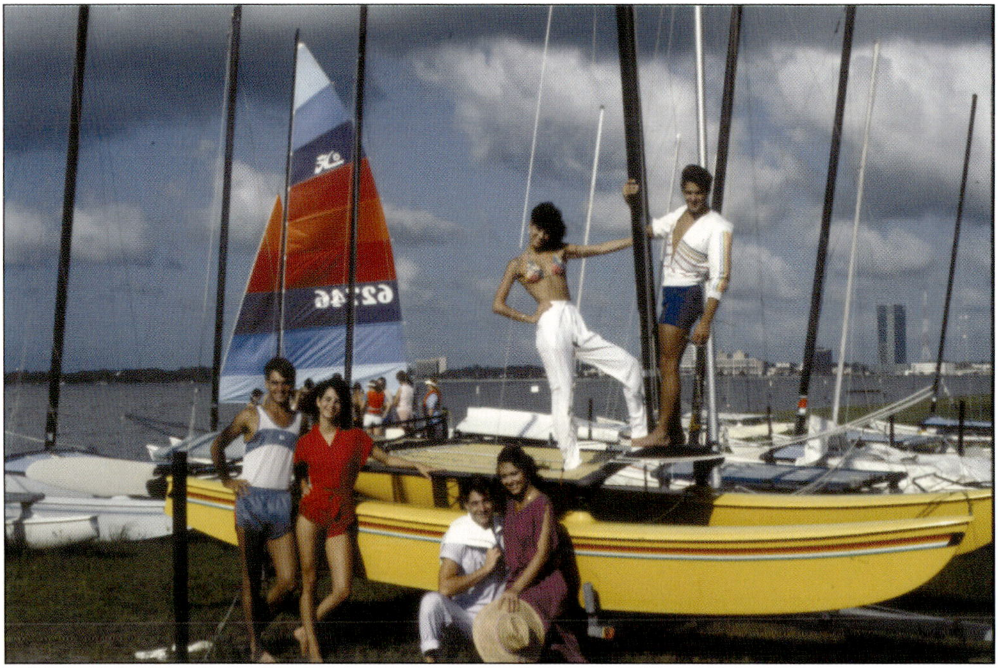

Lake Charles Yacht Club built a clubhouse and docks at the western end of North Beach. In addition to Wednesday-night sailing races around the lake, members participate in races and regattas with other yacht clubs along the Gulf Coast. This group of sailors is showing off its catamaran back in 1983.

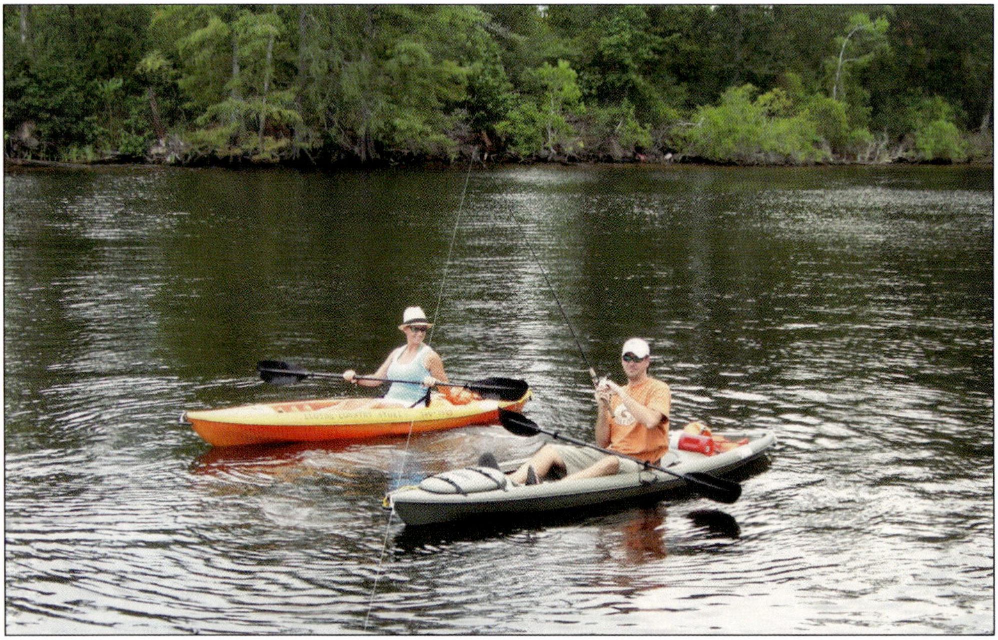

Kayaking, fishing, and crabbing are some of the ways residents enjoy the area's lakes, rivers, and bayous. Fish can include redfish, speckled trout, and sand trout. Many parks in Calcasieu Parish lie along the river with fishing docks and boat launches for those who want to spend time on the water. (Courtesy of www.visitlakecharles.org.)

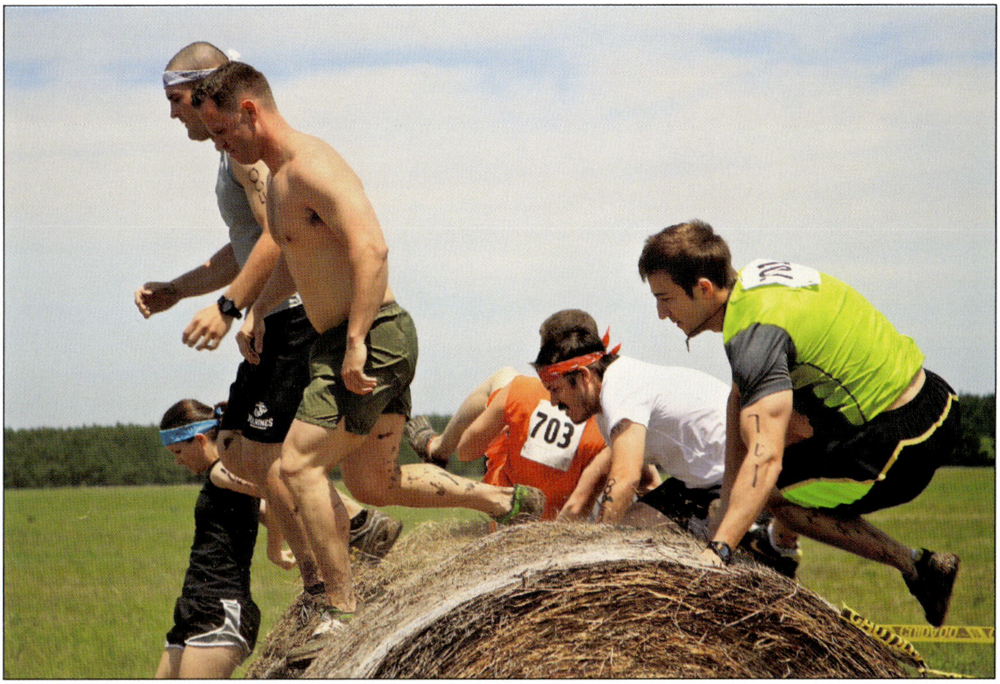

Lake Charles has an active running community that includes Go Run and Lake Area Runners. Races accompany every major festival, and they are often held as fundraisers. This 2013 photograph shows runners in the ReALLIEty Challenge, an obstacle-filled race organized by Allie Ieyoub that drew hundreds of runners from many states. (Courtesy of www.visitlakecharles.org.)

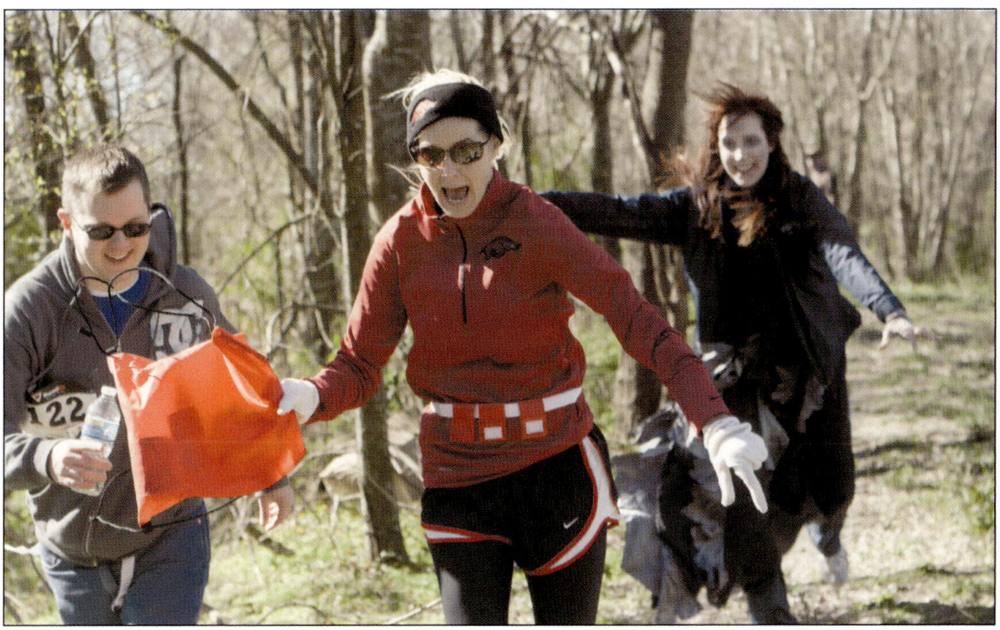

The End of the Human Race in 2013 is another example of events geared toward the active community in Lake Charles. Designed as a fundraiser for Fusion Five, a local young professionals' association, this race was held in northeast Lake Charles on Camp Edgewood Road. (Courtesy of Daniel Castro Photography.)

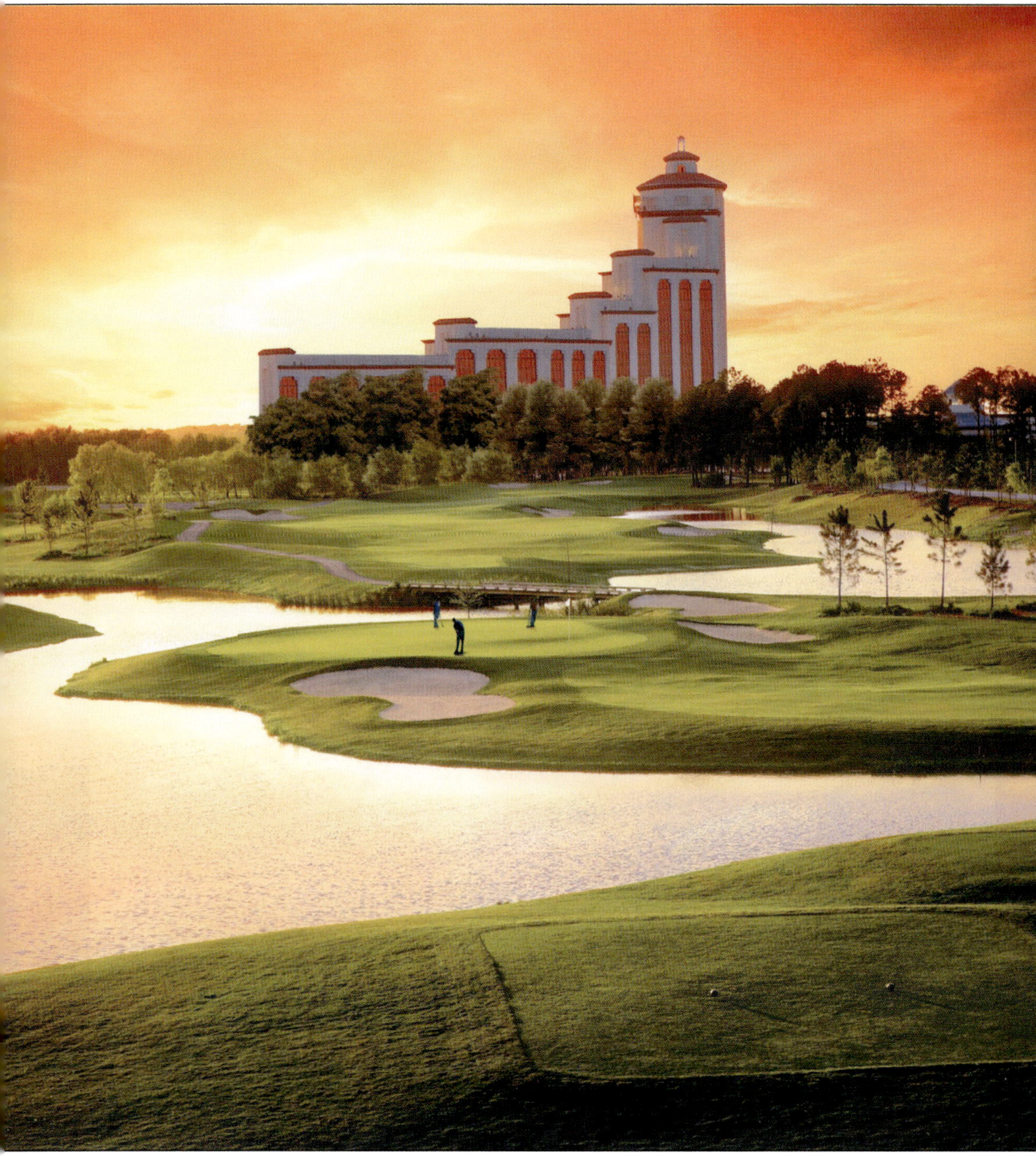

Contraband Bayou Golf Club at L'Auberge du Lac is an award-winning golf course designed by renowned golf architect Tom Fazio. Other local public golf courses include Gray Plantation in the southwest part of Lake Charles and the city's original municipal course, Mallard Cove Golf Course, which opened in 1976 near Chennault. (Courtesy of L'Auberge du Lac.)

Six

FOOD AND FESTIVALS

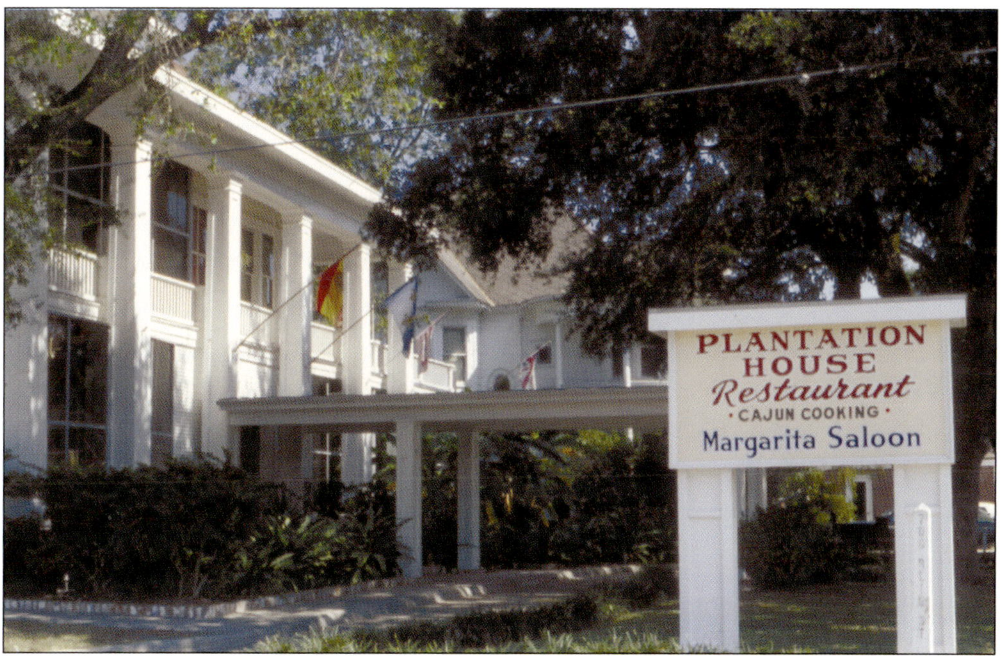

Ward's Plantation House Restaurant was opened at 903 Broad Street by Pearl and Axel Ward in 1964. The restaurant was known for fine Southern cooking, including chicken fried steak and seafood platters. The decor of the Plantation House included multiple fireplaces and red velvet curtains, and it is remembered as a place to celebrate special occasions or to impress a date.

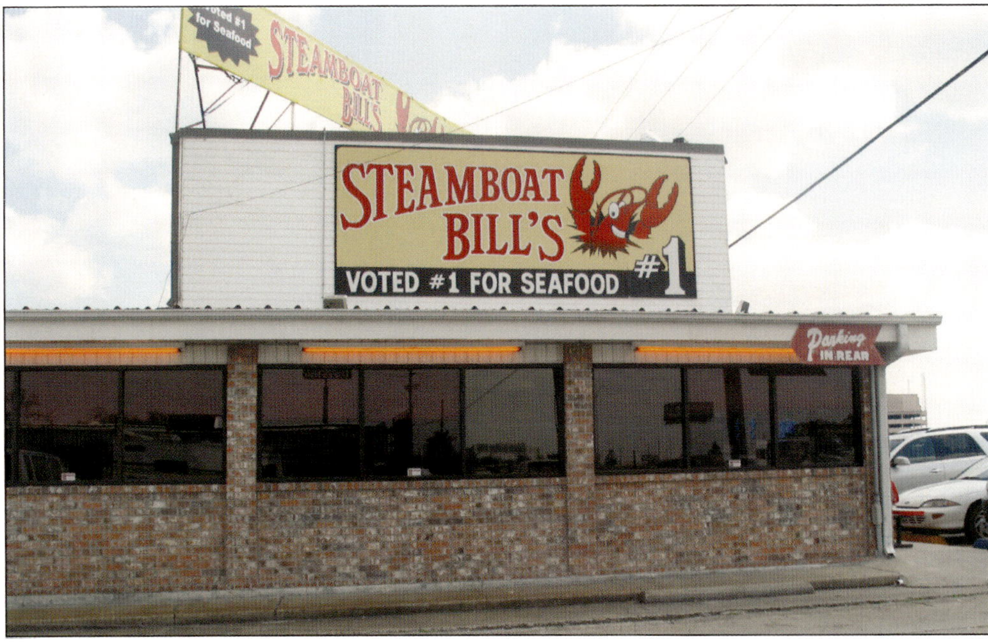

Kathi Kocik Bonamici came to Lake Charles in 1982 from Chicago and began selling shrimp. Her business grew to include her own shrimp dock and plant, and she opened Steamboat Bill's in 1985. The restaurant is famous for its boiled crawfish, shrimp, and crabs, and it features authentic Cajun dishes, including jambalaya and etoufee. (Courtesy of www.visitlakecharles.org.)

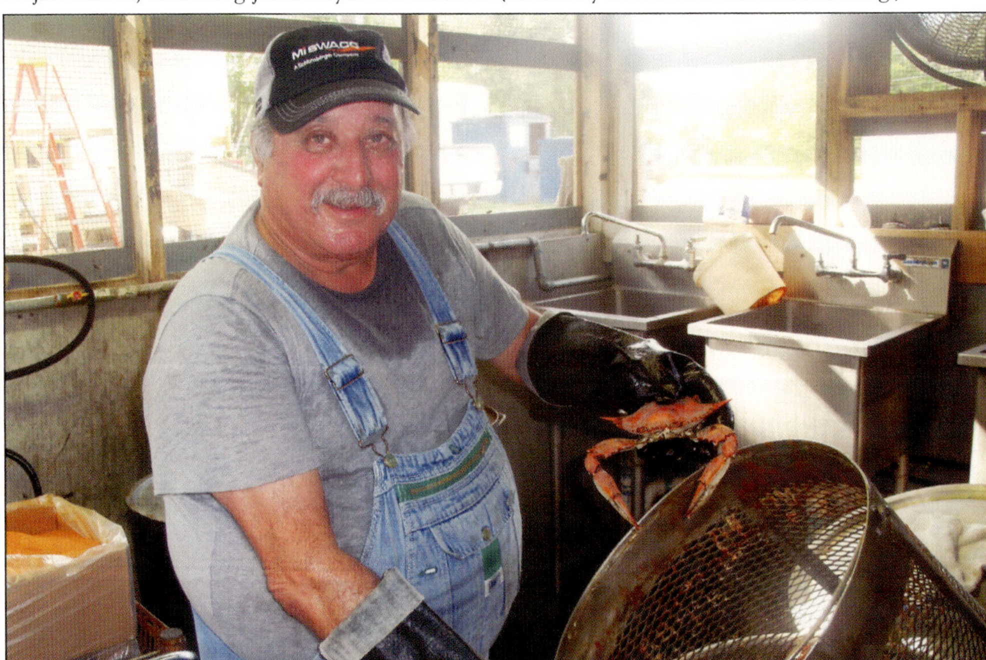

Paul Papania holds a blue crab over the boiling pot at Seafood Palace on Enterprise Boulevard, the former Crab Palace. The restaurant is owned by David Papania, and David and Paul come from a family of Lake Charles restaurateurs. Their father and mother, Frank and Louise, ran Papania's on the corner of Highway 14 and Broad Street.

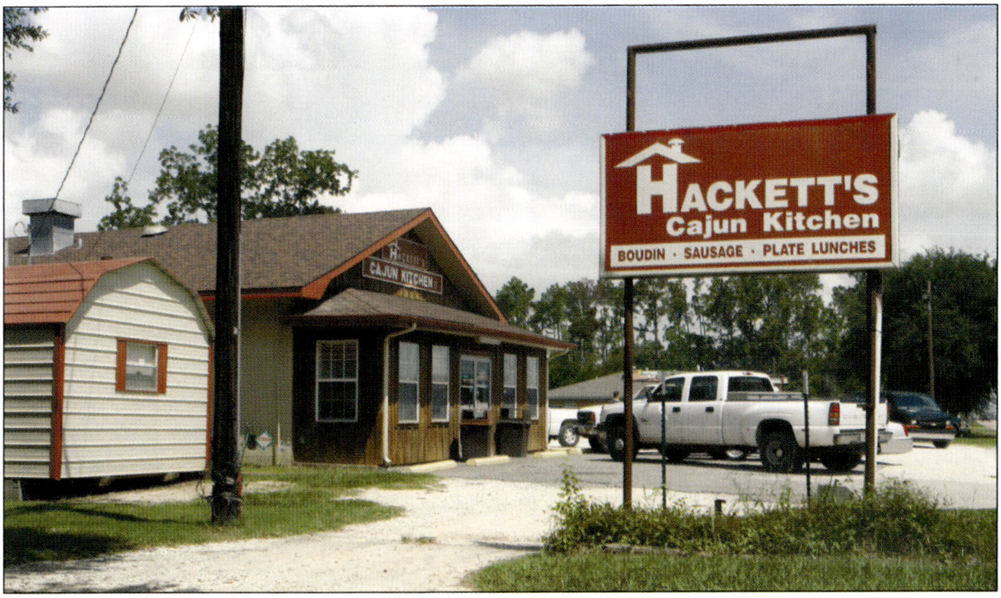

Charlie and Karen Hackett opened Hackett's Cajun Kitchen in 1988. It is one of several popular places to not only have a home-style plate lunch, but also purchase foods unique to this part of the state, including boudin, tasso, cracklins, and smoked sausage varieties such as andouille, alligator, and crawfish with pork. (Courtesy of www.visitlakecharles.org.)

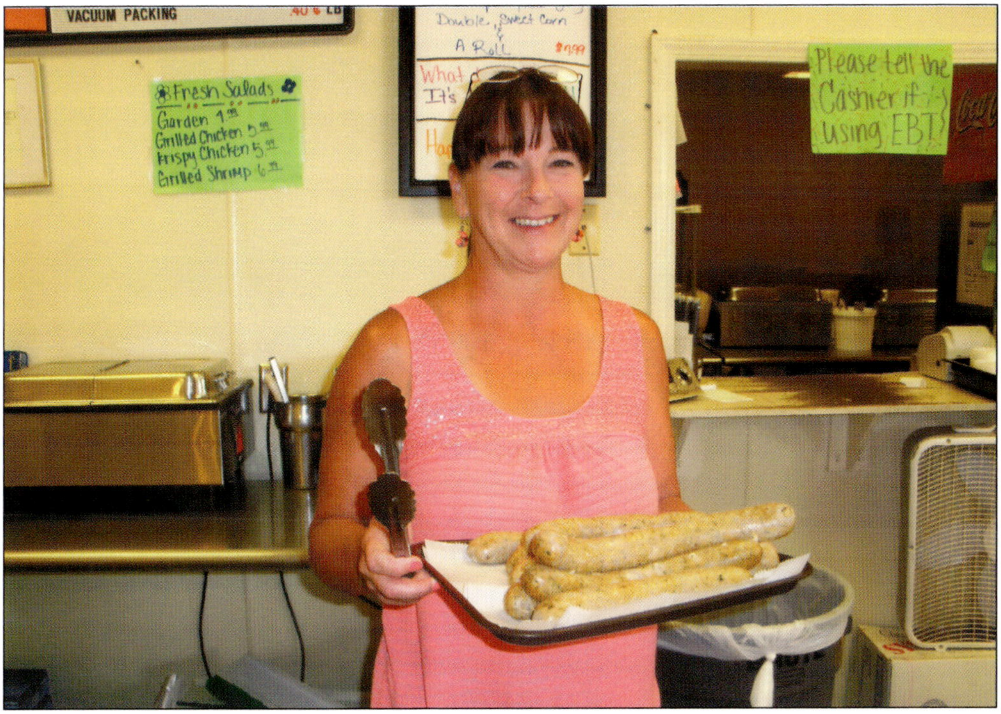

Boudin is a sausage casing filled with a mixture of pork, rice, liver, onions, and spices, but a butcher could use crawfish, green onion, shrimp, or even alligator. Ledra Marburger from Billedeaux's Cajun Kitchen holds some fresh boudin in this 2014 picture. Billedeaux's is part of the Boudin Trail of Southwest Louisiana, which showcases the best boudin producers in the region.

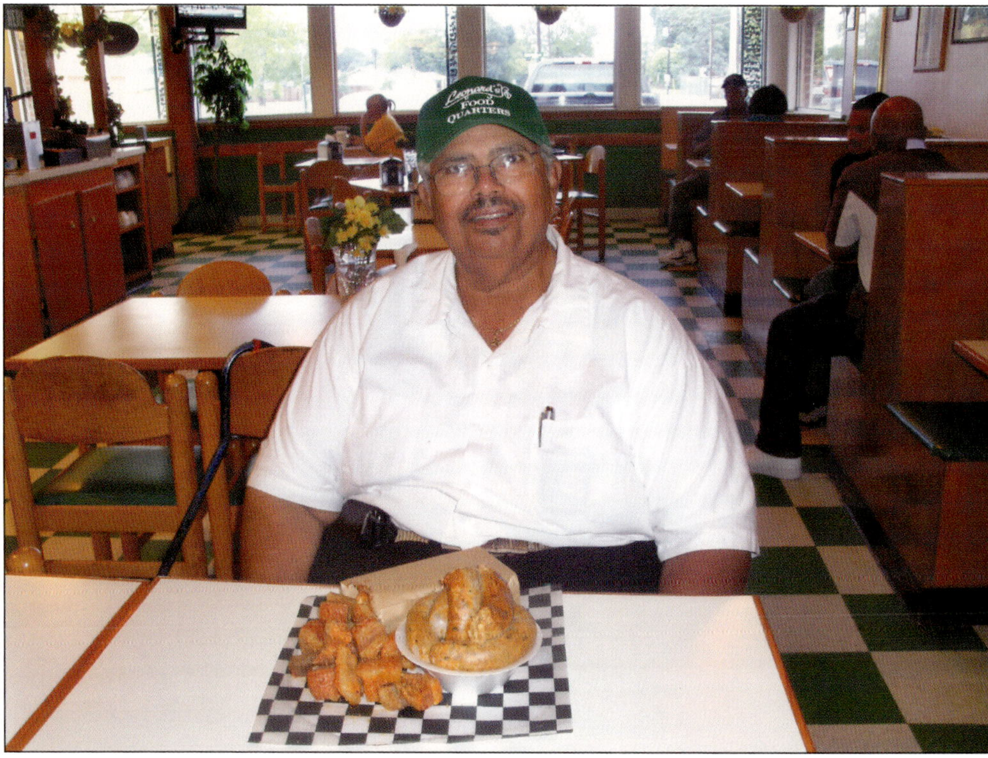

Leonard's Food Quarters at Highway 14 and Legion Street is owned and operated by Leonard Fusilier and his sons Marlon and Troy. Featuring Louisiana fare like red beans and rice and gumbo, the restaurant also serves pizza, something Leonard learned to cook when he worked at Tony's Pizza during his youth. Leonard is pictured here in 2014 with his restaurant's famous cracklins and boudin.

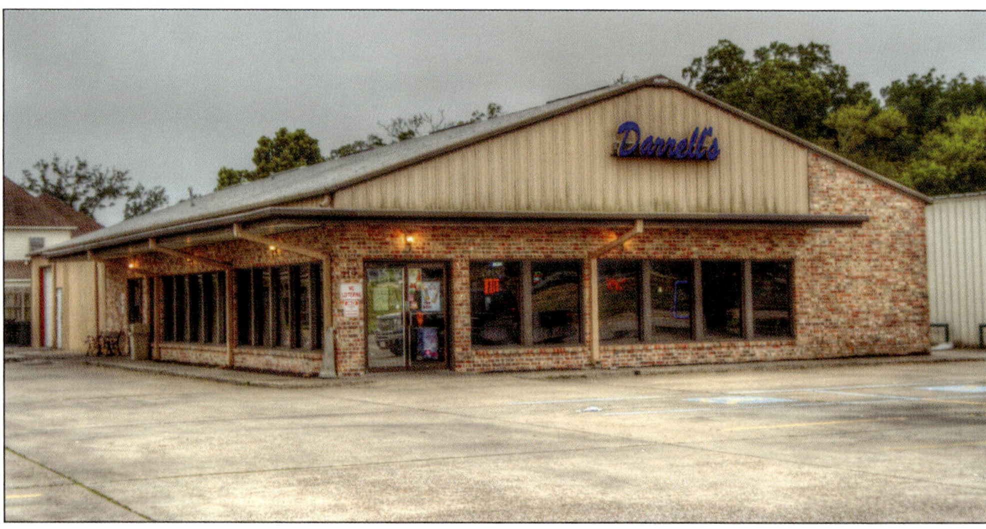

Darrell DeRouen opened his bar on Ryan Street in 1985, but his famous sandwiches came years later. He moved to his College Street location, pictured here, in 1996. Now serving a simple menu of eight po'boys, the most popular item is the Darrell's Special with ham, turkey, roast beef, and cheese with gravy and jalapeno mayo. (Courtesy of Dennis Thibodeaux.)

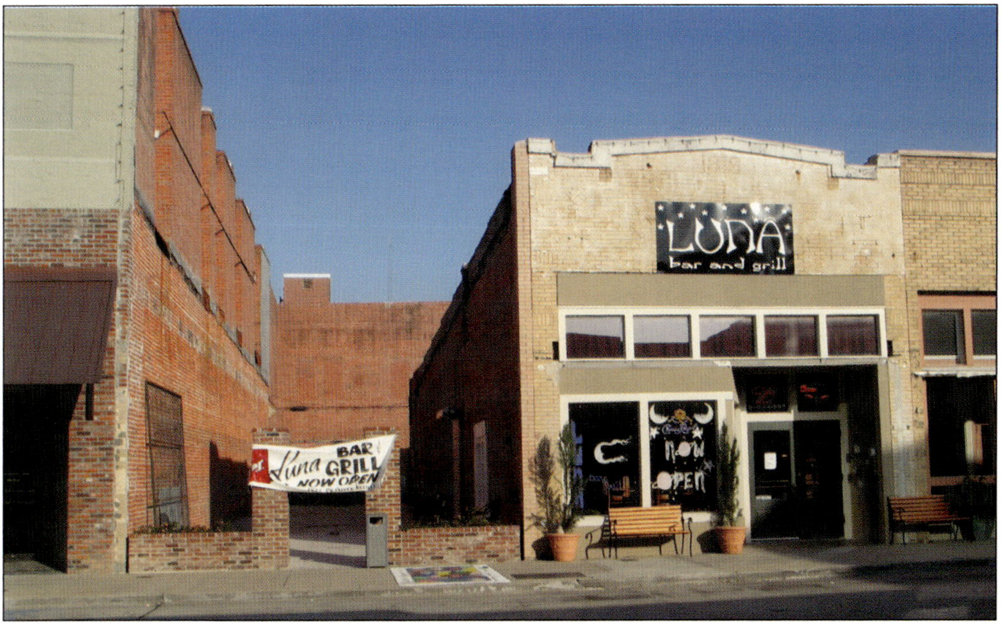

Dave Evans opened Luna Bar and Grill in October 2004 on Prewett Street, but Hurricane Rita destroyed the building in September 2005. Evans reopened three months later at the current location pictured here on Ryan Street. He comes from a family of Lake Charles restaurateurs, including his parents, who owned and operated Normandy Lounge and Dave's Oyster House. (Courtesy of www.visitlakecharles.org.)

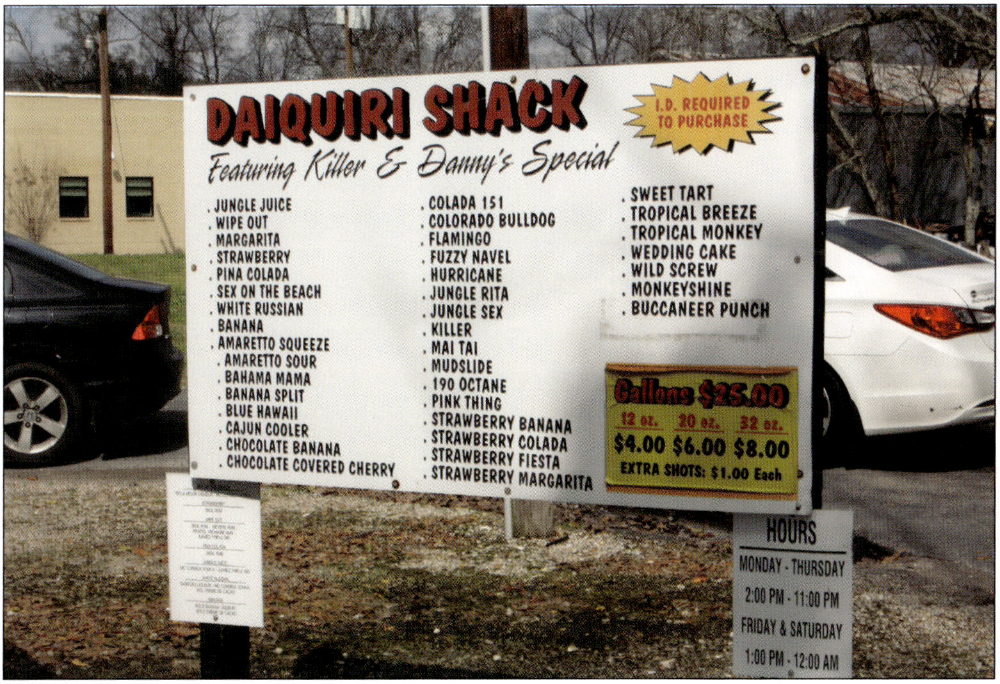

One of South Louisiana's most unique offerings is the drive-through daiquiri stand. The Daiquiri Shack on Ryan Street is one of several in the city where drivers can purchase the frozen drink with its signature strip of masking tape across the lid. (Courtesy of Doug Hill.)

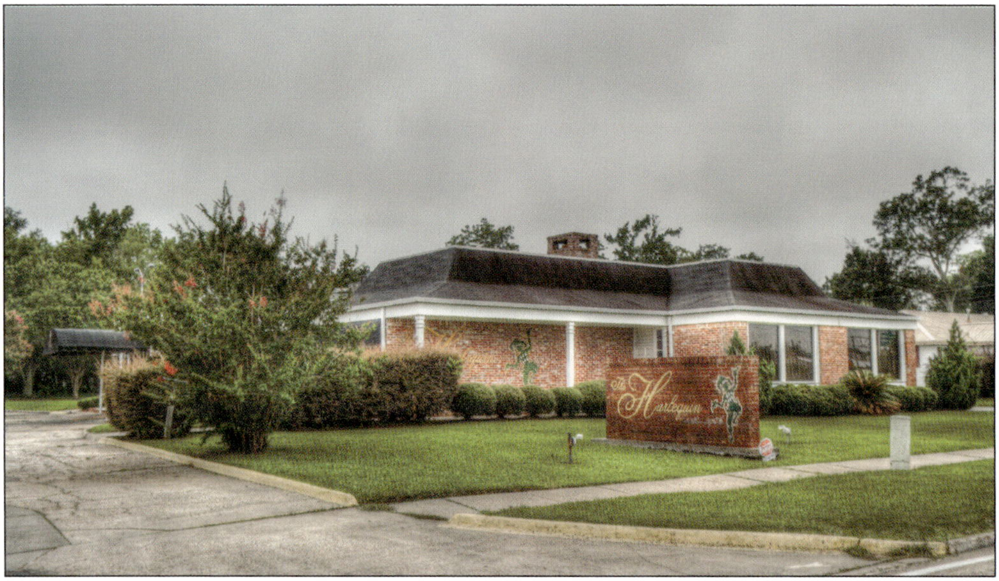

Edward and Lucille Hunter opened Harlequin Steak House and Cocktail Lounge in 1956 on Highway 14 and Legion Street. Harlequin is the city's oldest family-owned restaurant, and it is currently operated by the Hunters' grandson Nicholas Hunter. He moved it to its current location on College Street, pictured here, in 2004. (Courtesy of Dennis Thibodeaux.)

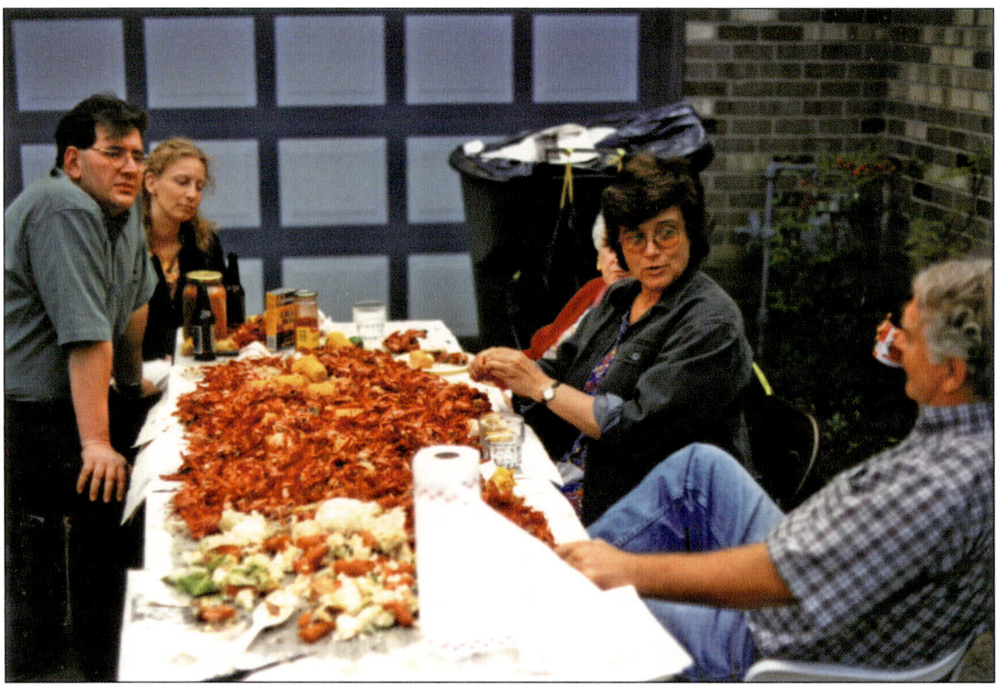

This is a picture of a typical home-style crawfish boil. Crawfish go from the boiling pot into ice chests so they retain their heat. The crawfish are then scooped onto long tables lined with newspaper. Heavily seasoned, crawfish are often boiled with corn, potatoes, sausage, and vegetables. Pictured is Carrie Chrisco (second from the right) with her mother and fellow members of the Banners Arts and Humanities Committee.

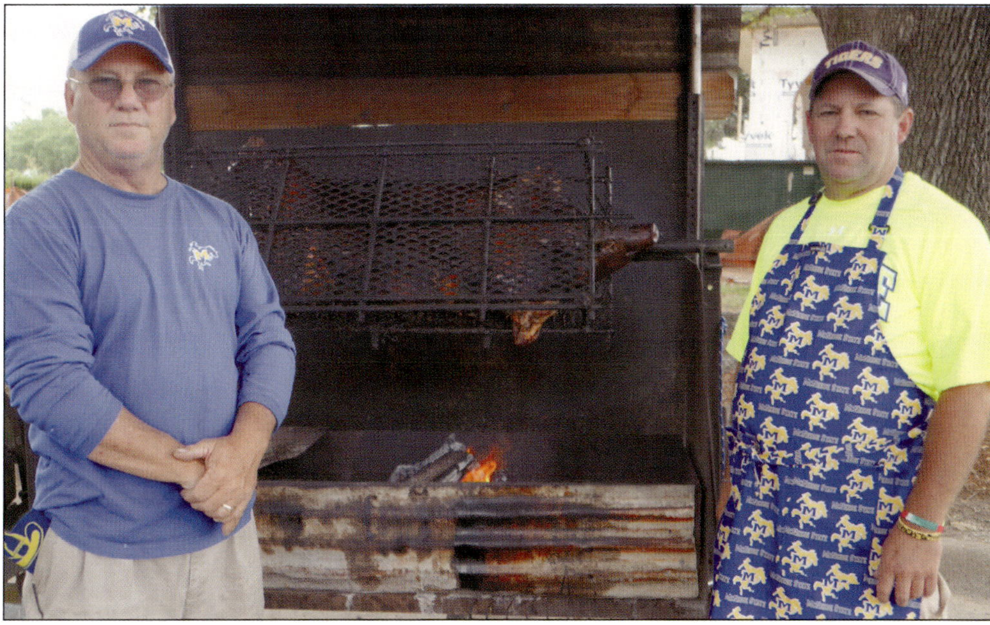

Cochon de lait, French for "pig in milk," describes the traditional Cajun method of roasting a suckling pig over an open fire. These days, a pig might be up to 100 pounds and roasted over a fire pit, in a cooking shed, or in a Cajun microwave roasting box. Darald Bubba Doga and Troy Viator prepare this pig at the McNeese Alumni Center. (Courtesy of Joyce Patterson.)

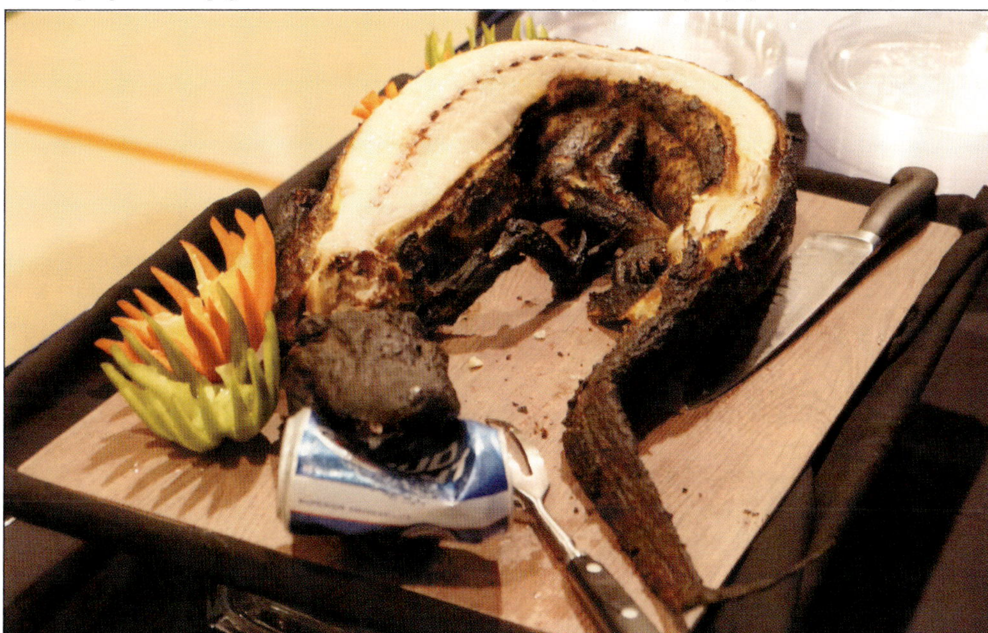

The Louisiana Department of Wildlife and Fisheries manages the annual harvest of Louisiana alligators, which are often used in sausage, boudin, and other popular South Louisiana recipes. Roasting or smoking an entire alligator is an impressive display reserved for big events, such as the Crocodile Specialist Group Conference in 2014 at McNeese State University, pictured here. (Courtesy of Joyce Patterson.)

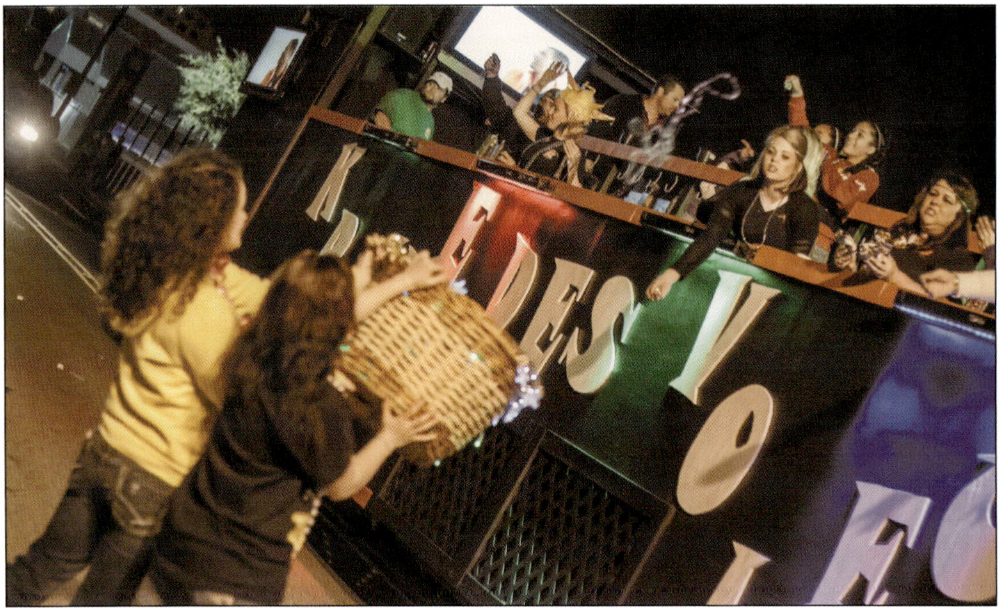

The Mardi Gras of Imperial Calcasieu group organized the first Merchants Parade in 1990. Held on Friday night before Shrove Tuesday, the Merchants Parade is the first to roll through Lake Charles during the Mardi Gras holiday. Members of area businesses and social organizations ride on floats and throw beads, doubloons, plastic cups, and other items to the crowd. (Courtesy of Daniel Castro Photography.)

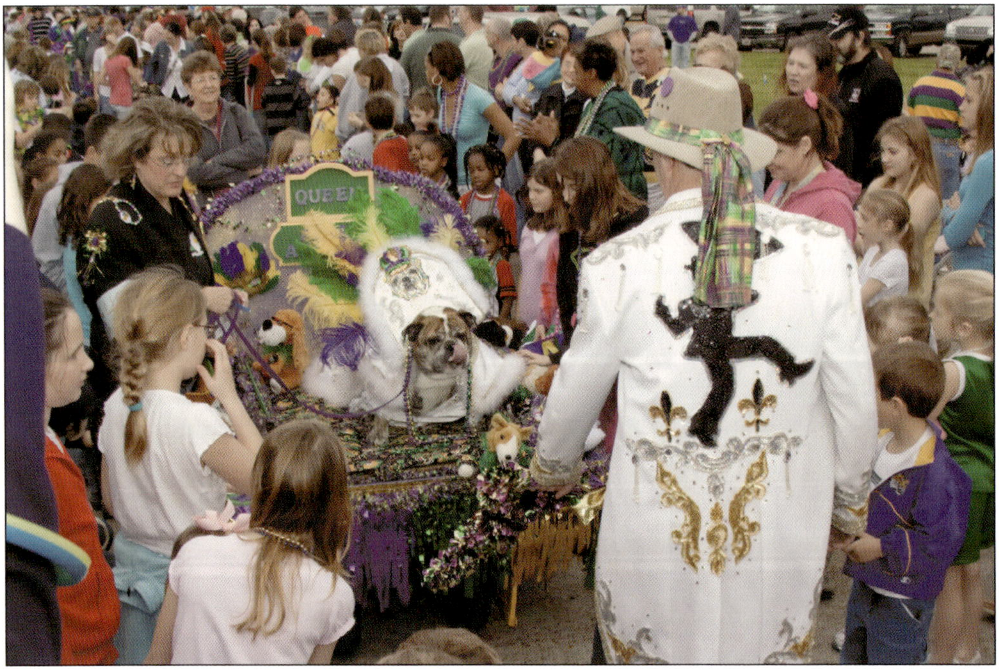

The Krewe of Barkus Parade has been a popular Lake Charles Mardi Gras tradition since 1996. Dogs and their owners dress in Mardi Gras regalia or other costumes and parade along Bord du Lac Drive near the lakefront. The title of "Mystical Dog" is awarded to the dog with the finest costume. (Courtesy of Dennis Thibodeaux.)

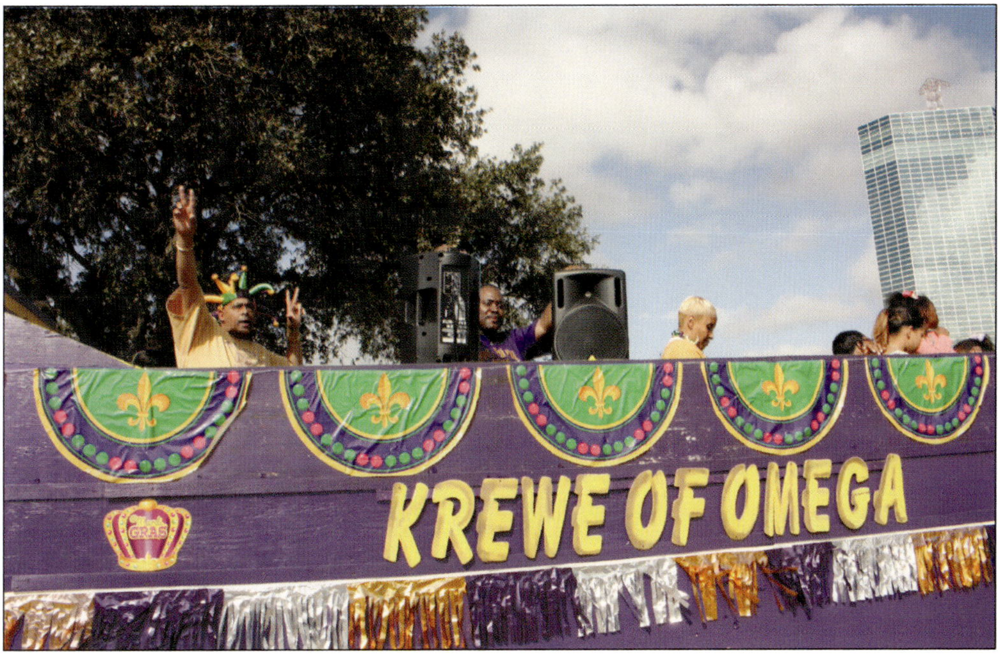

The Krewe of Omega was formed in 1970 as a community service organization benefiting the young and elderly. Many members of the Krewe of Omega are also members of the Rho Chi chapter of Omega Psi Phi. It is the only krewe in Southwest Louisiana to hold its own parade. (Courtesy of Doug Hill.)

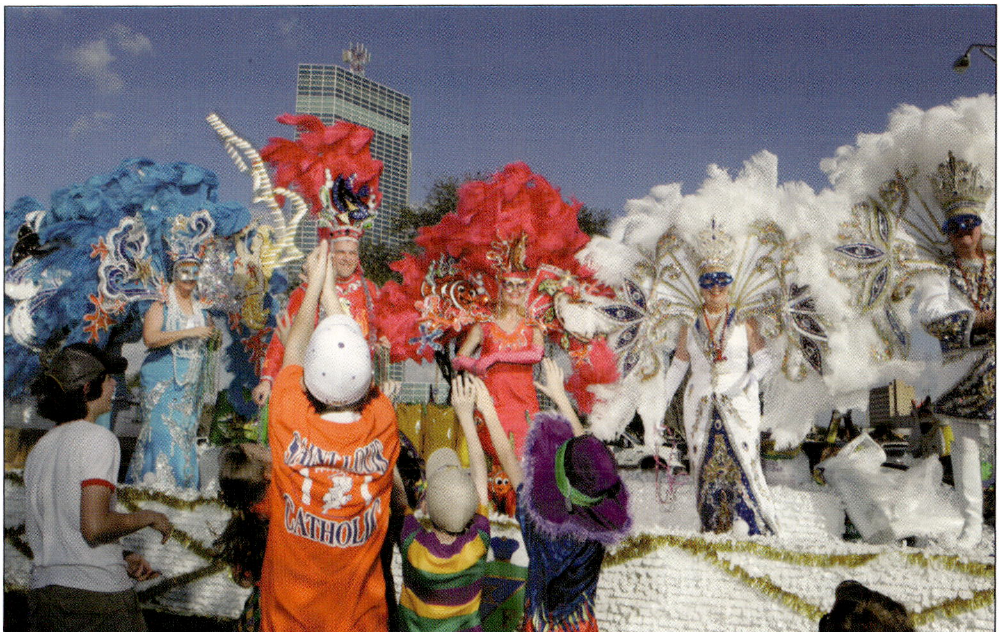

Under the leadership of Anne Monlezun, the Krewe of Krewes formed in 1979 as a way to bring all of the local krewes together for a Mardi Gras parade. Every Fat Tuesday, the Krewe of Krewes Parade provides a lavish finale to the series of Mardi Gras festivities held in Lake Charles. (Courtesy of monsoursphotography.net.)

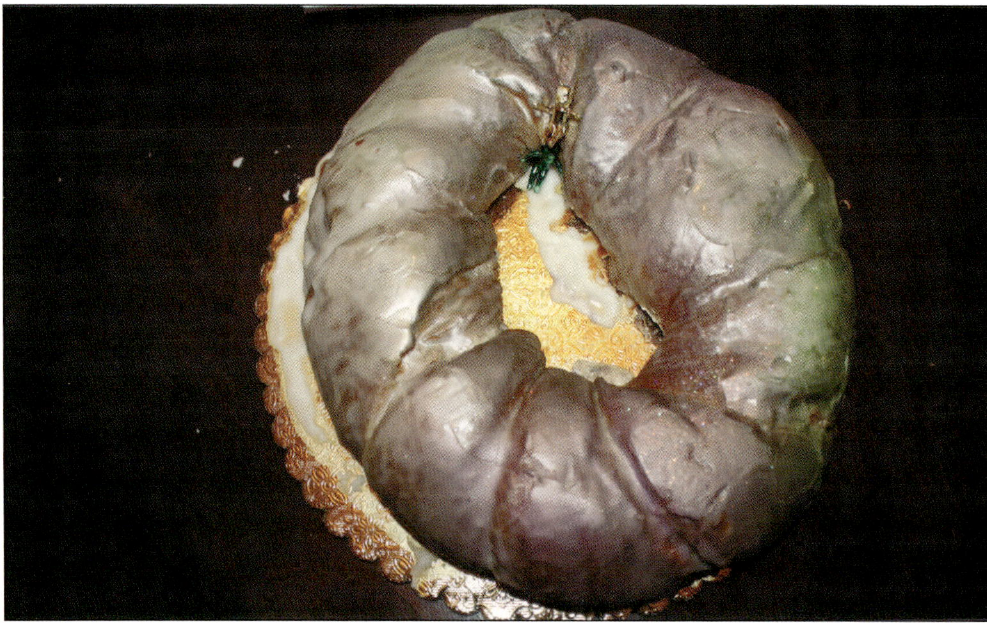

King cakes appear in grocery stores and bakeries from Twelfth Night in January until Mardi Gras before the start of Lent. A small plastic baby is inserted in the cake, and the person who receives the baby in their piece must buy the king cake for the next party. (Courtesy of Doug Hill.)

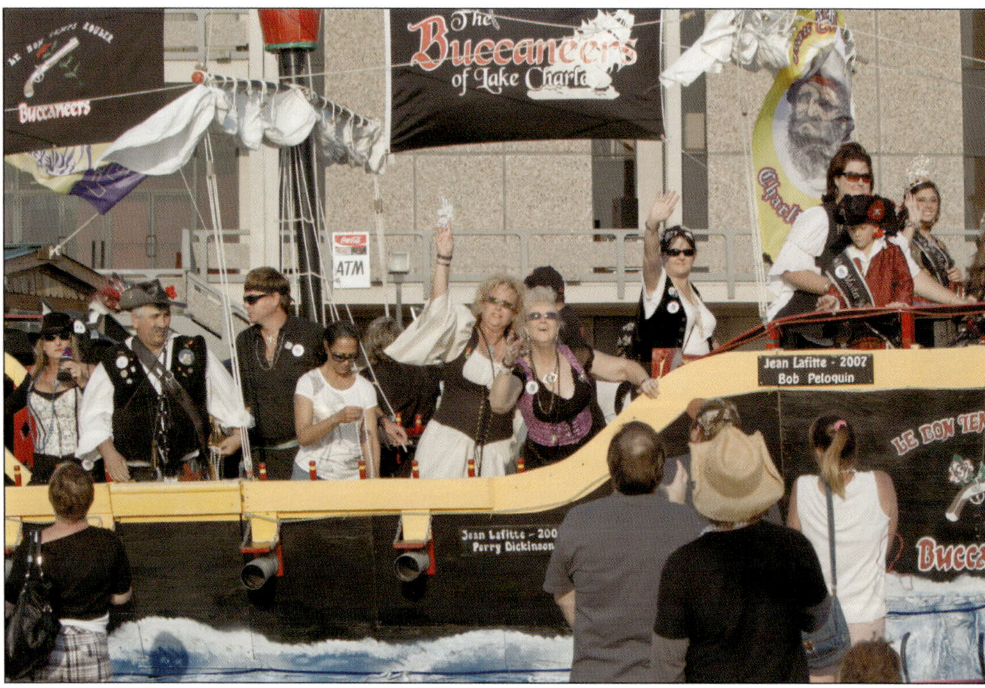

The Buccaneers is a social club in Lake Charles created to promote the city's annual festival, Contraband Days. This 2011 photograph shows a Buccaneer parade float near the Lake Charles Civic Center, where the festival is held each spring. Buccaneers roam around the festival in costume handing out beads and doubloons, as well as participating in daily festival events. (Courtesy of Dennis Thibodeaux.)

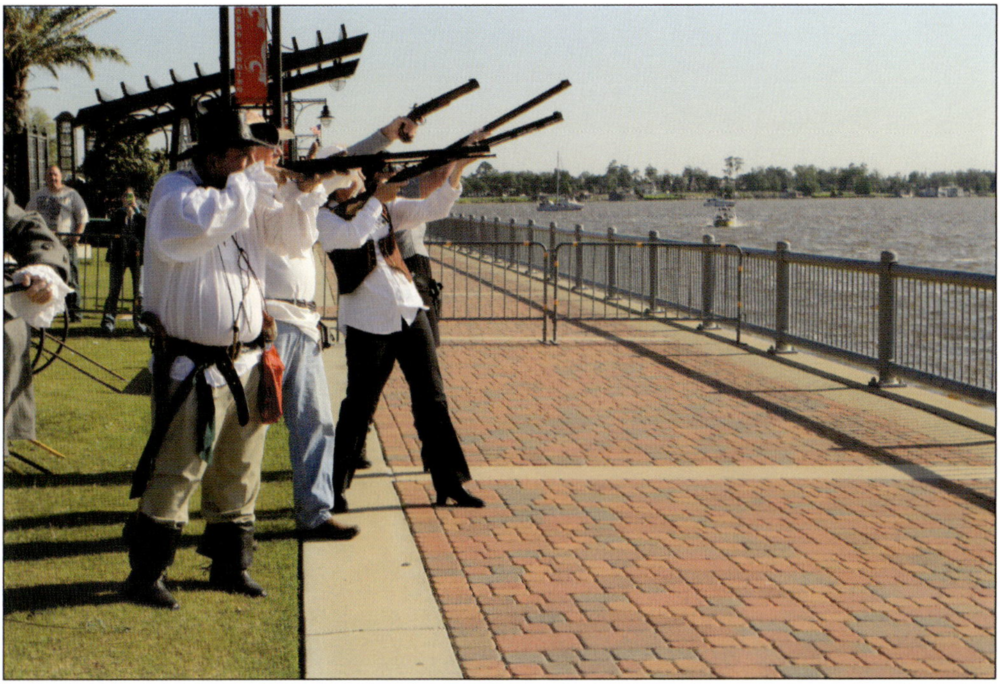

Contraband Days begins with the invasion of a fleet of Buccaneers on the lakefront. This 2013 photograph shows the "city militia" trying to prevent the Buccaneers from landing. Contraband Days began in 1958 as a one-day festival of water events, and it has grown to include over 100 events covering 12 days in May. (Courtesy of Parker Brand Creative.)

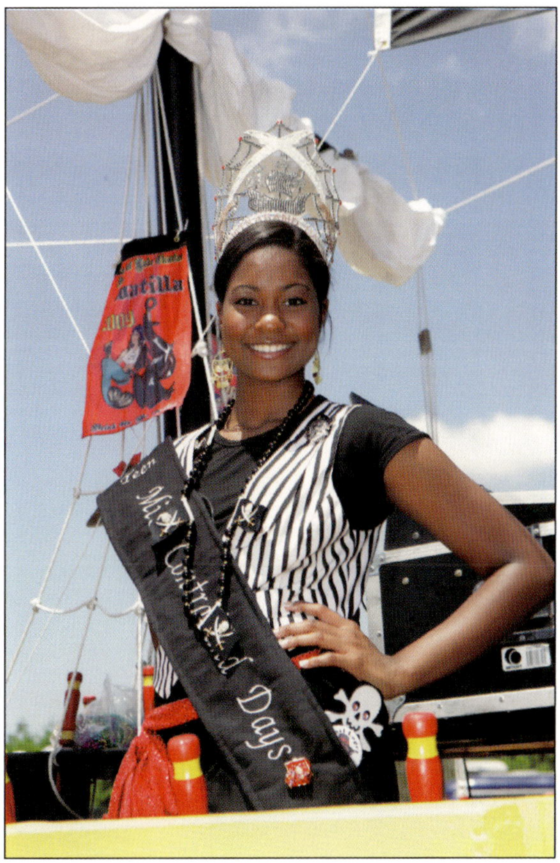

Maaliyah Papillion was the 2009 Teen Miss Contraband Days at the annual pageant that began in 1956 as the Miss Lake Charles contest. Other events during the festival include a pirogue-building contest, an arm wrestling tournament, and a barbecue cook-off. (Courtesy of monsoursphotography.net.)

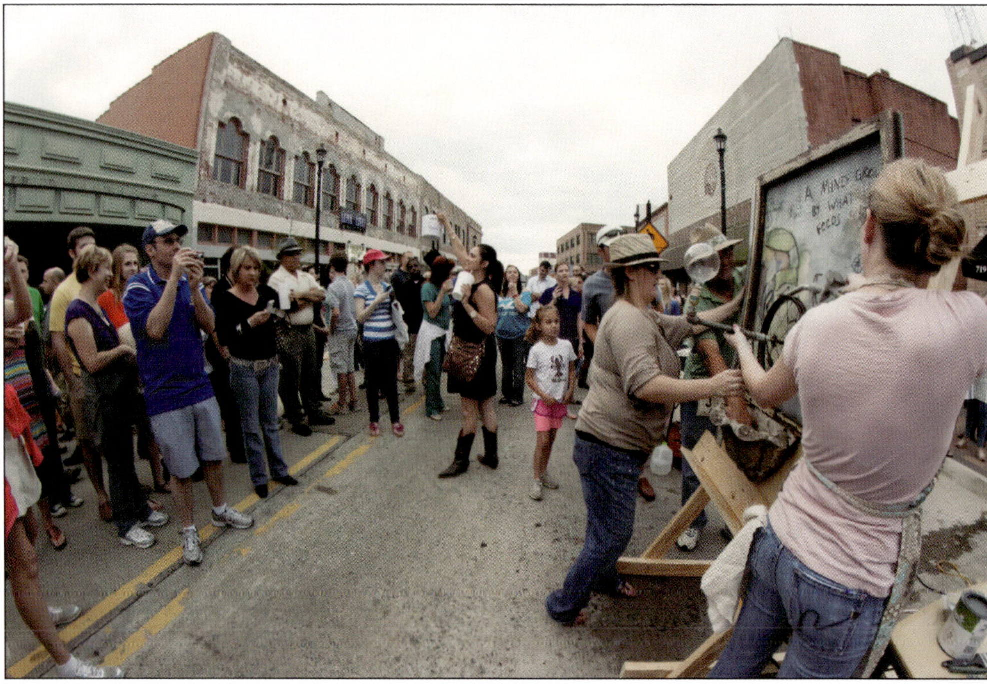

The Spring Art Walk was begun in 2006 by the Arts and Humanities Council of Southwest Louisiana as a downtown event featuring local artists and galleries. The Art Battle was added in 2011, and it challenges individual artists or teams to create a mural in one hour in front of a live audience. (Courtesy of Daniel Castro Photography.)

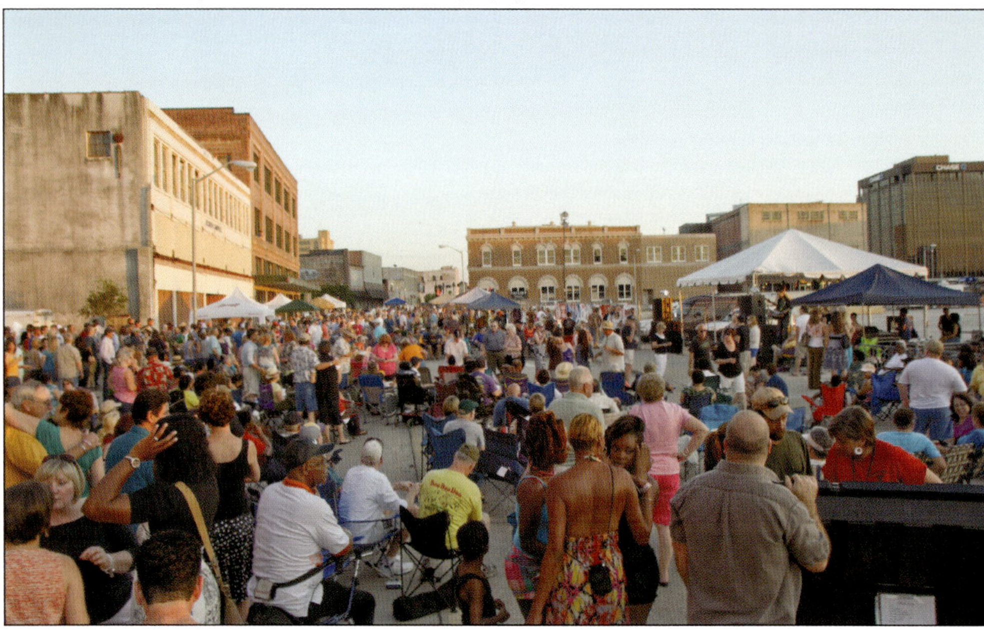

Downtown at Sundown began in 1999 as a way to attract people to the downtown area and showcase local artists, musicians, and restaurants. The Lake Charles/Southwest Louisiana Convention and Visitors Bureau organizes the annual block party–style event with proceeds benefitting the Arts and Humanities Council of Southwest Louisiana. (Courtesy of Dennis Thibodeaux.)

Begun in 2006, Rouge et Blanc is a decadent wine and food festival held each October. It has grown into a series of wine seminars and dinners that lead to the four-hour Grand Tasting featuring dozens of wines and cuisine from area restaurants. The event is a fundraiser for Banners Arts and Humanities Series. (Courtesy of www.visitlakecharles.org.)

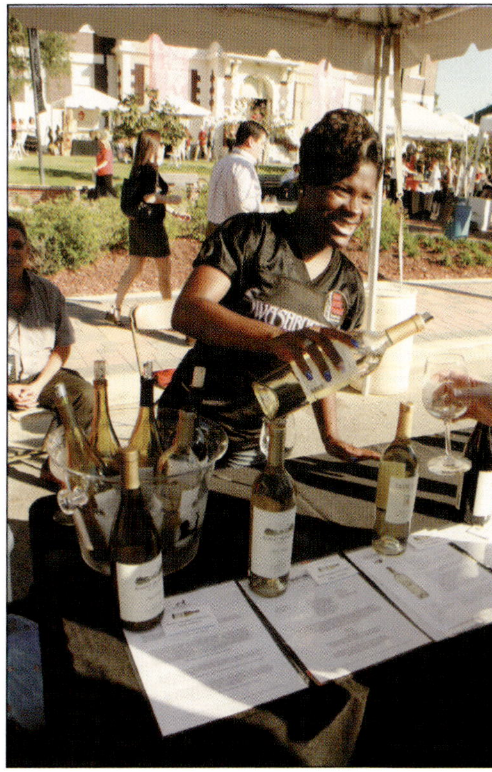

Lake Charles Pride is an organization promoting the recognition and equal treatment of Southwest Louisiana's gay, lesbian, bisexual, and transgendered citizens. This photograph was taken at the 2012 Pride Festival at L'Auberge du Lac. Pictured are the 2012 Lake Charles Pride board members, from left to right, Adam Manuel, Whitney Akers, Megan Norris (founder), and Rita Costello. (Courtesy of Rita Costello.)

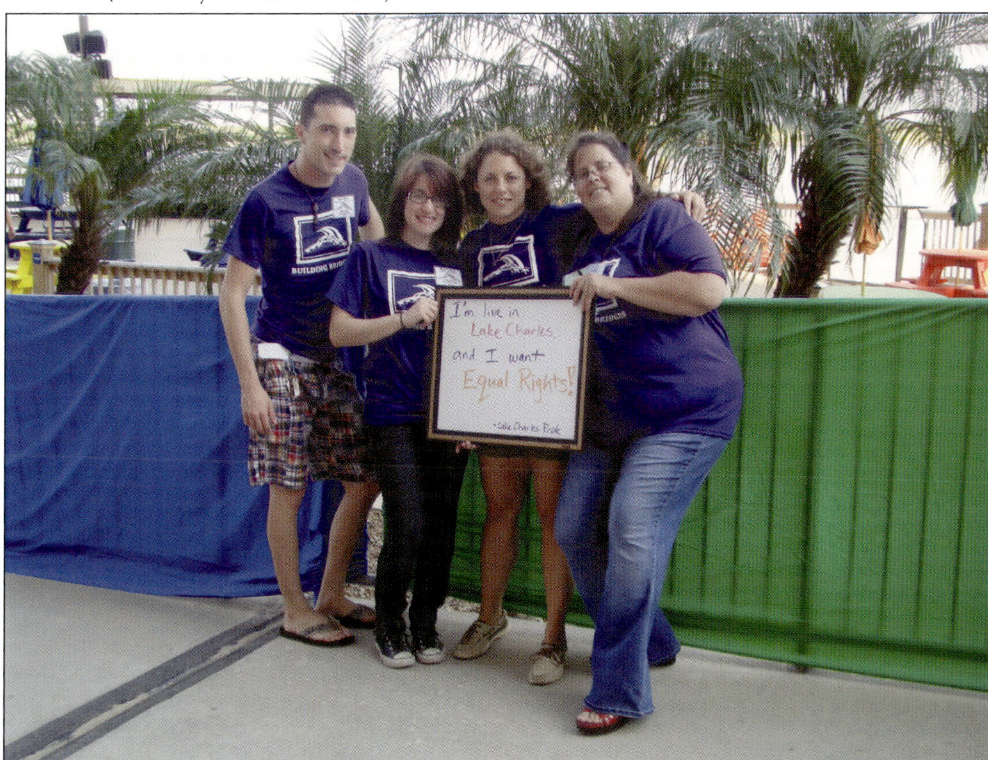

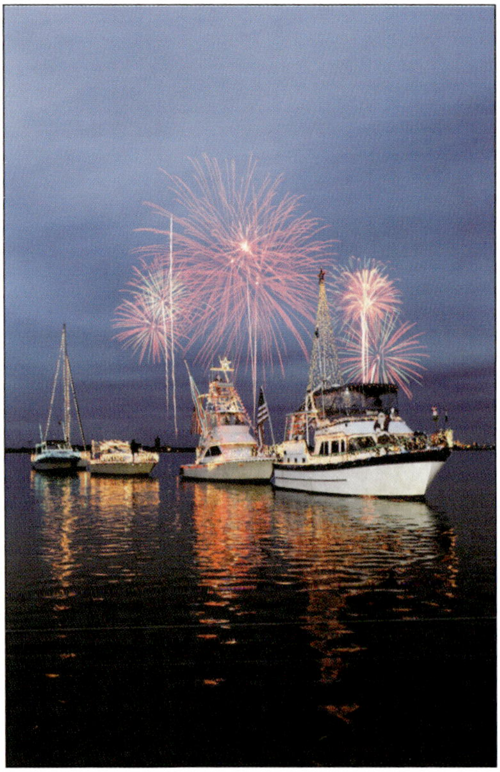

Boat parades and fireworks displays over Lake Charles are popular attractions during many festivals and holidays throughout the year, including Mardi Gras, Contraband Days, Fourth of July, and Christmas. This photograph shows the annual Light Up the Lakefront Boat Parade, which has been a part of local Christmas celebrations since 1987. (Courtesy of monsoursphotography.net.)

McNeese president Dr. Phillip Williams celebrates India Nite with Sanjeeta Dhakal and Dr. Pankaj Chandra, mechanical engineering professor at McNeese and past president of the India Association of Lake Charles. Lake Charles is home to approximately 100 Indian families, and India Nite has allowed them to share their rich culture with Lake Charles. (Courtesy of Dr. Pankaj Chandra.)

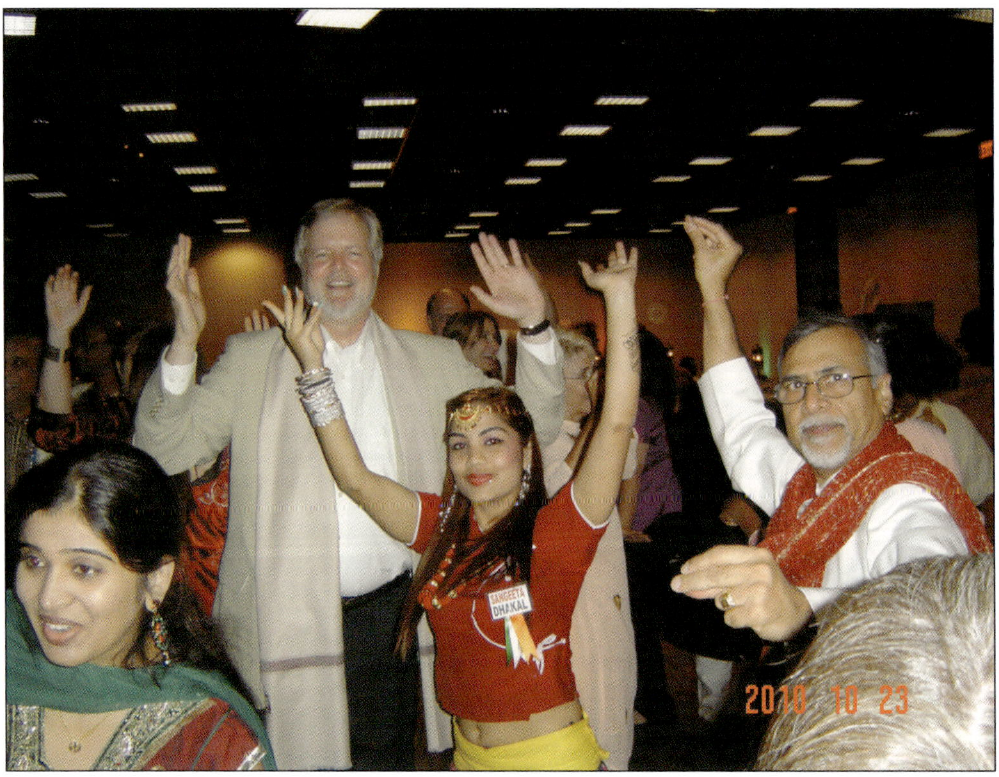

Seven

LAKE CHARLES TODAY

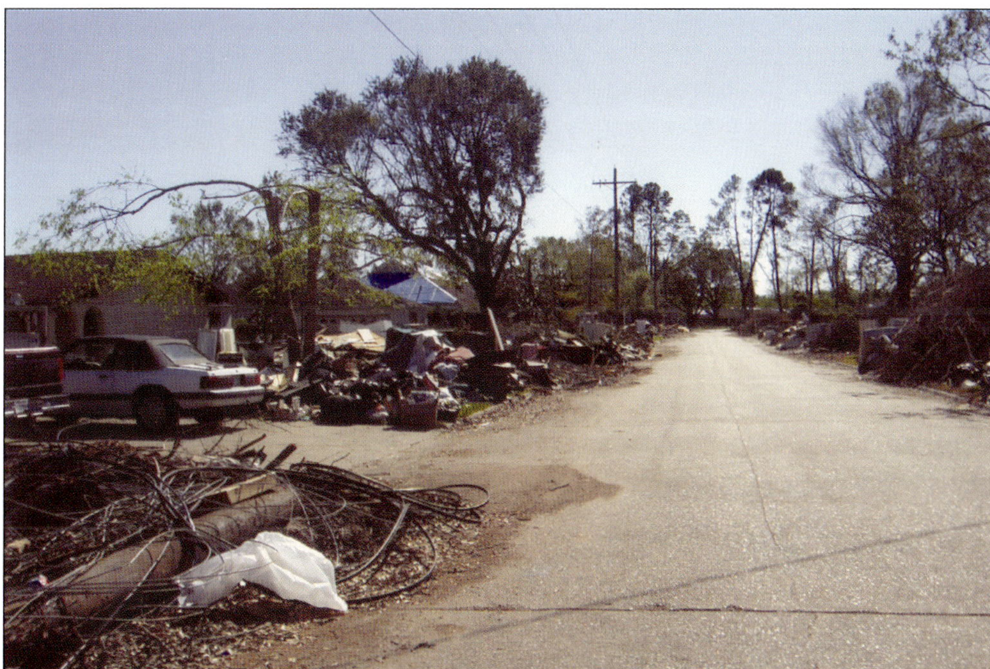

Hurricane Rita was a category 5 storm that roared through Southwest Louisiana in late September 2005. Throughout Lake Charles and surrounding areas, trees fell on homes, businesses, vehicles, and power lines. Emergency crews and citizens worked to clear the streets and remove the trees and debris with chainsaws, trucks, cranes, and grappling machines. This photograph is from Audubon Street soon after the storm (Courtesy of Brenda Bachrack.)

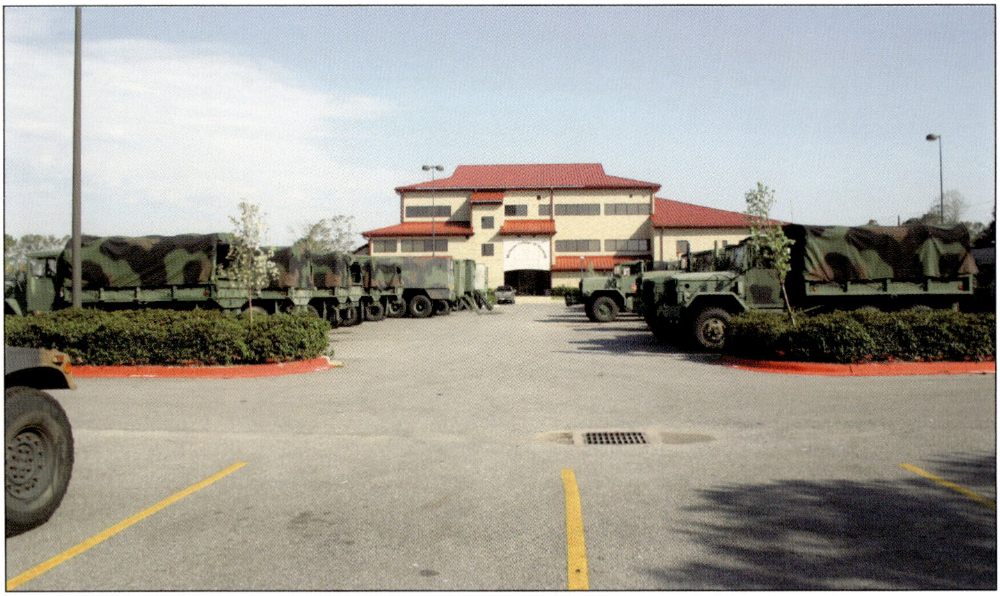

National Guard troops from across the nation came to Lake Charles to assist in the aftermath of Hurricane Rita. Troops gave residents relief supplies from FEMA distribution centers, including MREs (Meals Ready to Eat), water, and ice. They enforced a 7:00 p.m.–6:00 a.m. curfew and patrolled town to prevent the looting that was seen weeks earlier in New Orleans after Hurricane Katrina. This photograph shows their vehicles in the parking lot of the College of Nursing at McNeese. (Courtesy of McNeese State University.)

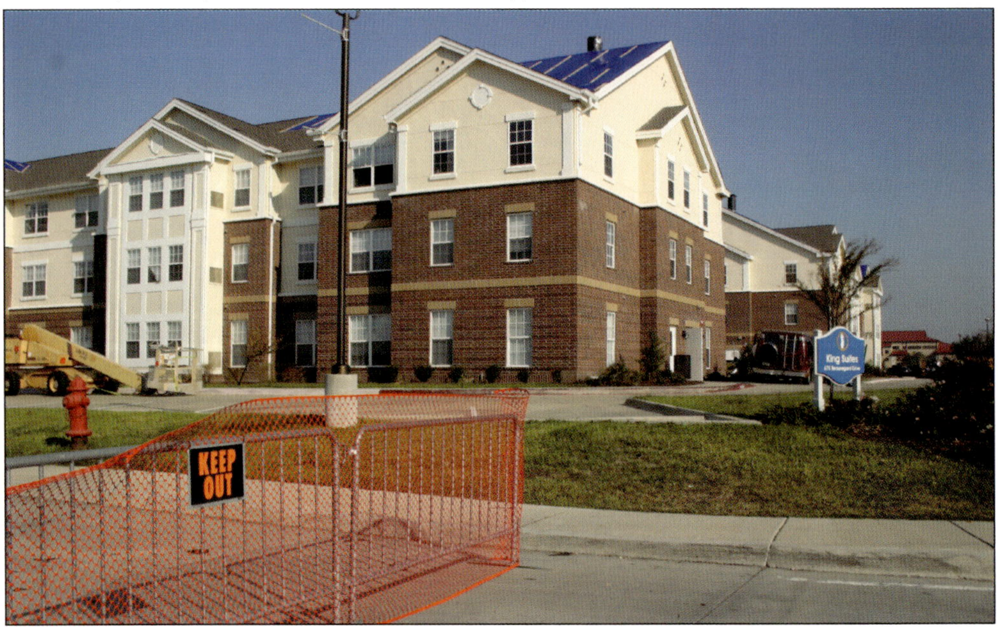

This photograph shows the McNeese apartments at the intersection of Common Street and McNeese Street with the iconic blue tarp covering the roof damage. During the immediate aftermath of the hurricane, FEMA affixed blue tarps to the damaged roofs of homes and businesses throughout Southwest Louisiana. The theme for McNeese's homecoming that fall was dubbed the "Blue Tarp Tour." (Courtesy of McNeese State University.)

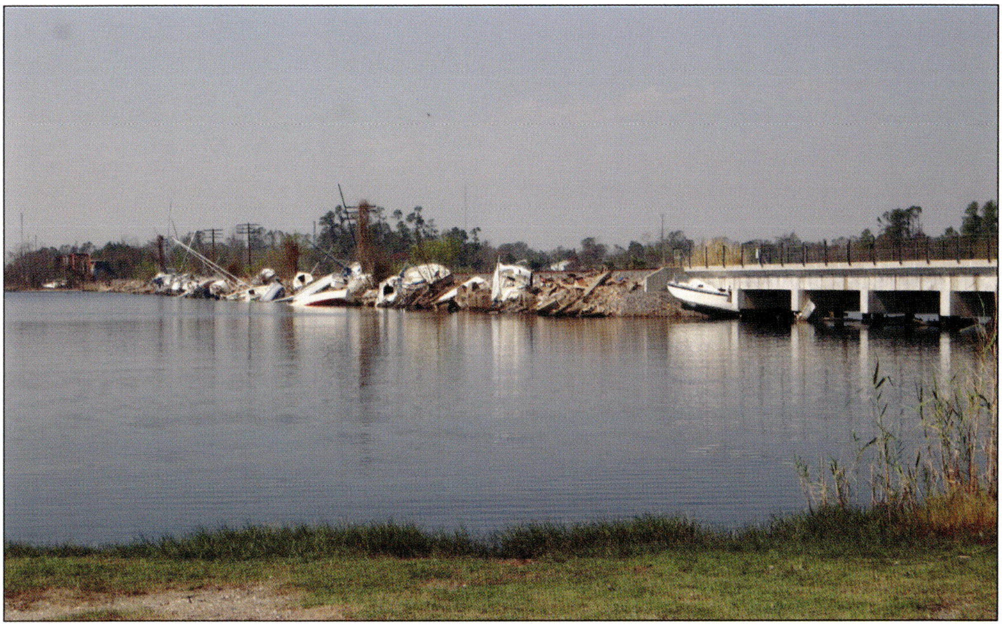

The powerful storm surge and winds from Hurricane Rita destroyed the Lake Charles Yacht Club and carried its sailboats from North Beach to the bank of the railroad tracks north of the Interstate 10 Calcasieu River bridge. Yacht club members began removing the damaged boats the following month. (Courtesy of McNeese State University.)

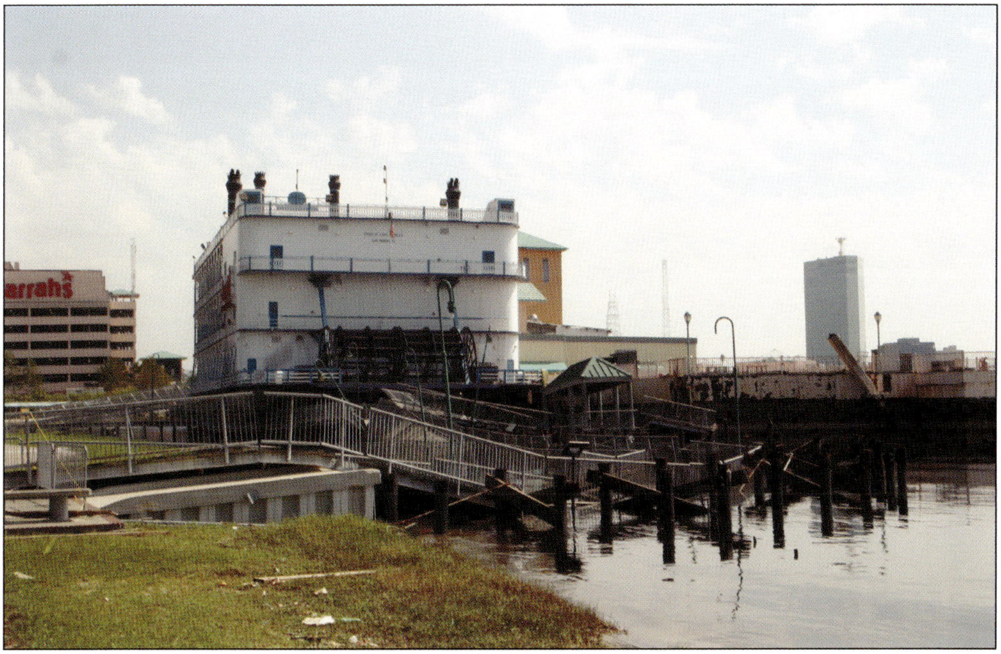

This photograph shows part of the extensive lakefront damage following Hurricane Rita. Two riverboats belonging to Harrah's Casino were beached during the storm, and the island barge on which the casino sat was destroyed. Harrah's sustained millions of dollars in damage and never reopened. Demolition of the twisted and collapsed sections of the boardwalk commenced the following May. (Courtesy of McNeese State University.)

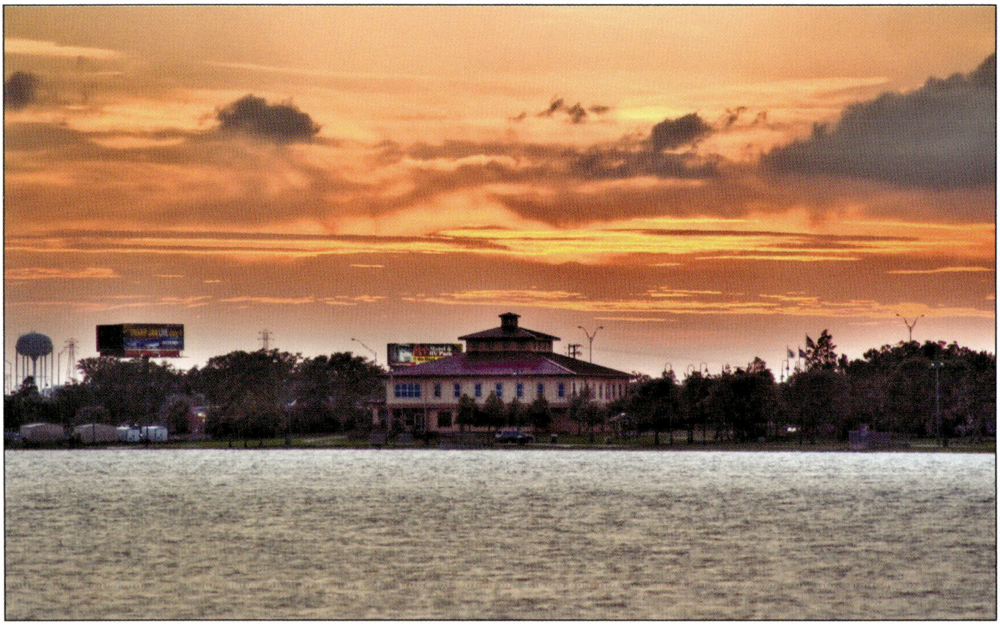

Lake Charles/Southwest Louisiana Convention and Visitors Bureau was originally named Lake Charles–West Calcasieu Parish Convention and Tourist Commission when it was established in 1972. Its operations include marketing and public relations, assisting with planned events for large groups, and operating the visitors center on Lakeshore Drive, pictured here. (Courtesy of Dennis Thibodeaux.)

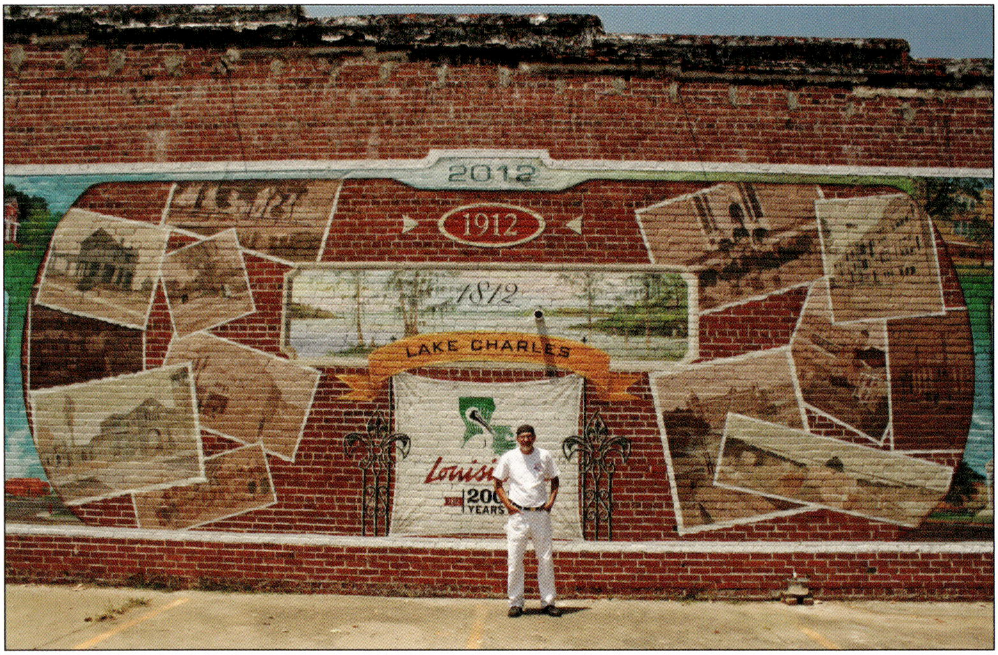

Local artist Fred Stark stands in front of his 2012 mural celebrating Louisiana's bicentennial. Commissioned by the Southwest Louisiana Arts and Humanities Council, the mural has three layers depicting scenes from the early days of the area's settlement, 1912 following the Great Fire, and the redeveloped downtown landscape of 2012. (Courtesy of www.visitlakecharles.org.)

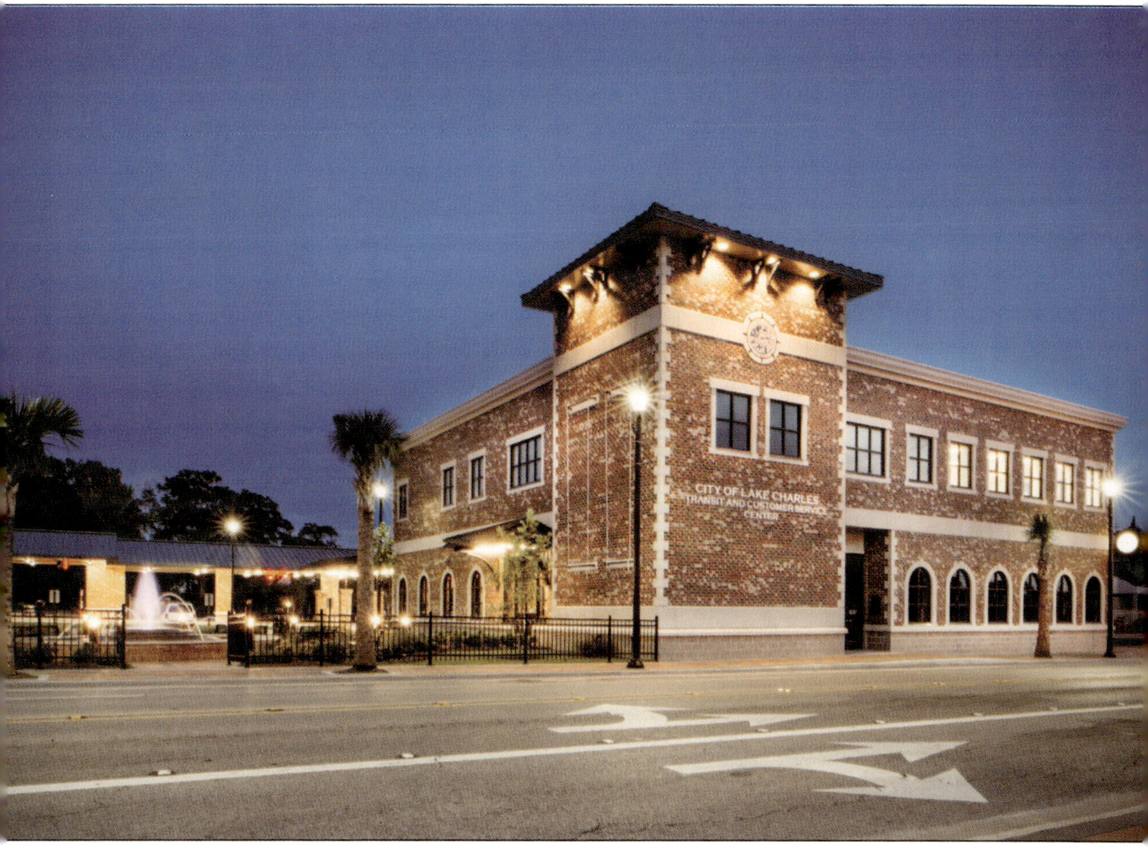

The City of Lake Charles Transit and Customer Service Center on the corner of Clarence and Ryan Streets opened its doors in 2012 in a building that sat vacant for many years before the city's downtown renewal. When this building was constructed in 1960, it housed Calcasieu Savings and Loan Association, and it later housed the Lake Charles Office of Motor Vehicles. In addition to office space for transit operations, the facility features a large bus-transfer canopy and a landscaped outdoor area with a fountain and a pavilion. The facility's design complements other renovations throughout downtown Lake Charles and along the lakefront. Each weekday, the Lake Charles Transit System operates five routes throughout the city that span from Nelson and Country Club Roads in the south to Highway 171 and Colfax Street in the north. (Courtesy of Lindsey Janies.)

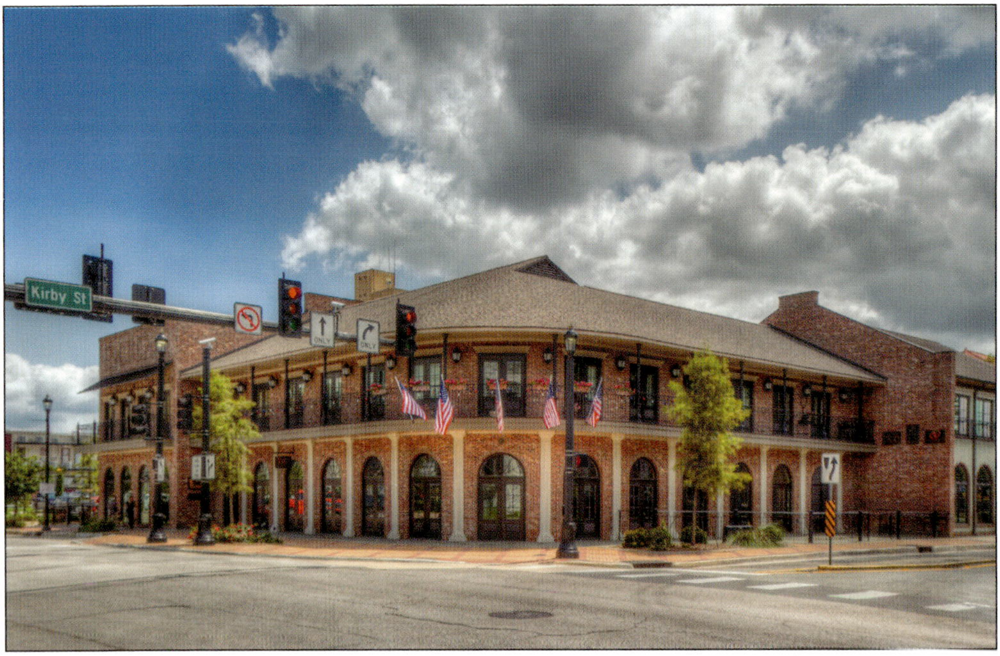

The Phoenix Building at the intersection of Ryan and Kirby Streets opened in 2010, a century after the great fire of 1910 destroyed most of downtown Lake Charles. The building is a project of Empire of the Seed, and it provides office and retail space for local businesses. (Courtesy of Dennis Thibodeaux.)

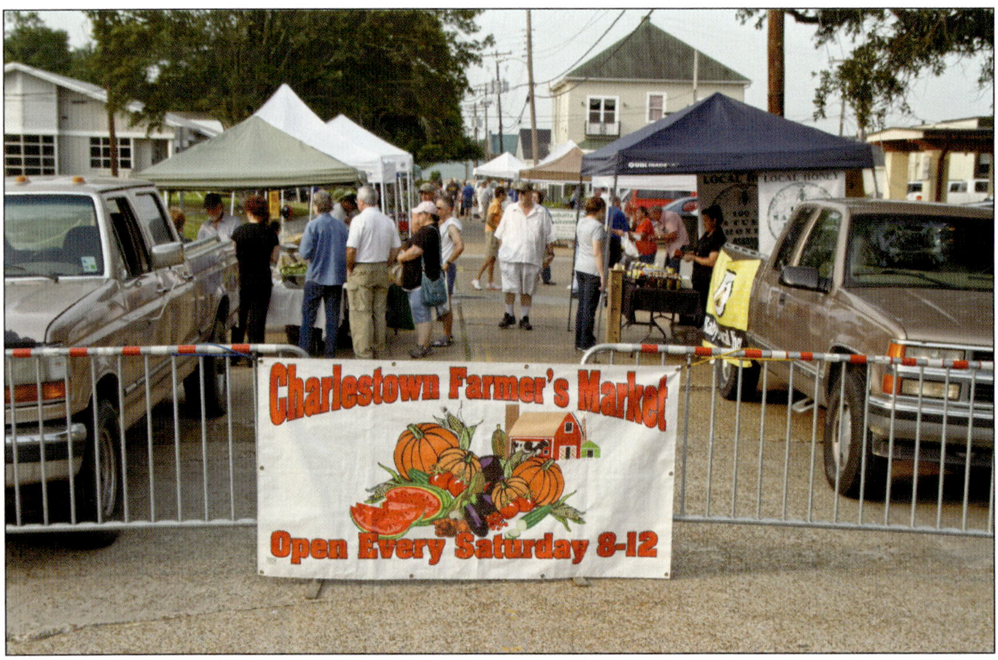

Charleston Farmers Market began in March 2005, and it is held every Saturday morning behind the 1911 city hall on Bilbo Street. Visitors can find handmade crafts, locally grown produce, meats, rice, and many types of handmade baked goods and products. On rainy days, the market moves into the first floor of the old city hall. (Courtesy of Dennis Thibodeaux.)

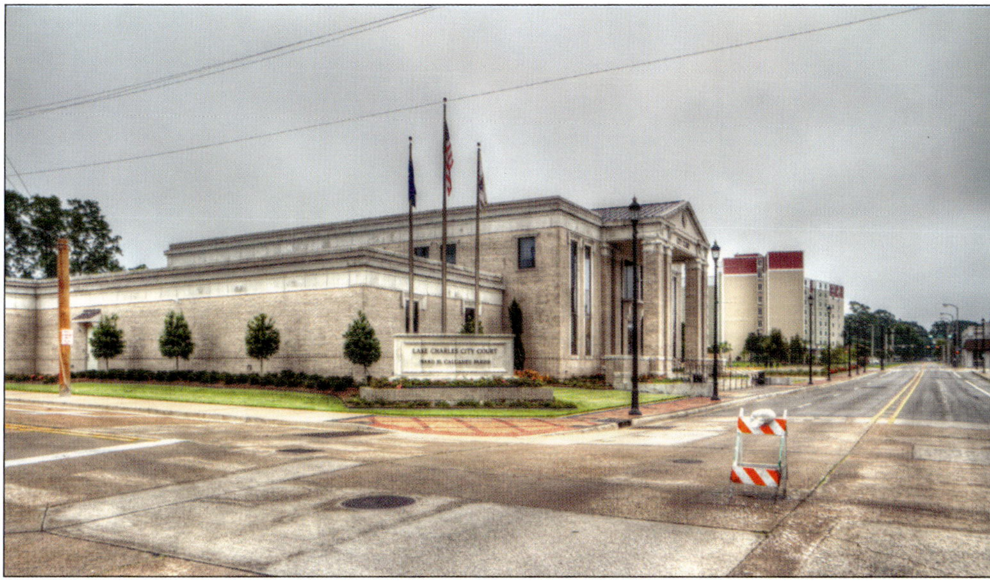

The Lake Charles City Court on Mill Street serves all of Ward 3 in Calcasieu Parish. The building opened in 2013 and was paid for through court costs at no additional taxpayer expense. The lobby and courtroom furniture was made by inmates from Louisiana Prison Enterprises. (Courtesy of Dennis Thibodeaux.)

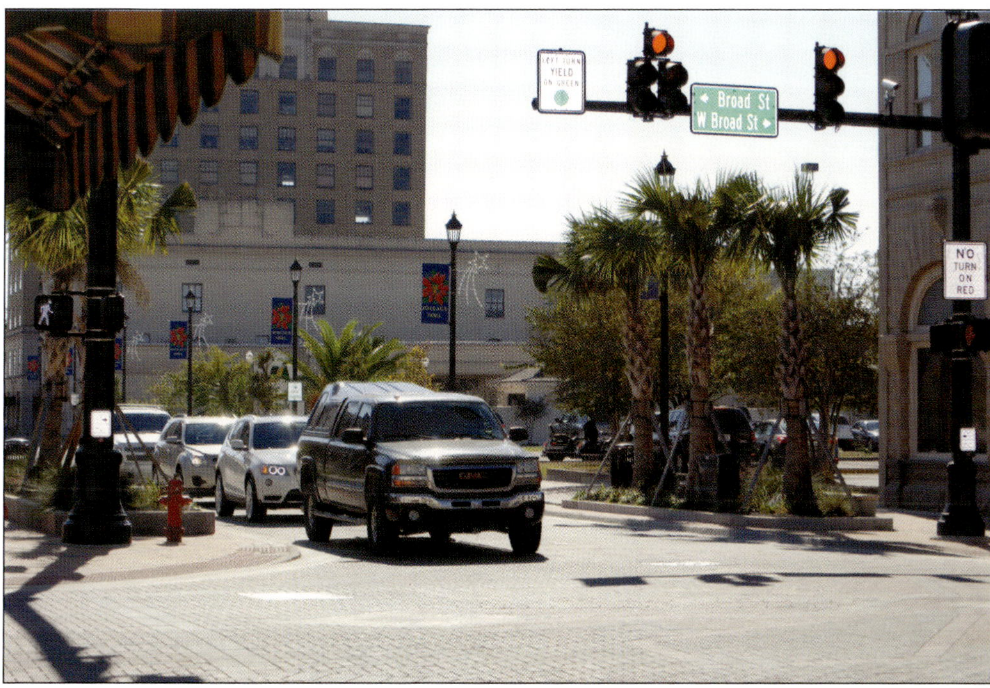

The post-Rita improvements to downtown Lake Charles include a renovated streetscape with decorative paving, new landscaping, signage, streetlamps, and benches. The project's aim was to encourage downtown development by easing traffic and providing pedestrian-friendly enhancements. (Courtesy of www.visitlakecharles.org.)

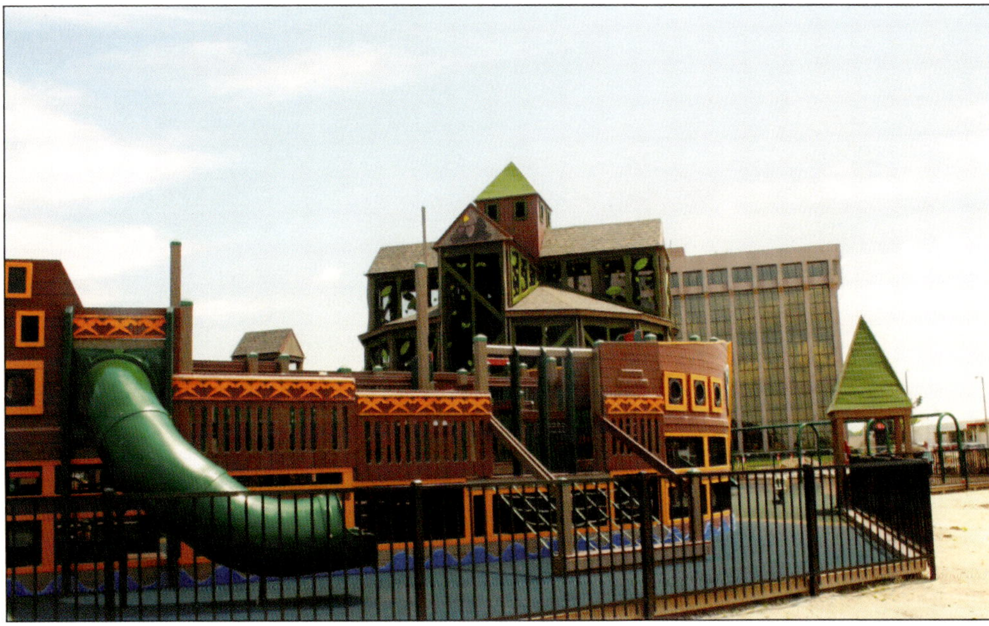

Millennium Park, located at the intersection of Clarence Street and Lakeshore Drive, was destroyed by an arsonist in January 2011. The park reopened in March 2013 thanks to the efforts of the Rebuilding of Millennium Park Fundraising Committee. The park features several Lake Charles motifs, including pirate ships and crossed pistols. (Courtesy of www.visitlakecharles.org.)

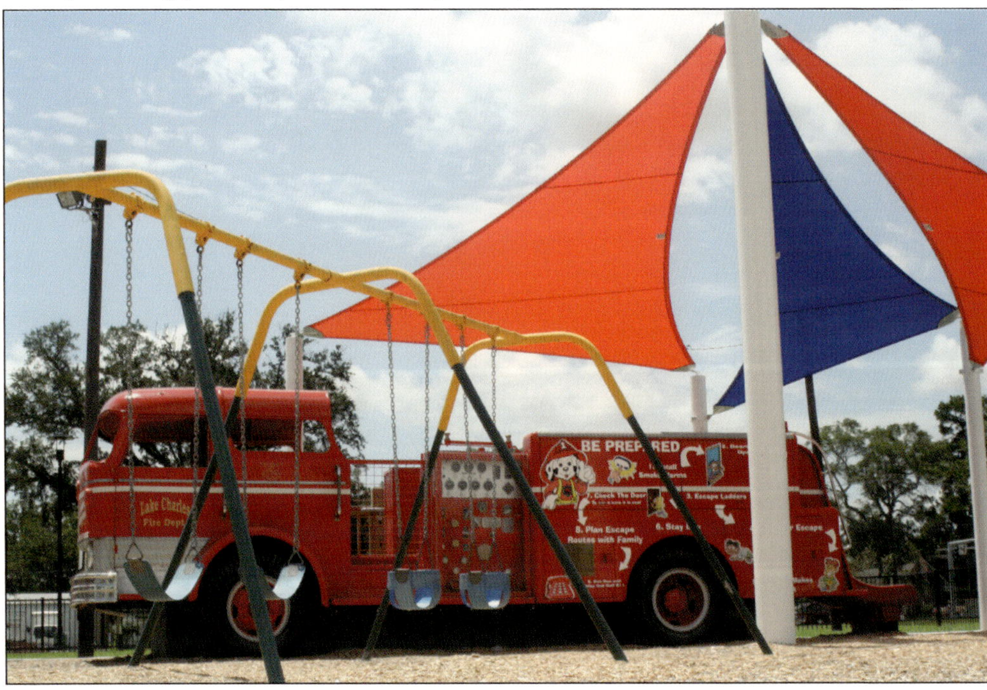

Lock Park, located at Ryan and Seventh Streets, is one of seven city parks that underwent refurbishing during the Parks Improvement Program that started in 2008. Improvements included canopy shading, new playground equipment and landscaping, and easier park access. This fire truck was converted into a safe piece of playground equipment for Lock Park. (Courtesy of www.visitlakecharles.org.)

The Charpentier Historic District features grand homes built during the late 19th and early 20th centuries, when Lake Charles experienced a lumber boom. This area of town was admitted to the National Historic Register in 1990 and subsequently experienced a slow rebirth as people worked to refurbish the homes after years of neglect. (Courtesy of monsoursphotography.net.)

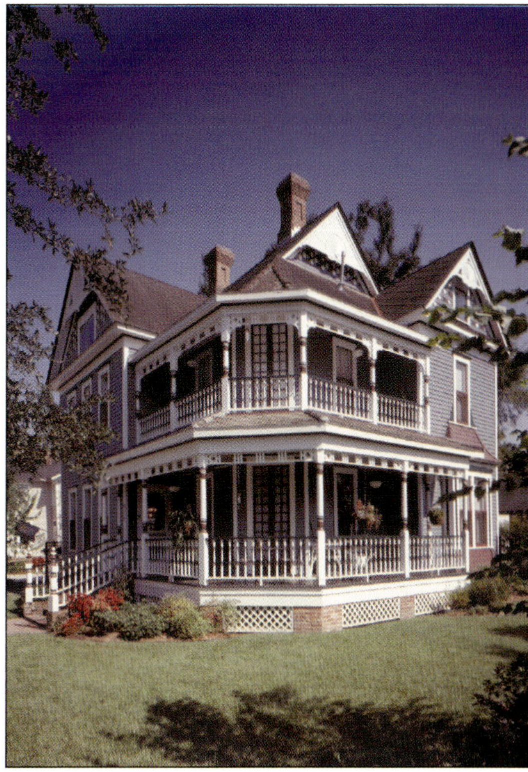

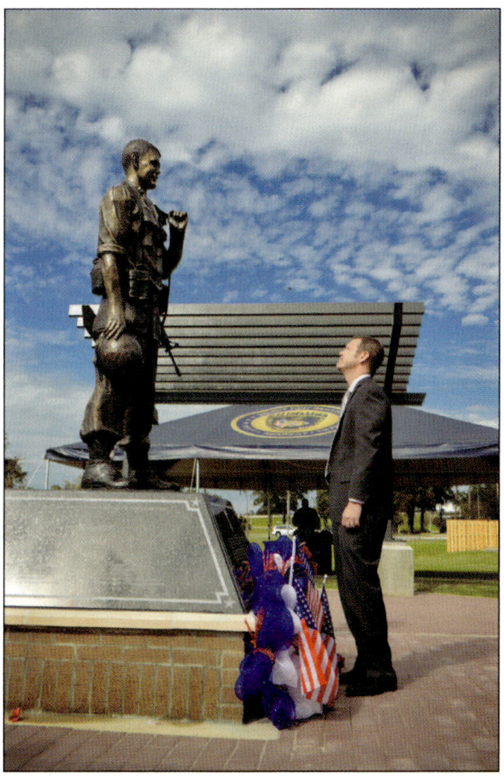

The Memorial to Peace, erected in 1968, evolved into Veterans Memorial Park. The newest addition to the park is this statue of 1st Lt. Douglas B. Fournet, a Medal of Honor recipient from Lake Charles who lost his life in the Vietnam War. Fournet's son, Bill, admires the statue at its unveiling in 2013. (Courtesy of Lindsey Janies.)

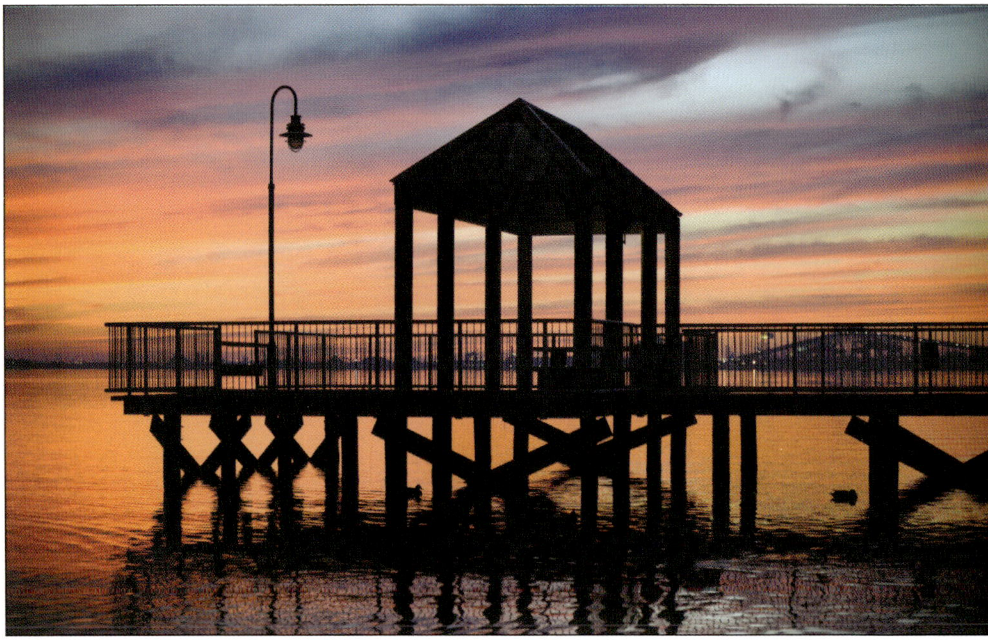

Lakefront development during Mayor Willie Mount's tenure included the construction of a boardwalk that connected the Lake Charles Civic Center to Veterans Memorial Park and continued around part of the lake. The boardwalk included several walkways and pavilions constructed over the water, as pictured here. Much of the boardwalk was destroyed during Hurricane Rita in 2005. (Courtesy of Lindsey Janies.)

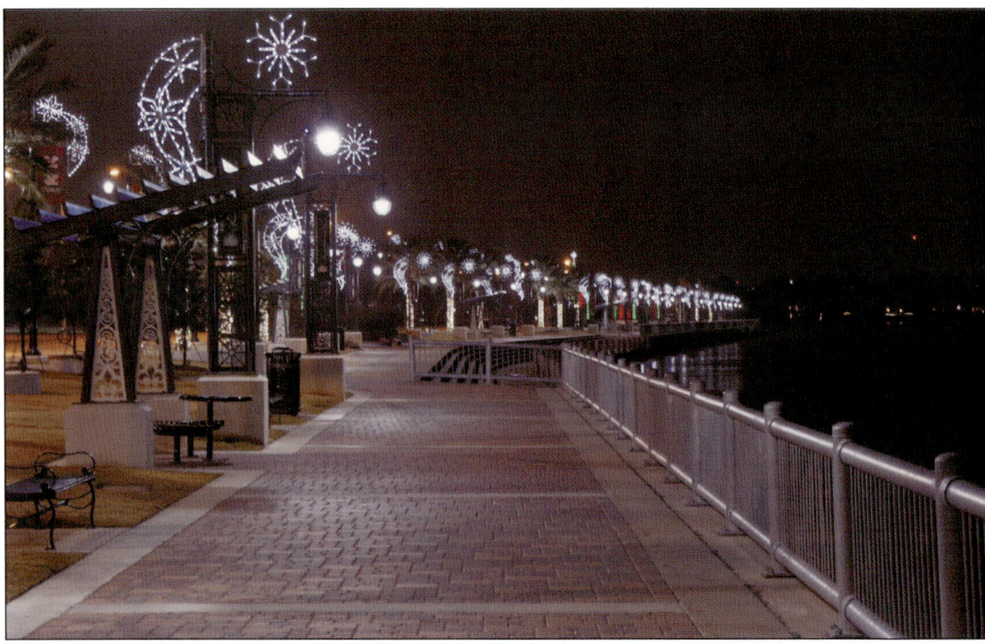

The Lakefront Promenade on Bord du Lac Drive and the Bord du Lac Marina was completed in 2012, and the area features landscaping, lighting, seating areas, and a new fountain with a sculpture. Mayor Randy Roach, city council officials, and the Downtown Development Authority were leaders of the lakefront projects. (Courtesy of Dennis Thibodeaux.)

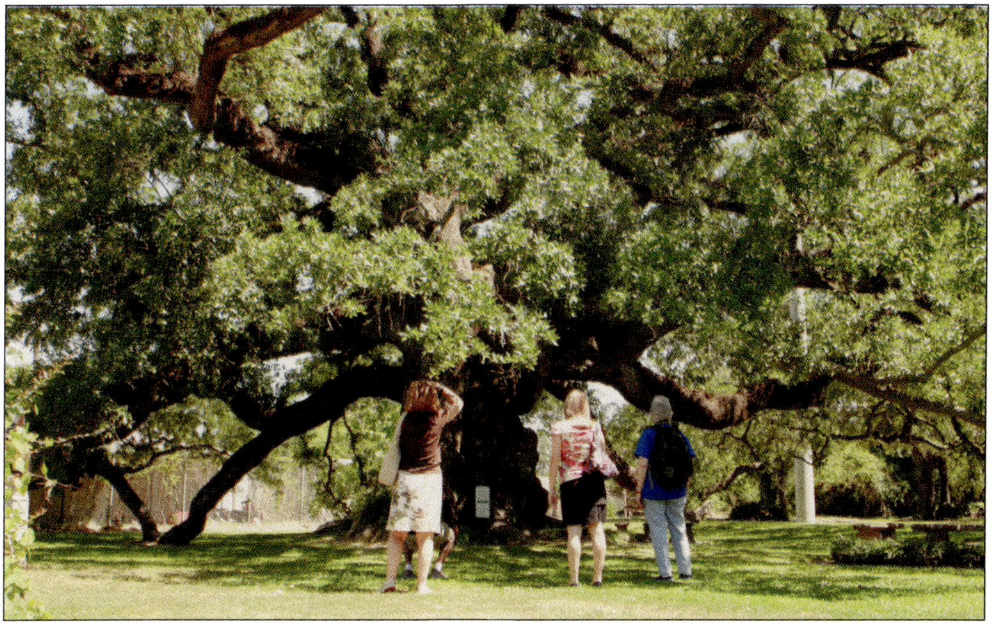

Sallier Oak is an old, beloved tree behind the Imperial Calcasieu Museum. The tree is said to be located on the original property of Charles Sallier, the early lakefront settler for whom Lake Charles is named. Chains used to bind the tree after it split during the 1918 hurricane have become deeply embedded and can still be seen. (Courtesy of www.visitlakecharles.org.)

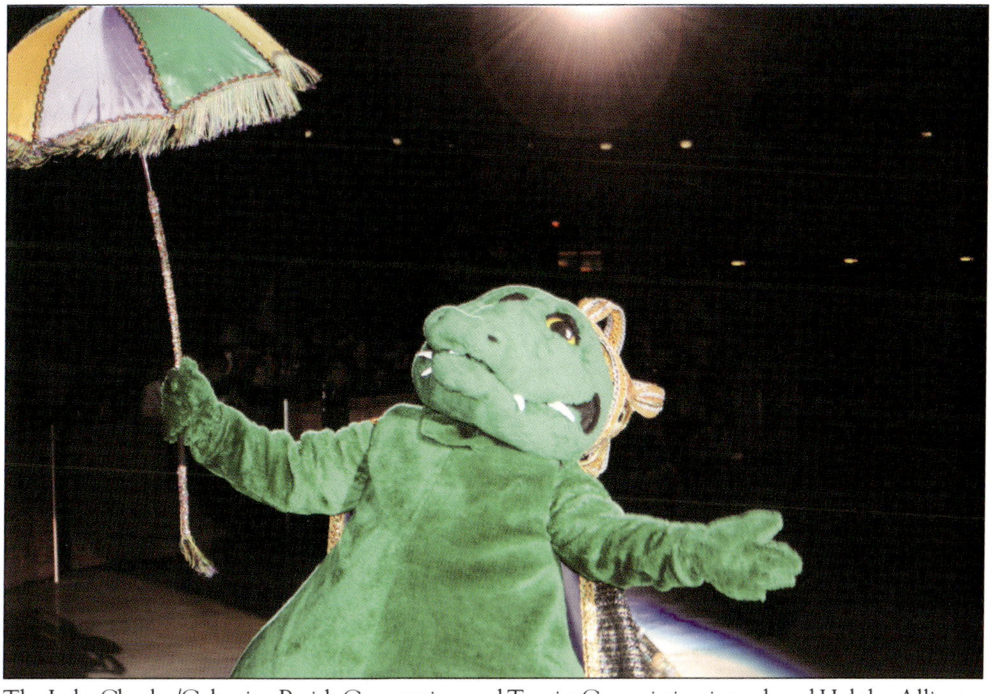

The Lake Charles/Calcasieu Parish Convention and Tourist Commission introduced Hal the Alligator in 1978 by featuring him holding a knife and fork on a billboard that said, "We'd like to have you for dinner in Lake Charles." Renamed Gumbeaux Gator later that year, he is the official mascot and goodwill ambassador of Southwest Louisiana. (Courtesy of www.visitlakecharles.org.)